Ultimate Swift Handbook for iOS Developers

A complete Guide to native app development
for iOS, macOS, watchOS, tvOS, and visionOS

Dúóng Đình Báo (James) Thăng

Orangeava.com

First published: October 2023
Published by: Orange Education Pvt Ltd, AVA™
Address: 9, Daryaganj, Delhi, 110002

ISBN: 978-93-88590-93-8
www.orangeava.com

Dedicated to

My beloved parents:
Dúóng Kim Húóng
Lê Thi Thu Hà

About the Author

Dúóng Đình Báo (James) Thăng's journey through the tech world is a testament to the idea that anyone can follow their passion and acquire new skills. While his educational background lies in Finance and Economics, he felt a compelling drive to explore the dynamic realm of app development. The potential of it is that anyone in this modern world now has a smartphone with them and spends most of their daily time on it. With dedication and self-education, he transitioned into a seasoned iOS developer and then a professional one, accumulating over 3 years of valuable industry experience.

His proficiency extends to both UIKit and SwiftUI, enabling him to create intuitive and user-friendly applications. He has successfully conceptualized, developed, and launched eight distinctive applications. These projects span a wide spectrum of domains, including finance, augmented reality, gaming, educational technology, and point-of-sale systems. Each of these apps has made a lasting positive impact, benefiting thousands of users.

As the author of this SwiftUI book, he has had the privilege of delving even further into this cutting-edge framework. This book not only reflects his passion for SwiftUI but also his commitment to helping others unlock their full potential. Through comprehensive insights and practical guidance, he aims to empower both aspiring and experienced developers to harness the power of SwiftUI and navigate the ever-evolving landscape of iOS development.

His motivation derives from an unwavering passion for innovation. He is deeply committed to crafting apps that not only meet but exceed user expectations, pushing the boundaries of what is possible in the iOS ecosystem. This journey has taught him that self-education is a powerful tool, and he is eager to inspire and empower others to embark on their learning journeys and achieve their aspirations in the ever-evolving world of iOS development through this book.

About the Reviewers

Catalin Patrascu is an experienced iOS Engineer and Mobile Technologist with over 13 years of experience developing mobile applications for various startups and mid-size companies as a freelancer.

Since the first iPhone was released, he has been developing iOS apps, transitioning from Windows development to mobile.

While Catalin has always been a goal-oriented, data-driven developer, in recent years he has shifted his focus towards building maintainable apps that are both robust and scalable. He has developed a keen interest in prioritizing the testability of the code and has become an expert in system design, refactoring, and automated testing.

He is now a content creator who shares insights on building maintainable iOS apps through system design, refactoring, and automated testing.

Nilesh Jha has over 8 years of experience in Software industries and has been using iOS frameworks since 2014. Nilesh currently works for a Consulting firm in London and also creates videos on YouTube under the channel App Developer. When he's not working on technology and the weather is nice, he likes to go near sea beaches.

Acknowledgement

I would like to express my gratitude to a few people who have provided me with continuous and ongoing support throughout the writing of this book. First and foremost, I would like to thank my parents for their continuous encouragement in writing the book – I could never have completed this book without their support.

I gratefully acknowledge Mr. Catalin Patrascu for his kind technical support for this book and Miss Sonali for her support from the very first chapter. Special thanks to Paul Hudson and his online blog, Hacking with Swift.

I extend my gratitude to the team at Orange Education for being supportive enough to provide meample time to write and refine this book.

Preface

This book is your comprehensive guide to iOS SwiftUI app development in a rapidly evolving landscape. From the foundational principles of Swift programming to advanced topics like networking, data persistence, and data visualization, this book equips you with the skills needed to create robust and engaging iOS applications.

With each chapter, you'll delve deeper into the world of app development, gaining practical insights and hands-on experience. In the opening chapters, we explore Swift programming language and SwiftUI, Apple's revolutionary framework for building user interfaces.

Then, we venture into essential aspects like networking, data persistence, and data visualization, providing you with the tools to create feature-rich and responsive apps. Whether you're an aspiring app developer or a seasoned coder looking to enhance your skill set, this book offers a structured pathway to success. Our aim is not just to teach you how to write code but to empower you to build innovative and user-centric apps that make a difference. Join us on this exciting journey, and let's create outstanding iOS applications together.

Chapter 1: In the opening chapter, readers will embark on a journey into the world of Swift, the powerful programming language for iOS, macOS, watchOS, and tvOS development.

By the end of this chapter, readers will have gained a solid understanding of the key concepts and tools they'll need to start their journey into Swift programming, setting a strong foundation for the chapters that follow.

Chapter 2: In this chapter, we will learn about the Layout concept and ideas in SwiftUI and understand how to break out complex UI into small and reusable pieces.

By the end of Chapter 2, readers will have gained a solid grasp of SwiftUI's core concepts and tools. They'll be equipped to create user interfaces with SwiftUI, laying the groundwork for more advanced UI development covered in subsequent chapters.

Chapter 3: This chapter will seamlessly continue from Chapter 2. This chapter focuses on the intricate details of how SwiftUI handles the layout of views and provides readers with a comprehensive understanding of the layout system.

By the end of Chapter 3, readers will have gained a deep understanding of how SwiftUI handles layout decisions, along with practical knowledge of fundamental View Modifiers, the coordinate system, positioning versus alignment, and life cycle methods. This knowledge will empower them to create complex and responsive user interfaces in their iOS apps.

Chapter 4: State and Property Wrapper are like the backbone of SwiftUI. They allow developers to manage the data that powers their app's user interface in a clean and efficient way. We will learn through these concepts in this chapter, and along the way, we will combine all of the previous knowledge to build a very familiar App from scratch: The Calculator.

Chapter 5: This is a pivotal chapter, as it delves into the world of software design patterns and specifically focuses on the MVVM (Model-View-View Model) pattern within the context of iOS development. This chapter equips readers with the knowledge and tools to create well-structured and maintainable iOS applications.

Chapter 6: In this chapter, we will be looking at commonly found elements and UI designs in a modern mobile application. Theyhavemultiple screens with different user stories. The tab bar and navigation bar are two important elements of modern user interface design. We will see how they work and recreate them in SwiftUI. Later, we will learn about compositional layout and how to make a modern complex layout like the Instagram or Spotify app.

Chapter 7: This is a critical chapter of the book, as it explores the essential topic of networking within the context of SwiftUI and iOS app development. In this chapter, readers will gain valuable insights into how to communicate with remote servers, retrieve data, and integrate it into their SwiftUI applications.

Chapter 8: This is a continuation of your exploration into networking concepts within SwiftUI and iOS app development. In this chapter, you will go through the development of a real-world application, providing practical insights into working with external APIs, handling authentication with OAuth 2.0, and integrating UIKit components into SwiftUI.

Chapter 9: In this chapter, we will learn about local storage, its meaning, and the purpose of using it.

Local storage is a crucial aspect of iOS app development, enabling the storage and retrieval of user-specific data within an application. In SwiftUI development, there are various techniques and frameworks available for local storage implementation, including UserDefaults, CoreData, and File Manager. Each of these options offers distinct features and capabilities to handle different types of data.

Chapter 10: With iOS 16, Apple introduced their solution built in SwiftUI to make charts. This framework works seamlessly combining SwiftUI with the declarative syntax. And this year, it even received more updates with iOS 17.

In this chapter, we will explore Swift Charts and recreate some of the most commonly used charts ranging from bar charts, line charts, pie charts to donut charts. During the process, we will make a simple application of expense tracking, which will visualize the spending data in different kinds of charts.

Downloading the code bundles and colored images

Please follow the link to download the
Code Bundles of the book:

https://github.com/OrangeAVA/Ultimate-SwiftUI-Handbook-for-iOS-Developers

The code bundles and images of the book are also hosted on
https://rebrand.ly/9b4056

In case there's an update to the code, it will be updated on the existing GitHub repository.

Errata

We take immense pride in our work at Orange Education Pvt Ltd and follow best practices to ensure the accuracy of our content to provide an indulging reading experience to our subscribers. Our readers are our mirrors, and we use their inputs to reflect and improve upon human errors, if any, that may have occurred during the publishing processes involved. To let us maintain the quality and help us reach out to any readers who might be having difficulties due to any unforeseen errors, please write to us at :

errata@orangeava.com

Your support, suggestions, and feedback are highly appreciated.

DID YOU KNOW

Did you know that Orange Education Pvt Ltd offers eBook versions of every book published, with PDF and ePub files available? You can upgrade to the eBook version at **www.orangeava.com** and as a print book customer, you are entitled to a discount on the eBook copy. Get in touch with us at: **info@orangeava.com** for more details.

At **www.orangeava.com**, you can also read a collection of free technical articles, sign up for a range of free newsletters, and receive exclusive discounts and offers on AVA™ Books and eBooks.

PIRACY

If you come across any illegal copies of our works in any form on the internet, we would be grateful if you would provide us with the location address or website name. Please contact us at **info@orangeava.com** with a link to the material.

ARE YOU INTERESTED IN AUTHORING WITH US?

If there is a topic that you have expertise in, and you are interested in either writing or contributing to a book, please write to us at **business@orangeava.com**. We are on a journey to help developers and tech professionals to gain insights on the present technological advancements and innovations happening across the globe and build a community that believes Knowledge is best acquired by sharing and learning with others. Please reach out to us to learn what our audience demands and how you can be part of this educational reform. We also welcome ideas from tech experts and help them build learning and development content for their domains.

REVIEWS

Please leave a review. Once you have read and used this book, why not leave a review on the site that you purchased it from? Potential readers can then see and use your unbiased opinion to make purchase decisions. We at Orange Education would love to know what you think about our products, and our authors can learn from your feedback. Thank you!

For more information about Orange Education, please visit **www.orangeava.com**.

Table of Contents

CHAPTER 1
Swift Language

Introduction

Swift is a powerful and modern programming language that was introduced by Apple in 2014. It has quickly gained popularity among developers due to its simplicity, safety, and performance. Swift is designed to be easy to learn and use, even for those who have never coded before, yet it is also a language that can be used to develop complex applications for iOS, macOS, watchOS, and tvOS. With its concise syntax and advanced features, such as optionals and closures, Swift is a versatile language that can be used for a wide range of applications. In this era of mobile and desktop computing, Swift is a language that every programmer should consider learning to stay competitive in the industry.

Structure

In this chapter, the following topics will be covered:

- Setting up Xcode
- Variable and constant
- Type and Optional Type in Swift
- Common ways to unwrap Optional Type

- Logical operators
- Conditional statements
- Array vs dictionary
- Scope and function
- Struct vs class

Downloading Xcode

On your Mac, go to the **AppStore** => Search for **Xcode** => **Install it**. Depending on your Wi-Fi, this will take around one to a couple of hours. When you are done and ready, let's take a quick tour of it.

Xcode 14.2 is used at the moment of writing this book. Now, let's make our first Programming Project: "**Hello World**".

Launch Xcode from your Mac, and then on the top left, select **File** => **New** => **Project**:

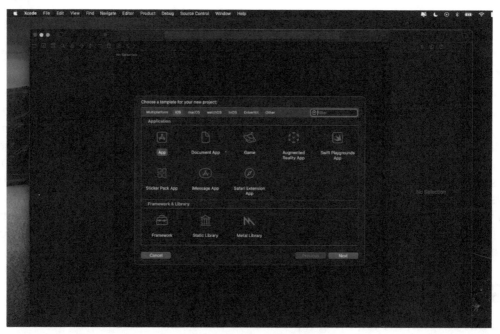

Figure 1.1: *Launching Xcode*

In this book, we will only be using the App category for iOS, and most iOS developments will choose this Option to start a New Project. While there are other things to explore, they are just templates with pre-setups. The option App will provide a clean New one to start. Now, click **Next**.

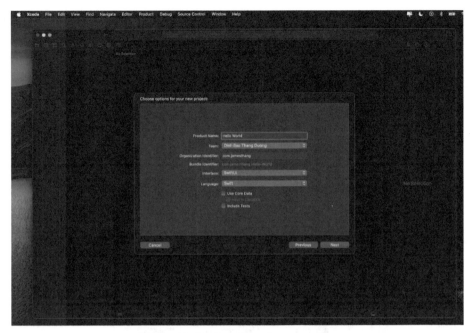

Figure 1.2: *Setting of project metadata*

- Here we will be setting the Project important metadata. The Name of this Project which will be Hello World. The Team here is the Developer Team. Now if you want to ship App to AppStore then you will need to buy yearly Subscription which will be $99 for Individual and $199 for Corporation. But if you just doing it for your own in the Personal Computer then just register your team with your personal Apple ID. One of the best advice here is just keep building and learning until you are fully ready then consider buying a real Developer Program.

Next is the Organization Identifier, which has to be a Unique String (Sentence). As you can see, the Organization Identifier and the Product Name will be used to generate the Bundle Identifier of the Project. The purpose of the Bundle Identifier is to uniquely identify one Project from many others App on the AppStore. The common practice here is to use the Reverse of your own Website Domain. If you don't have one, then we suggest this format: `com.your_name.your_birthday.your_app_name`. Anyway, make sure it is Unique.

For the Interface, make sure to select SwiftUI. Storyboard is for UIKit development, which won't be covered in this Book. The Programming language is Swift, and also, uncheck Core Data and Tests options. Those are not needed right now.

Then, hit **Next** to choose where you want to Save this Project. We will Save it on the Desktop for now. Let's see what we got for the first Project:

Figure 1.3: *Development Environment*

Here is our Project on Xcode, and we can clearly categorize them into four sections. Let's go one by one from left to right:

- Within the Red Rectangle Section is our File Management. We will mostly spend time create New Files and Navigate between the File System here. There also more important functionalities on this Tab like: Searching through Project, Information about Memory Usage, Perform Testing and Location of debuggers.

- Within the Yellow Rectangle will be our Coding Space. As you can see the File named Content View been selected from the left. This is the Code inside it and we will be writing Swift Code here.

- Next inside the Blue Area is our Live Preview which is only available for SwiftUI projects. Here will appear exactly what is written from the code from the Blue Rectangle. There are an Image of a globe and a text "Hello World". And as we code and modify, the Live Preview will change automatically to reflect what it is look like on real device. And it is also interactive too. Actions will work like button click or the logic of the App. Pretty great as this is one of the game changers compare to the older ways.

- Now we have the Green one on the right side. It is like a quick, convenient interface Toolbox. Like where you select font, color, alignment on Words or brusher and effects on Photoshop.

- You may also notice there is a small Purple down there at the bottom-right corner of the Blue section. Well, that button will open up another Area which is the Debug Area. But more on it later when we are making projects. Now let's learn some Swift first.

Defining variable

In a programming language, a variable is a storage location in a computer's memory that has been given a name and a data type, and it can be used to store a value of that data type. The value of a variable can change during the execution of a program, which makes it a useful tool for storing data that can be manipulated and used to solve problems. Variables are an essential part of programming and are used in almost every program that is written.

Here's an abstract example: think about a Variable like a box that has enough space to contain something. You store the value by assigning it to the Variable with the = syntax. The value can be a Number or a text message that will be stored inside that box. Then, later whenever that value is needed, you can always open the Box to take it out and use it.

Open Xcode to the Playground, and let's declare some variables.

File => **New** => **Playground** => choose the MacOS tab with the blank option. This is just a convenient way to write plain code and see what happens:

Figure 1.4: *Variable versus Constant*

We declare three variables here: greeting, **myName**, and **myAge**. You can see their inside value on the left side. First, let's distinguish between a variable and a constant. Both are used to store value, but as the name implies, a variable is a value that is expected to change, like **myAge** here because I am getting older and older. But my name does not change over time, so it should be a Constant. As you will see later, it is totally fine when we try to change **myAge,** but it is an error when we try to change **myName**. We use **var** to declare a Variable and **let** to declare a constant. Now, you may ask, then why we don't just use var all the time for everything? Well, the answer is performance optimization. It's generally a good idea to use constants whenever possible because they can help to prevent accidental changes to important values that could affect the behavior of a program. Constants also make it easier to understand the code because the values they represent are clearly marked as being fixed.

Also, one thing to remember is that we use **//** to write a comment in our Swift Code. A comment is a piece of text in a code file that is not executed as part of the program. Comments are used to explain/clarify the code, or to add notes or suggestions for other developers/or your future self who may be reading/rereading the code.

Now let's shift our focus to the part after the variable / constant name, where we see **:String** and **:Int**. These are Type Annotation used to specify the type of a variable or constant. They can be very useful for providing clarity and for catching type-related errors at compile time. The code in the aforementioned example can be interpreted as follows: we want to create two variables, greeting and **myName,** which will be of type **String** (for Text), and 1 constant, **myAge,** which will be of type **Int** (for a whole number).

It's generally a good idea to use type annotations whenever the type of a variable or constant is not immediately obvious from the context, or the value being assigned. However, it's important to keep in mind that type annotations are not required in Swift, and, in many cases, the type can be inferred from the value being assigned.

If you are completely new to programming, you will be confused here about Type: What is it and what does it mean?

In Swift, a Type is a classification of values that determines what operations can be performed on those values. Every value in Swift has a type, which is specified when the value is created. For example, the string literal "**Hello, playground**" is a value of type **String**, the integer literal 26 is a value of type **Int**, and the floating-point literal pi 3.14159 is a value of type **Double**.

In Swift, there are two main categories of types as follows:

- **Nominal types**: It include user-defined types such as classes (**class**), structures (**struct**), enumerations (**enum**), and protocols (**protocol**).

- **Structural types**: It include all other types, such as the built-in types like Integer (**Int**), floating number (**Double**), true false value (**Bool**), and for text (**String**), as well as compound types like tuples and optional types.

We will soon see and use all of these in later chapters.

Each **Type** in Swift defines a set of characteristics that determine how values of that type can be used. For example, the String type defines methods and properties for working with strings, the **Int** type defines methods and properties for working with integers, and so on.

Types are an important concept in Swift because they help to ensure that values are used correctly and safely in your code. They also enable the Swift compiler to optimize the performance of your code by generating efficient machine code for the different types of values.

Swift is a type-safe language, which means the language helps you to be clear about the types of values your code can work with. If part of your code requires a String, type safety prevents you from passing it an Int by mistake. Likewise, type safety prevents you from accidentally passing an optional String to a piece of code that requires a non-optional String. Type safety helps you catch and fix errors as early as possible in the development process:

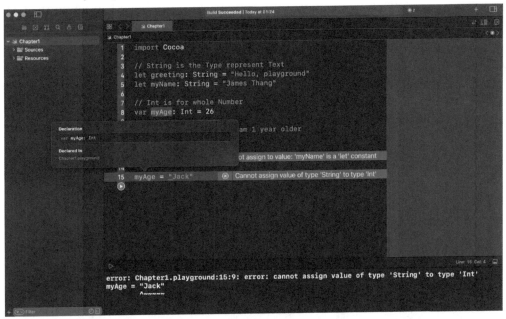

Figure 1.5: *Swift is Type strict*

We try to change **myAge** to "**Jack**", and Xcode auto notify us with a very descriptive error that it cannot assign a **String** to a type **Int** variable. Here is one of the most effective shortcuts to remember: on your Mac, hold the Option key + right click on the variable name => you will be able to check which Type it is supposed to be: **myAge** should be an **Int** here.

Some people find it difficult and not convenient with Type-Safe Language. However, it makes our code predictable, less Buggy, and better compile time. Type-safe languages help prevent type errors, which are errors that occur when a value has a different type than what is expected. These errors can be difficult to spot and can lead to unexpected behavior in a program. By ensuring that all values have the correct type, type-safe languages can help make code more predictable and easier to debug. Additionally, type-safety can help improve the performance of a program, as the compiler can optimize code more effectively when it knows the types of variables at compile time. Finally, type-safety can also make it easier to reason about code, as it can help ensure that values are used consistently and in ways that are compatible with their intended purpose.

Optional Type and nil

In Swift, there is also one value that any variable/constant can be: **nil**. Nil here means nothing, an unknown value, or the absence of value. Why can a variable be in this state? For various reasons such as wrong decoding, missing data, or because we purposely want it to be because we don't have the value of it yet when we declare it.

An **optional** is a type that can either hold a value or hold nil, indicating that the value is absent. Optionals are used to represent values that may be absent or unknown. We can have an optional Int, which can be **Int** or **nil**, option String, or of any other type. Optionals are denoted using a ? after the type name:

```
// Current Temperature, not know yet because data is being calculate
var temperature: Int?                                        ▣ nil

// Now we have data, which is 26 Celcius
temperature = 26                                             ▣ 26

if let temperature {
    print("Current temperature is \(temperature)")           ▣ "Current temperature is 26\n"
}

// Data is recalculate, so set to unknown
temperature = nil                                            ▣ nil

if let temperature {
    print("Current temperature is \(temperature)")
} else {
    print("We are recalculating, please wait")               ▣ "We are recalculating, please wait\n"
}
```

Figure 1.6: Unwrapping

To use the value of an Optional, we need to unwrap it. There are some ways but here we are using the if let closure. Again, Swift is type-safe language, so we cannot have a nil value when it is supposed to use/receive an Integer.

Now, let's look at some common ways to unwrap optional types in Swift.

Common ways to unwrap Optional Type

In Swift, there are several ways to unwrap optional types, depending on the situation and your preference for handling potential nil values. Here are the most common ways to unwrap optionals:

Forced Unwrapping

This method is denoted by adding an exclamation mark "!" after the optional variable or property. It forcefully unwraps the optional, assuming that it has a non-nil value:

```
// Force unwrapping
let optionalValue: Int? = 42
let unwrappedValue = optionalValue!
```

Figure 1.7: Force unwrapping

However, if the optional is nil at runtime, it will cause a runtime crash (a "*fatal error: unexpectedly found nil while unwrapping an Optional*" error). Because of it, this is not a recommended way in practice.

Optional Binding with `if let`:

Using the **if let** construct, you can conditionally unwrap an optional and assign its non-nil value to a new variable within the scope of the **if** block. This method avoids crashes and allows you to handle the case where the optional might be **nil**:

```
let optionalValue: Int? = 42

if let unwrappedValue = optionalValue {
    // Use unwrappedValue safely here
} else {
    // Handle the case when optionalValue is nil
}
```

Figure 1.8: Optional binding with if-let

Optional Binding with `guard let`:

Similar to if let, **guard let** is used to conditionally unwrap an optional and assign its non-**nil** value to a new variable. It is usually used within functions to exit early if the optional is **nil**, making the rest of the function safe to use with the unwrapped value:

```swift
func processValue(_ optionalValue: Int?) {
    guard let unwrappedValue = optionalValue else {
        return // Exit early if optionalValue is nil
    }
    // Use unwrappedValue safely here
}
```

Figure 1.9: *Optional binding with guard-let*

Nil Coalescing Operator ??

The nil coalescing operator provides a way to provide a default value when an optional is nil. It unwraps the optional if it has a value, or returns the default value specified on the right-hand side if the optional is **nil**:

```swift
let optionalNilValue: Int? = nil                              ▣ nil
let unwrappedNilValue = optionalNilValue ?? 0 // If optionalValue is    ▣ 0
    nil, unwrappedValue will be 0
```

Figure 1.10: *nil coalescing operator*

Optional Chaining

Optional chaining is a way to call methods, access properties, or call subscripts on an optional that might be nil. If the optional is nil, the entire expression evaluates to nil without causing a runtime crash:

```swift
struct SomeStruct {
    var value: Int
}

let optionalStruct: SomeStruct? = SomeStruct(value: 42)
let result = optionalStruct?.value
// result will be an Int? containing 42, or nil if optionalStruct is nil
```

Figure 1.11: *Optional chaining*

We will learn about Struct later in this chapter. Each of these methods has its use cases, and the choice of which one to use depends on the scenario and how you want to handle potential nil values.

Optionals are a powerful feature of Swift and are used extensively in the language, particularly when working with optional values or when handling errors.

Logical operators

In the Swift programming language, operators are special symbols or characters that perform specific operations on one or more values and return a result.

Swift supports a variety of operators, including arithmetic operators, comparison operators, logical operators, assignment operators, range operators, and more.

Here are some examples of common operators in Swift:

- **Arithmetic operators**: + (addition), - (subtraction), * (multiplication), / (division)

- **Comparison operators**: == (equal to), != (not equal to), > (greater than), < (less than), >= (greater than or equal to), <= (less than or equal to)

- **Logical operators**: && (and), || (or), ! (not, opposite)

- **Assignment operators**: = (assign a value to a variable or constant), += (add and assign), -= (subtract and assign), *= (multiply and assign), /= (divide and assign)

- **Range operators**: ..< (half-open range), ... (closed range)

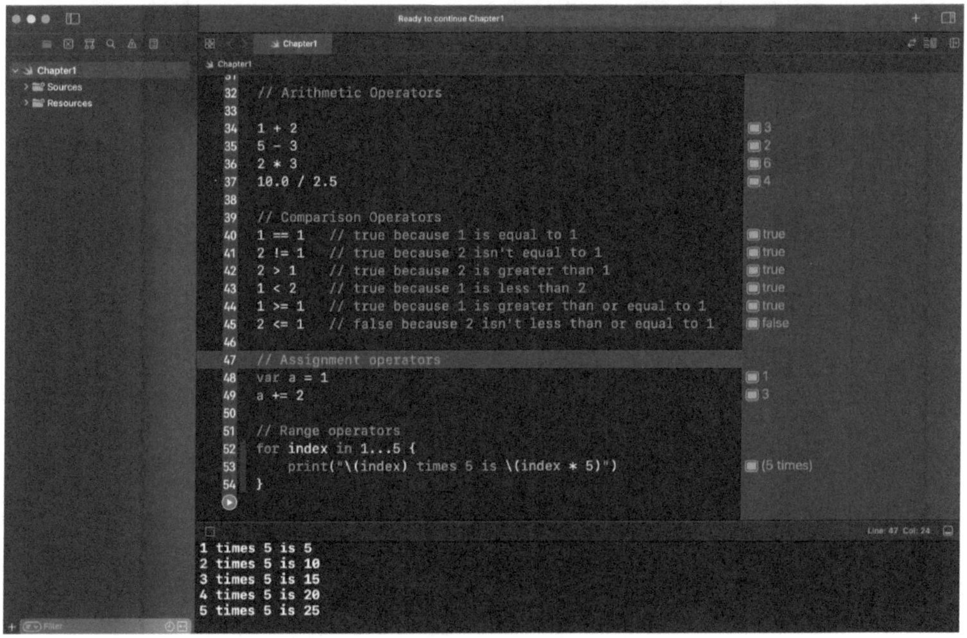

Figure 1.12: *Swift operators*

Operators in Swift can be used in expressions and can be combined with other operators with **Logical Operators** to create more complex expressions. Because SwiftUI is a declarative programming style, we will be using a lot of operators when developing using it.

Conditional statements

Sometimes, it is useful to execute different sections of code based on certain conditions. This can include running additional code when an error occurs or displaying a message when a value becomes too high or low or when it's true or false. To achieve this, you can make certain parts of your code conditional.

In Swift, there are two ways to add conditional branching to your code: the **if** statement and the **switch** statement. The **if** statement is generally used for evaluating simple conditions with a limited number of possible outcomes, while the **switch** statement is better for more complex conditions with multiple potential combinations and can be helpful in cases where pattern matching can aid in selecting the appropriate code branch to execute. The best practice is to consider using **switch** statement when there are more than three different states.

Here is an example, both will have the same result:

```
// Time in 24 hour format
var time = 8                                        ▨ 8

if time <= 12 {
    print("Good morning")
} else if time <= 18 {                              ▨ "Good morning\n"
    print("Good afternoon")
} else {
    print("Good evening")
}

switch time {
case 0...12:
    print("Good morning")                           ▨ "Good morning\n"
case 13...18:
    print("Good afternoon")
default:
    print("Good evening")
}
```

Figure 1.13: *if else vs switch case*

Sometimes, what we want is not just one condition alone. This is where the use case of Logical Operators comes in: **&&** means and, **||** mean or, **!** means the opposite of it. These will become very handy in coding later, especially when we want a different appearance when some conditions are satisfied.

Here are the examples:

```
56   // Time in 24 hour format
57   var time = 8                                              8
58   var weather = "raining"                                    raining
59
60   if time <= 10 && weather == "raining" {
61       print("Book a Car to work because it is raining")      "Book a Car to work\n"
62   }
63
64   if !(weather == "raining") {
65       print("It is not raining, we can go outside and play.")
66   } else {
67       print("It is raining, we should stay inside.")          "It is raining, we should stay inside.\n"
68   }
69
70   let hungry = true                                          true
71   let thirsty = false                                        false
72
73   if hungry || thirsty {
74       print("Let's get something to eat and drink.")          "Let's get something to eat and drink.\n"
75   } else {
76       print("We are not hungry or thirsty.")
77   }
```

Figure 1.14: *Example of conditions*

Now, there is one important concept to note here: The Ternary Condition Operator.

The ternary conditional operator is a special operator with three parts, which takes the form: **question ? answer1 : answer2**.

It is a shorthand way to write an if statement that returns a value. Both the following codes are the same:

```
97    let b = 5                       5
98    let c = 10                      10
99
100   var min = b < c ? b : c         5
101   print(min)                      "5\n"
102
103   if b < c {
104       min = b                     5
105   } else {
106       min = c
107   }
108   print(min)                      "5\n"
```

Figure 1.15: *Ternary condition operator*

Because of the way SwiftUI code work, we will be purposely using a lot of ternary conditional operator. So, it is better to get used to it.

Collection Type: Array

There will be times when we find ourselves needing a collection of related data, not just a single one. For example, 7 days of the week or all 30 days of the month. This is why we need Collection Types in every Programming Language. In Swift, there are several different types of collections, including array, dictionary, and set. We will talk about **Array** and **Dictionary** since they are commonly used.

Definition: An array is an ordered list of values. The same value can appear in an array multiple times at different positions. All of the elements inside it must be of the same Type. You can use an array to store a list of items, such as strings, numbers, or even other arrays.

Here's an example of how you can create an array in Swift:

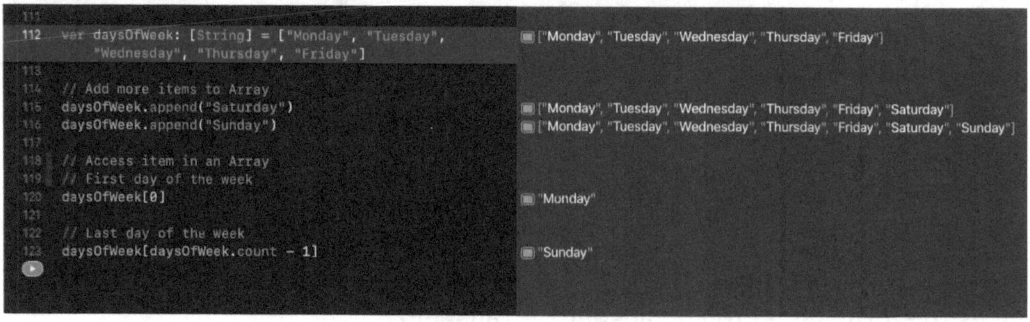

```
111
112  var daysOfWeek: [String] = ["Monday", "Tuesday",      ▣ ["Monday", "Tuesday", "Wednesday", "Thursday", "Friday"]
         "Wednesday", "Thursday", "Friday"]
113
114  // Add more items to Array
115  daysOfWeek.append("Saturday")                         ▣ ["Monday", "Tuesday", "Wednesday", "Thursday", "Friday", "Saturday"]
116  daysOfWeek.append("Sunday")                           ▣ ["Monday", "Tuesday", "Wednesday", "Thursday", "Friday", "Saturday", "Sunday"]
117
118  // Access item in an Array
119  // First day of the week
120  daysOfWeek[0]                                         ▣ "Monday"
121
122  // Last day of the week
123  daysOfWeek[daysOfWeek.count - 1]                      ▣ "Sunday"
```

Figure 1.16: Create an array

When dealing with collection types, the actions that are frequently used include accessing, modifying, and iterating through all values. Let's explore those now for an Array.

Remember that an array is an ordered list, and we can access the value we need by its index. Each **Element** of an **Array** will have an index representing its current position, and the starting index will always be 0:

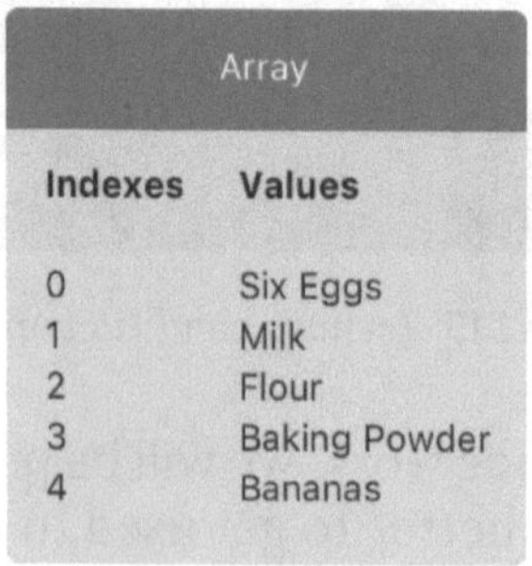

Array	
Indexes	**Values**
0	Six Eggs
1	Milk
2	Flour
3	Baking Powder
4	Bananas

Figure 1.17: Array visualization

It's such a famous concept that we programmers have a joke that we start counting from 0, not 1. We access an array value by the syntax: **ArrayName[index]**. And if we want to change its inside value, we just use the assign operator: **ArrayName[index] = newValue**. We also use **count – 1** to access the last index: .count is a property available with all Collection Types and will return the length of it. We substract 1 because Array index starts from 0.

We use **.append()** above to add more items to the end of an Array. There are other modifications such as adding more items or removing item(s) from an Array. All are available inside Swift Language, and you will easily find them with just a simple search on Google.

One more thing to note here is that if we want to modify or change the value of an Array, we must declare it as a Variable with **var** syntax.

When using Collection Types, most of the time, there will always be one that we want to iterate through every Element of it. In Programming, we can do this with the help of Loop.

A loop is a control flow construct that allows a block of code to be executed repeatedly. There are several types of loops in Swift, including for loops, while loops, and repeat loops.

Here is an example of using a **for** loop to iterate through our weekdays Array:

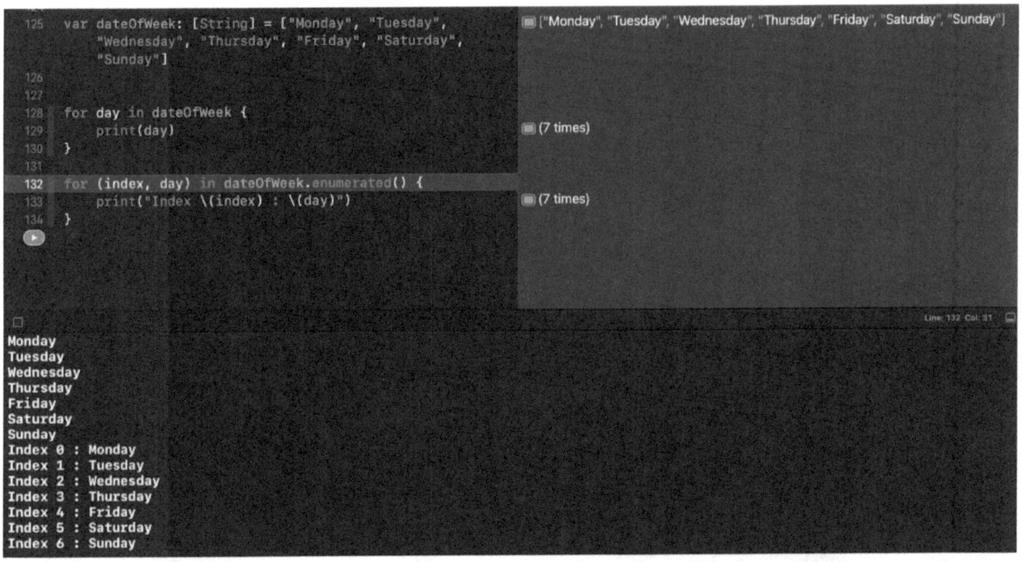

```
125    var dateOfWeek: [String] = ["Monday", "Tuesday",        ["Monday", "Tuesday", "Wednesday", "Thursday", "Friday", "Saturday", "Sunday"]
              "Wednesday", "Thursday", "Friday", "Saturday",
              "Sunday"]
126
127
128    for day in dateOfWeek {
129        print(day)                                           (7 times)
130    }
131
132    for (index, day) in dateOfWeek.enumerated() {
133        print("Index \(index) : \(day)")                     (7 times)
134    }


Monday
Tuesday
Wednesday
Thursday
Friday
Saturday
Sunday
Index 0 : Monday
Index 1 : Tuesday
Index 2 : Wednesday
Index 3 : Thursday
Index 4 : Friday
Index 5 : Saturday
Index 6 : Sunday
```

Figure 1.18: For loop

There are two ways to use a **for** loop here. One is where we only need the value, and the other is where we also need its index position. And we can get both returned to us by `.enumerated()`. These two ways are the most use cases, so, keep that in your mind. Now, let's move on to discuss our next Collection Type: Dictionary.

Collection type – Dictionary

Definition: The first thing to imply here is that, unlike an Array, a Dictionary is an unordered list. This means the value we store in them will not be in the same order each time we retrieve them.

Each element of a Dictionary will be a key-value pair. Each value is associated with a unique key, which acts as an identifier for that value within the dictionary. You use a dictionary when you need to look up values based on their identifier, in much the same way that a real-world dictionary is used to look up the definition for a particular word. Dictionaries are a powerful tool for storing data, and they're particularly useful when you need to look up values quickly:

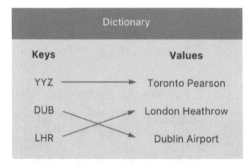

Figure 1.19: *Dictionary visualization*

Here's an example of how to create a dictionary in Swift:

```
// Favourite Fruit of our friends
var names: [String : String] = ["Anna": "Apple",      ["Craig": "Coconut", "Anna": "Apple", "Brian": "Banana"]
    "Brian": "Banana", "Craig": "Coconut"]

// Anna Favorite Fruit
let favoriteFruit = names["Anna"]                      "Apple"

// Check mine, unexisted yet
let myFavoriteFruit = names["James"]                   nil

// Adding my Favorite Fruit
names["James"] = "Watermelon"                          "Watermelon"
names                                                  ["Craig": "Coconut", "Brian": "Banana", "James": "Watermelon", "Anna": "Apple"]

// Update Anna favourite fruit
names["Anna"] = "Orange"                               "Orange"
names                                                  ["Craig": "Coconut", "Brian": "Banana", "James": "Watermelon", "Anna": "Orange"]

// Remove Brian favourite fruit
names["Brian"] = nil                                   nil
names                                                  ["Craig": "Coconut", "James": "Watermelon", "Anna": "Orange"]
```

Figure 1.20: *Dictionary example*

In this example, the dictionary is a collection of names and their corresponding favorite fruits. The keys are the names (Anna, Brian, and Craig), which are of type **String**, and the values are the favorite fruits ("Apple", "Banana", and "Coconut"), which are also **String**.

We can then access and check the inside value using a specific key. If it is does not exist yet, like in my case, then Swift will return **nil**. Later, there are commonly used actions, just like in an Array, including adding, updating, and removing value. Now to iterate through a Dictionary, we can use the same syntax with a **for** loop, just like we have already done with an Array. However, because a Dictionary is an unordered list, every time we run the loop, the order of each element will be different. And instead of an index to find where the value is located, Dictionary will have a key to do that.

There are several key differences between Array and Dictionary that can influence when you might choose to use one over the other. Here are some factors to consider:

- **Access time**: Arrays are index-based, so you can access elements in an array quickly by their position in the array. Dictionaries, on the other hand, are key-based, so you access values by looking up the key. In general, it's faster to look up a value in a dictionary than it is to search through an array for a particular value.

- **Ordering**: Arrays maintain the order of their elements, so if you need to preserve the order of your items, an array might be a better choice. Dictionaries, on the other hand, do not maintain the order of their key-value pairs.

- **Uniqueness**: Arrays can contain multiple copies of the same value, but dictionary keys must be unique. If you need to ensure that there are no duplicate values in your collection, a dictionary might be a better choice.

Overall, you should choose an array when you need an ordered collection of values that may contain duplicates, or when you need to store values of different types. You should choose a dictionary when you need to look up values quickly using a unique key, or when you need to ensure that there are no duplicate keys in your collection.

There is one more Collection Type in Swift: Set. We won't be covering it here, but if you have time, take a look at it. It has some very interesting and special characteristics.

And well, that's quite a whole lot of knowledge. So, take some rest before we jump into one of the most important building block Concept of Programming: Function.

Function

So far, we have discussed ways of storing Data. In App Development and Programming itself, almost everything we do can be simplified into either Storing Data or Processing Data.

Data can be created and stored in a variety of formats, such as variables, arrays, dictionaries, databases, or in some kind of complicated Data Structure. Programmers use different Data Structures to store data efficiently and retrieve it quickly. There is no such perfect solution, each has pros and cons. And being able to choose the suitable one for the specific circumstance is a crucial skill of a good programmer.

Processing data is another crucial aspect of programming. After being created or stored, Data then is often processed to make it more useful or to perform some action. Common operations include sorting, searching, filtering, and transforming data. This step is the main purpose of Function.

Definition: In programming, a function is a block of code that performs a specific task. Functions are often used to encapsulate a specific piece of functionality, making it easier to understand and maintain large and complex codebases.

We have already seen and used some of Swift's built-in functions previously, such as **append()**, which receives an Element and performs the action to add it at the end position of an Array.

When coding, just like with variables, we will frequently make our own function. We give a function a name that identifies what it does, and this name is used to *call* the function to perform its task when needed. Functions can take one or more inputs (also called parameters or arguments) and return one or more outputs (or return values).

Here's an example of a function that can append two elements at the same time:

```
157   var alphabetArray = ["a", "b", "c"]                           ["a", "b", "c"]
158
159   // Define a Function that can append 2 Element
160   func append2Element(element1: String, element2: String) {
161       alphabetArray.append(element1)                            ["a", "b", "c", "d"]
162       alphabetArray.append(element2)                            ["a", "b", "c", "d", "e"]
163   }
164
165   // Execute by calling it
166   append2Element(element1: "d", element2: "e")
167   alphabetArray                                                 ["a", "b", "c", "d", "e"]
```

Figure 1.21: define and call a function

Again, because Swift is a type-safe language, when declaring two input parameters (**element1** and **element2**) for this function, we have to specify which type they are.

A function can return one or more outputs (or return values) after its execution. We do this by using the **return** keyword:

```
169    // Define a function to add 2 value
170    func add2ValueWithReturn(a: Int, b: Int) -> Int {
171        return a + b
172
173        // Won't be execute
174        a * b                        ⚠ Code after 'return' will never be executed
175    }
176
177    let result1 = add2ValueWithReturn(a: 1, b: 2)
178    result1
179
180    func add2ValueNoReturn(a: Int, b: Int) {
181        a + b
182    }
183
184    let result2 = add2ValueNoReturn(a: 1, b: 2)  ⚠ Constant 'result2'...
185    result2
```

Figure 1.22: *Using return keywords with function*

Many newcomers have some confusion about the return concept. So here are two examples of adding two value functions: one with return and another without. In both cases, the action of a + b is being executed. The difference depends on whether we want to save/store the result for later usage: **result1** will have a value, and **result2** will not. Because after execution, things will be lost unless we return and store them. Also, do notice the syntax of **add2ValueWithReturn**, after the closing **)**:

-> Int. This means that this function will return an Int value. Just like parameters, a return value must have a specific Type when we define a function.

Anything after the **return** keyword won't be executed. Because of this characteristic, when combined with the if-else condition, things become very neat and flexible.

Another benefit of using functions is that they allow you to organize your code into logical, reusable blocks. You can use functions to group together related code and then call that function whenever you need to perform that specific task. This is the DRY principle (Don't repeat yourself), which is a software development principle that states that similar or identical code should be refactored into a single function or class, rather than duplicated. This can make your code more readable, maintainable, and testable.

Functions can also be nested, meaning a function can call another function within it to create more complex logic. In the preceding example, **append()** is also a function being called inside our custom one.

In Swift, functions are first-class citizens, which means they can be treated like any other value, such as an Integer or a String. This means that functions can be assigned to variables, passed as arguments to other functions, and returned as the output of a function. This allows for powerful functional programming constructs, such as higher-order functions and closures.

Bear in mind that it will be difficult to grasp this Concept even for experienced programming. The important part to take away here is that Swift function can be used just like a variable.

Here is an example:

```
188   func doSomething(fn: (Int) -> Int, x: Int) -> Int {
189       let result = fn(x)                                    ◼ 20
190       return result                                         ◼ 20
191   }
192
193   // This is the function that will be passed as an argument
194   func double(x: Int) -> Int {
195       return x * 2                                          ◼ 20
196   }
197
198   // Now we can call `doSomething` and pass the `double` function
          as an argument
199   let resultsOfDoSomething = doSomething(fn: double, x: 10)  ◼ 20
200   resultsOfDoSomething                                      ◼ 20
201   // Output: Result: 20
```

Figure 1.23: *use function as a parameter of another function*

In this example, the **doSomething** function takes two arguments as follows:

- a function fn that takes an **Int** and returns an **Int**
- an Int x

When we call **doSomething(fn: double, x: 10)**, we pass the double function as the argument for **fn** and 10 as the argument for x. Inside the **doSomething** function, we call the **fn** function with the argument x and assign the result to a variable result. Finally, we return the result.

Once again, this is a hard-to-grasp concept and will require a lot of practice in coding. So, for now, let's focus on the question: Why are we doing this? What are the benefits we have when function are first-class citizens? It's always best to understand the Purpose before jumping into learning and doing.

There are several benefits of using functions as first-class citizens in a programming language, such as the ability to pass functions as arguments to other functions. Some of the key benefits include:

- **Code Reusability**: You can write a function that takes other functions as arguments, and use that function in multiple places in your code, making your code more reusable.

- **Code Composability**: You can write small, simple functions that do one thing well, and then compose them together to create more complex functionality. This allows for a more modular and maintainable codebase.

- **Abstraction**: By passing functions as arguments, you can abstract away the implementation details of a certain piece of functionality, making it easier to reason about and understand.

- **Declarative Programming**: By expressing computation in terms of function composition, it allows you to focus on what you want to accomplish rather than how to accomplish it, making your code more readable and maintainable.

- **Functional Programming**: The ability to pass functions as arguments is a key feature of functional programming, which is a programming paradigm that emphasizes immutability, pure functions, and function composition. Functional programming can make your code more predictable, easier to test, and less prone to errors.

These are just a few examples of the benefits of using functions as first-class citizens in a programming language. It can be a powerful tool for writing clean, maintainable, and reusable code.

Now, remember earlier when we introduced SwiftUI, that it is a Declarative framework. To be able to achieve it, Functional Programming is the crucial part. We will see it all over the place when we do SwiftUI coding. However, there is one more Concept.

Closure: In Swift, a closure is a self-contained block of functionality that can be passed around and used in your code. A function is also a closure in Swift. Closures can be defined using the { } syntax and can capture variables from the surrounding context:

```
197
198    // Now we can call `doSomething` and pass the `double` function as an
           argument
199    let resultsOfDoSomething = doSomething(fn: double, x: 10)        ▣ 20
200    resultsOfDoSomething                                             ▣ 20
201    // Output: Result: 20
202
203    // Now with Closure, we can pass it Directly without have to define a
           double function
204    let resultsOfDoSomethingClosure = doSomething(fn: { (x: Int) in return x   ▣ (2 times)
           * 2 }, x: 10)
205    resultsOfDoSomethingClosure                                      ▣ 20
```

Figure 1.24: *Use closure as a parameter of another function*

We redo the same example using a closure. With it, we don't have to predefine the double function. In Swift, closure comes with many syntactic sugars, and things can get pretty complex. Here is still the same code:

```
203   // Now with Closure, we can pass it Directly without have to define a
         double function
204   let resultsOfDoSomethingClosure = doSomething(fn: { $0 * 2 }, x: 10)    ▨ (2 times)
205   resultsOfDoSomethingClosure                                             ▨ 20
   ▶
```

Figure 1.25: *Syntactic sugar for closure*

This will be also hard to grasp and will take a lot of practice. But don't worry about those shortcuts if they confuse you, those two are the same. The most important thing is readability, which is a priority for us programmers. Over time, every programmer will learn that code is written to be read by ourselves or our peer programmers in the future. So, don't confuse your future self and write clear, easy-to-read code, and add comments for better understanding. No one blames you for a couple of more lines. Now, let's understand the benefits that closure brings.

Closures have several benefits in Swift programming as follows:

- **Conciseness**: Closures allow you to write concise, expressive code that is easy to read and understand. They can also help to reduce the amount of boilerplate code you need to write.

- **Flexibility**: Closures can be passed around as arguments, making it easy to write code that can be reused in multiple places. This allows for more flexible and modular code.

- **Abstraction**: Closures can help to abstract away complex logic and make your code more readable. You can use closures to encapsulate a specific piece of functionality and then pass it around your codebase, making it easy to understand what the code is doing.

- **Asynchronous programming**: Closures are commonly used in asynchronous programming, such as in completion handlers and callbacks. Closures can be used to pass code that will be executed when an asynchronous task completes, making it easy to handle the results of the task.

- **Higher-Order Function**: Closures can be used in higher-order functions like map, filter, reduce, and so on, which makes the code more readable, shorter and easy to understand.

- **Memory management**: Closure capture list allows you to control the memory management of closure by specifying the relationship between the closure and the objects it references.

Well, this section sure has a lot to capture, and we are sure it will always be a great place to come back to later. This is because SwiftUI is a Declarative framework based on Functional Programming. We talked about Function and their importance. We used them to encapsulate a specific piece of functionality, making it easier to understand and maintain.

In Swift, functions are first-class citizens, which means they can be treated like any other value of a variable. A function can be a parameter of another function and can be passed around just like a Variable. Closure, in short, can be thought of as an anonymous function. A block of code being passed around without needing to be predefined. Let's talk about a related Concept to Function and Variable: Scope.

Scope

In programming, scope refers to the parts of the code where a variable, function, or other identifier is accessible. The scope of an identifier determines where it can be used and accessed.

In Swift, there are two main types of scope: global scope and local scope.

- **Global scope**: Identifiers defined at the global level, outside of any function or class, have global scope. These identifiers can be accessed from anywhere in the code.

- **Local scope**: Identifiers defined inside a function or class have local scope. These identifiers can only be accessed within the function or class where they are defined.

It's important to understand the scope of an identifier because it can have an impact on the way your code behaves and can also help you to avoid naming conflicts and other issues that can arise when multiple identifiers have the same name.

Figure 1.26 gives us an example of scope in Swift:

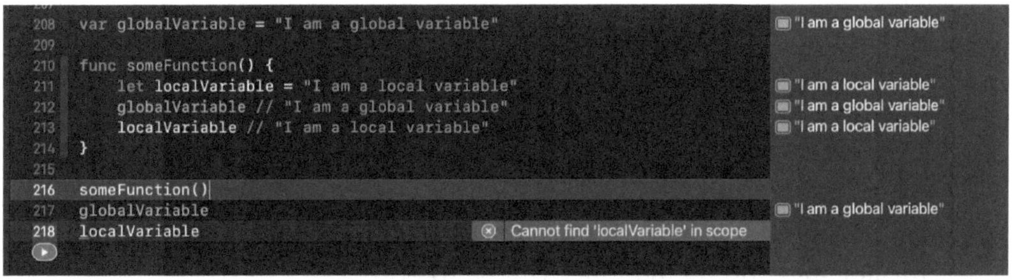

Figure 1.26: *Scope in Swift*

In this example, **globalVariable** is defined at the global level, outside of any function or class, and therefore has global scope. It can be accessed from anywhere in the code. **localVariable** is defined inside the **someFunction()** function and therefore has local scope. It can only be accessed within the function where it is defined.

When we try to access **localVariable** outside of the **someFunction()** function, we get an error because the variable is not defined in that scope.

Additionally, Swift has block-level scope, which means that identifiers defined inside a block of code, such as a loop or an if statement, have a scope that is limited to that block:

```
220  if true {
221      let blockVariable = "I am a block variable"          ■ "I am a block variable"
222      blockVariable // "I am a block variable"             ■ "I am a block variable"
223  }
224
225  // Error: blockVariable is not defined in this scope
226  blockVariable                    ⊗  Cannot find 'blockVariable' in scope
```

Figure 1.27: *Outside of scope*

In this example, **blockVariable** is defined inside the if statement block and can only be accessed within that block. Once the if statement is completed, the variable will not be available in the outer scope.

Simple but bringing many benefits to programming include:

- **Organization**: Scope helps to organize your code by keeping related identifiers together and separate from other identifiers that may have the same name. This makes it easier to understand and maintain your code.

- **Clarity**: By controlling the scope of identifiers, you can make your code more readable and clearer. This makes it easier to identify the purpose and use of each identifier, and can help to prevent naming conflicts and other issues.

- **Reusability**: By controlling the scope of identifiers, you can make your code more reusable. For example, by keeping the scope of a variable or function local, you can make it specific to a particular use case, and reuse it in other parts of the code.

- **Memory Management**: Block-level scope helps to manage the memory usage of the variable. Once the block is completed, the variable will be deallocated and the memory will be freed.

- **Modularity**: By controlling the scope of identifiers, you can make your code more modular. For example, by keeping the scope of a variable or function internal, you can make it accessible only within the module it is defined, and not outside of it, making the code more secure.

- **Encapsulation**: By controlling the scope of identifiers, you can use encapsulation to hide implementation details and protect the internal state of an object, making it more robust and less prone to errors.

The best practice here is to always avoid using global scope. Declare things at the scope level that is needed only. It sounds simple, and it really is. Just remember this whenever writing new code, all the benefits will come, from Better Performance to clarity and cleanliness of the codebase.

The scope of an identifier can also be controlled by the access level (`public`, `internal`, `fileprivate`, `private`) of the identifier, which defines the parts of the code where it can be accessed. We will cover all of these in the next section when we will discuss it.

Struct

Struct is an important concept of Swift Language and will be a crucial part when developing in SwiftUI. As a result of this, this section will require a lot of focus from you, readers.

Structures/Struct and later classes/class are general-purpose, flexible constructs that become the building blocks of our program's code. We define properties and methods to add functionality to our structures and classes using the same syntax we use to define constants, variables, and functions.

Previously, we have created a lot of variables to store Data. However, here is a case to think about: What if we want Data to store all the needed information about a Student? This includes their name, age, height, weight, all scores of the semester, and so on. Of course, we can create separate variables for each metric, but it will be hard to track them later. As a result, general-purpose Data Structures like Struct exist to store related data for us to freely customize. We will talk about struct first and then class later, and discuss their main differences.

Think about struct like our own customized type. Unlike Int, where we have to input an Integer, with struct, we declare what will be needed and package them in one place for later usage.

Here, we declare a **Student** struct as shown in *Figure* 1.28:

```
struct Student {
    let id: String              // Student ID
    let name: String            // Student Name
    let isMale: Bool            // Student gender: Male or Female
    var age: Int                // Student Age
    var scores: [String : Double]  // Ex: Math : 9.1
}

var studentJohn = Student(
    id: UUID().uuidString,
    name: "John",
    isMale: true,
    age: 23,
    scores: [
        "Math" : 9,
        "Physic" : 8.4,
        "Computer Science" : 8.5
    ]
)
```

```
id "F0DC3CBE-8E5F-4D30-9F06-E5E3935(
name "John"
isMale true
age 23
v ["Math": 9, "Physic": 8.4, "Computer Science
  > (key "Math", value 9)
  > (key "Physic", value 8.4)
  > (key "Computer Science", value 8.5)
```

Figure 1.28: *Define and use Struct*

We define a **Student** struct starting with the keyword struct. Inside it, we declare its properties, such as **id**, **name**, **isMale**, **age**, and **scores**. Then, later, we create **studentJohn**, which is an Instance of struct Student. Let's go through all these terms one by one.

Instance: an instance refers to a specific occurrence of a class or struct. It is an object created at runtime from a class or struct definition, with its own unique set of data and behavior. The properties and methods defined in the class or struct are available to be used by the instance. Instances are created using the initializer method of the class or struct.

For better visualization, think of a struct or class as a **Blueprint** from which you create objects. Here, a **Car** or **Student** struct/class is a blueprint that describes what it will have or need. Then, from it, we can create specific object/instances like **studentJohn** or **studentJames**, or an Audi card, Nissan car, and Volvo car (*Figure* 1.29).

Figure 1.29: *Struct / Class vs Instance / Object*

Properties associate values with a particular class or struct. Also, we can make them variables and constants. Again, avoid variable when it is unnecessary. We can get access to Instance properties using the "." syntax:

```
248
249
250                                                                      id "F0DC3CBE-8E5F-4D30-9F06-E5E3935(
251                                                                      name "John"
252                                                                      isMale true
253    studentJohn.age = 24                                              age  24
254    studentJohn.isMale = false    ⊙ Cannot assign to property: 'isMale' is a 'let' const  ["Math": 9, "Physic": 8.4, "Computer Scienc
255
256
257
258
```

Figure 1.30: *Accessing instance's properties*

Here, we access and change the age of John because it is a variable. However, we can't change **isMale** because we declare it as a constant.

Just like value, we can also associate specific functions with a particular class or struct. When this happens, we call those functions methods:

```
229    struct Student {
230        let id: String                    // Student ID
231        let name: String                  // Student Name
232        let isMale: Bool                  // Student gender: Male or Female
233        var age: Int                      // Student Age
234        var scores: [String : Double]     // Ex: Math : 9.1
235
236        func singASong() -> String {
237            return name + " sing a Song"                            "John sing a Song"
238        }
239
240        mutating func increaseAge(number: Int) {
241            age = age + number                                      Student
242        }
243    }
244
245    var studentJohn = Student(                                      Student
246        id: UUID().uuidString,
247        name: "John",
248        isMale: true,
249        age: 23,
250        scores: [
251            "Math" : 9,
252            "Physic" : 8.4,
253            "Computer Science" : 8.5
254        ]
255    )
256
257    studentJohn.singASong()                                         "John sing a Song"
258    studentJohn.increaseAge(number: 5)                             Student
259    studentJohn.age                                                 28
```

Figure 1.31: *Usage of mutating keyword*

Here, we define two functions, **singASong** and **increaseAge** , and call them with a **.** keyword. Note the difference here is the appearance of mutating syntax. Both functions are using their property, but when we want to change the properties of the **Instance: age** here, we have to mark the function increaseAge with the perquisite keyword mutating.

Now, remember from the previous section where we mentioned the five keywords: **open**, **public**, **internal**, **fileprivate**, **private** with accessing level. Let's have some discussion about them here.

In the Swift programming language, there are five levels of access control as follows:

- **Open**: The least restrictive access level, which allows entities to be sub classed and overridden within the current module and also in other modules that import the module where the entity is defined. This access level is typically used for public interfaces that need to be accessible outside the defining module.

- **Public**: Similar to **Open**, but it doesn't allow entities to be sub classed or overridden outside the module where they are defined. However, entities marked as **public** can still be accessed from other modules.

- **Internal**: The default access level if none is specified. Entities with internal access are accessible within the module where they are defined but not outside of it.

- **Fileprivate**: Entities marked with **fileprivate** are accessible only within the same Swift source file where they are defined. This is useful for restricting access to implementation details that should not be exposed outside the file.

- **Private**: The most restrictive access level, which limits access to the enclosing declaration (class, struct, or extension). Entities marked as **private** can only be accessed within the scope of the enclosing declaration.

By default, classes, structs, enums, and members are considered internal, unless explicitly specified otherwise.

Now, *Accessible from the same module* means that the class, struct, enum, or member can be accessed from any source file within the same module in which it is defined, but not from outside of that module.

In Swift, a module is a single unit of code distribution, such as a framework or application bundle, which can be imported by another module using the import keyword. It defines a namespace, and all the entities (types, functions, variables, and so on) defined within a module are scoped to that module.

For example, if you have an internal struct called **MyStruct** defined in a framework called **MyFramework**, other parts of **MyFramework** can access **MyStruct**. However, if you have another module that imports **MyFramework**, it won't be able to access **MyStruct**.

In summary:

- **open**: The most permissive access level in Swift, allowing entities to be subclassed and overridden both within the current module and other importing modules.

- **public**: Access level allowing entities to be accessed from other modules but not subclassed or overridden outside the defining module.

- **internal**: The default access level, enabling entities to be accessible within the same module but not from outside modules.

- **fileprivate**: Restricts access to entities within the same Swift source file.

- **private**: The most restrictive access level, limiting access to the enclosing declaration (class, struct, or extension).

Enumeration: **enum** is a very interesting concept that can be used very effectively with switch cases. We will talk and code about them in a later chapter.

Next, for the end of this chapter, we will briefly go through Class and discuss their main difference with struct. Class and **OOP (Object Oriented Programming)** are very important concepts in programming.

Class and Class vs Struct

Class is also a general-purpose, flexible construct and the blueprint for the Instance/Object. Let's make a Student with Class, similar to the above example:

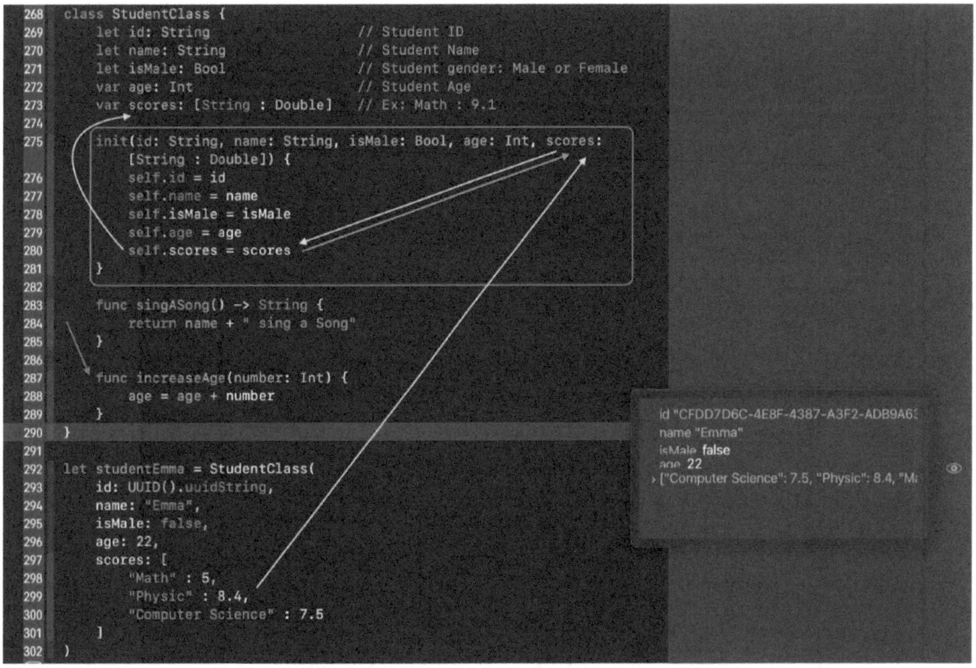

```
class StudentClass {
    let id: String            // Student ID
    let name: String          // Student Name
    let isMale: Bool          // Student gender: Male or Female
    var age: Int              // Student Age
    var scores: [String : Double]   // Ex: Math : 9.1

    init(id: String, name: String, isMale: Bool, age: Int, scores:
        [String : Double]) {
        self.id = id
        self.name = name
        self.isMale = isMale
        self.age = age
        self.scores = scores
    }

    func singASong() -> String {
        return name + " sing a Song"
    }

    func increaseAge(number: Int) {
        age = age + number
    }
}

let studentEmma = StudentClass(
    id: UUID().uuidString,
    name: "Emma",
    isMale: false,
    age: 22,
    scores: [
        "Math" : 5,
        "Physic" : 8.4,
        "Computer Science" : 7.5
    ]
)
```

id "CFDD7D6C-4E8F-4387-A3F2-ADB9A6{
name "Emma"
isMale false
age 22
> ["Computer Science": 7.5, "Physic": 8.4, "M{

Figure 1.32: *Define and use Class in Swift*

Here, we define **StudentClass** as a Blueprint of a Student, and just like **studentJohn** in the previous example, we can now create **studentEmma** with the same syntax, and everything looks just the same from the outside. Before we go into detail, let's point out two differences compared with the Struct declare syntax:

- Initialization: now both class and struct also require initialization. It is a method/function that is used to set up or prepare an object for use. "**init**" special keyword in Swift so we don't need the **func** keyword, but it is a function. Inside it we declare the required parameters for this class. Now inside a class or struct, the keyword **self** refers to the Instance/ Object of it. So, inside the init function on the left side follow the yellow arrow we are referring to its properties and assign it ("=") with the value on the right side follow the green one we are the parameters of the function. Later, we create studentEmma the init function will be call to set up all required data. The data will flow with the way of the three yellow arrows. So, the question you may ask here is why don't we write this **init** when we define **Student** Struct on previous Examples. The answer is that in Swift, struct comes with a prebuilt init for use so we don't have to rewrite it, quite convenient. And yes, if you want to write it yourself then you absolutely can.

- Noticing that we don't need the keyword mutating for the increaseAge function anymore. The functionality of these two are the same and both will increase the age. But the reason behind this is also one the main difference between Class and Struct. In Swift, Struct is **immutable** and Class is **mutable**. By this we mean whenever we change a property of an Instance of Struct, the old Instance will be destroyed and the new one will be created in replacement. On the opposite, the Instance of the Class is still the same when their properties value changed.

Here are some of the key differences between structs and classes in Swift:

- **Value vs Reference Type**s: Structs are value types, which means that when they are assigned to a variable or constant, a copy of the struct is made. Classes, on the other hand, are reference types, which means that when they are assigned to a variable or constant, a reference to the original class is stored.

- **Mutability**: By default, structs properties are considered to be immutable, while class properties are mutable.

- **Inheritance**: Structs do not have inheritance and cannot be subclassed, whereas classes can be subclassed and inherit from other classes.

- **Initializers**: Structs automatically get a memberwise initializer for initializing their properties, whereas classes do not. Classes require you to write your own initializer for initializing their properties.

- **Deinitializer**: Classes have deinitializer method, but structs do not.

- **Reference Counting**: Classes use reference counting to manage memory, whereas structs do not.

- **Efficiency**: Accessing properties of structs is generally faster than accessing properties of classes because of the value type nature.

Now, this is a must-have question in every iOS interview. So, it is a suggestion to all readers to take more time and research/dive deeper on this topic. In general, structs are best used for simple data structures that do not need inheritance or complex behavior, while classes are more appropriate for complex data structures that need inheritance and advanced behavior.

Well, that's a lot for this chapter. I hope this will be a great resource to come back to not only when you are reading this book but also later in development.

If you want to dive deeper into the Swift Language, then we highly suggest starting with Apple's Swift Language Book, Which is available for free at: **https://docs.swift.org/swift-book/**. You can also download it to your iPhone / iPad through the Book App.

In the next chapter, we will discover the most fundamental building block of SwiftUI: View.

CHAPTER 2
Introduction to View in SwiftUI

Introduction

In this chapter, we will learn about the Layout concept and ideas in SwiftUI and understand how to break out complex UI into small and reusable pieces. By the end of this Chapter, readers are expected to be comfortable when facing a new Scene or UI Element. Let's get started.

The magic sentence here to remember is: Building layout in SwiftUI is like Lego Blocks. We build each piece and assemble it.

Structure

In this chapter, the following topics will be covered:

- Fundamental views in SwiftUI
- Container views: VStack, HStack and ZStack
- Build a simple layout from SwiftUI components
- What is the view and protocol in SwiftUI?
- Introducing View Modifier and View Builder

Fundamental view

Let's start with a simple example. Let's say we want to create a Renting Card Component, which will have the following layout:

Figure 2.1: *The card layout*

This is the design we want, but where to get started? And how do we tackle any design layout in SwiftUI? Well, once again, think about it like Lego blocks. A big complex layout is a combination of many small pieces. To have a big piece, let's build each small piece:

Figure 2.2: *Behind the screen of the card*

Here, with the colors highlighted for better visualization, we can see how each small component is placed to form the final Design. Two red and yellow texts are placed vertically inside the green area. The orange image and blue circle are placed on top of each other. And those three green and blue areas are placed horizontally with each other.

This can be easily achieved with the help of the three most common and basic built-in View in SwiftUI: VStack, HStack, and ZStack.

These are three stack views in SwiftUI that are used to arrange views in a vertical, horizontal, and overlapping manner, respectively:

VStack (vertical stack) arranges views vertically, one after the other:

Figure 2.3: *Vertical stack*

HStack (horizontal stack) arranges views horizontally, side by side:

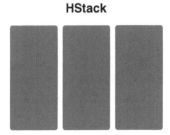

Figure 2.4: *Horizontal stack*

ZStack (z-axis stack) arranges views on top of each other, with the last view added being on top of the stack:

Figure 2.5: *Z-axis stack*

With this new knowledge, let's open up XCode and build this renting card:

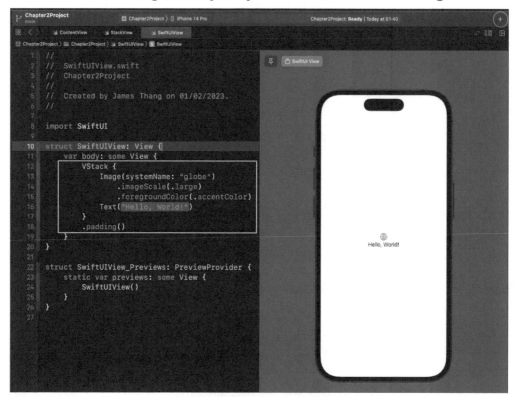

Figure 2.6: *New project*

This is how every new project initially appears when it is created. Now, we clearly understand what is going on here. There is a VStack containing an Image and a Text: "Hello, World!". And that's everything for now, and it is reflected in the live preview on the right side. And just like with VStack, Image and Text are built-in views for convenient usage in SwiftUI. Image is used for loading and displaying an image, and text is used to display a string.

Now, you may wonder how we knew about this. What about other built-in view and their usage? Well, see that plus button inside the red circle, you can click on it and explore more. Select the first tab, and there you have a list of all common built-in views with detailed documentation from Apple. There are also examples and detailed explanations. With SwiftUI, Apple has done a great job providing detailed documentation. So, explore and read around because there are many powerful components like **Button**, **Date Picker**, **Color Picker**, and those are the power of SwiftUI.

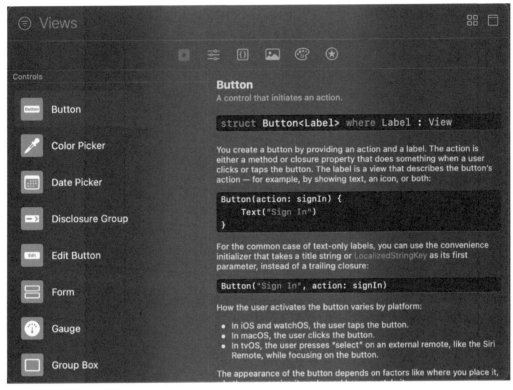

Figure 2.7: *SwiftUI documentation interface for views*

One more point to note here is that while developing an app or programming, there will be **times** when we want to build some feature but don't know where to start. Well, **just** Google it or ask on Stack Overflow. For example, instead of an Image, how **about** displaying a video? Well, just ask, and there will be an answer.

Now, let's **build our** renting card:

Figure 2.8: *The card*

We will start with the right green area, which contains two texts vertically.

```
VStack {
    Text("House for Rent")
        .font(.title)

    Text("#0xxx123456")
        .font(.caption)
        .fontWeight(.semibold)
}
.padding(.horizontal)
```

Figure 2.9: *The green area of the card*

Notice that we use `.font()`, `.fontWeight()`, and `.padding()`. These are called view modifiers. We will explain them in detail later, but think of them like features added to views. Here, we want the two texts to have different fonts, and the smaller one to be bold. The padding modifier is to give additional horizontal spacing, which is the green space on the left and right of the red text in the picture above.

Then, let's tackle the left side, which contains an image sitting on top of a blue circle.

```
ZStack {
    Circle()
        .fill(.blue.opacity(0.75))
        .frame(width: 50, height: 50)
    Image(systemName: "house")
        .foregroundColor(.white)
}
```

Figure 2.10: *The blue area of the card*

As we are already aware that SwiftUI is a Declarative programming, you can clearly see here that the code is very descriptive and self-explainable. We have a ZStack with a Circle and an Image, and the order of placement is in the direction of the red arrow, so the Image will stand on top of a circle.

Circle is a Shape, which is a special type of View. There are many convenient built-in Shapes in SwiftUI, such as Circle, Rectangle, RoundedRectangle, Capsule, Ellipse, etc. These have many use cases to create modern style design.

Image is used to load and represent an Image in SwiftUI. Here, we are loading a system Image named house and presenting it. Now, Apple has provided developers with a collection of vector icons that are very neat. App developers use a lot of icons in their apps. So, to see what is available to use, go to the App Store and download the SF Symbols App:

Figure 2.11: SF Symbol

Here are all the great icons with professional designs for you to use, and Apple's Developers have used them all in their apps. So, users are already familiar with them and their meanings.

Now, let's get back to our renting card. We have built the left and the right sides, and placing them horizontally is the purpose of HStack:

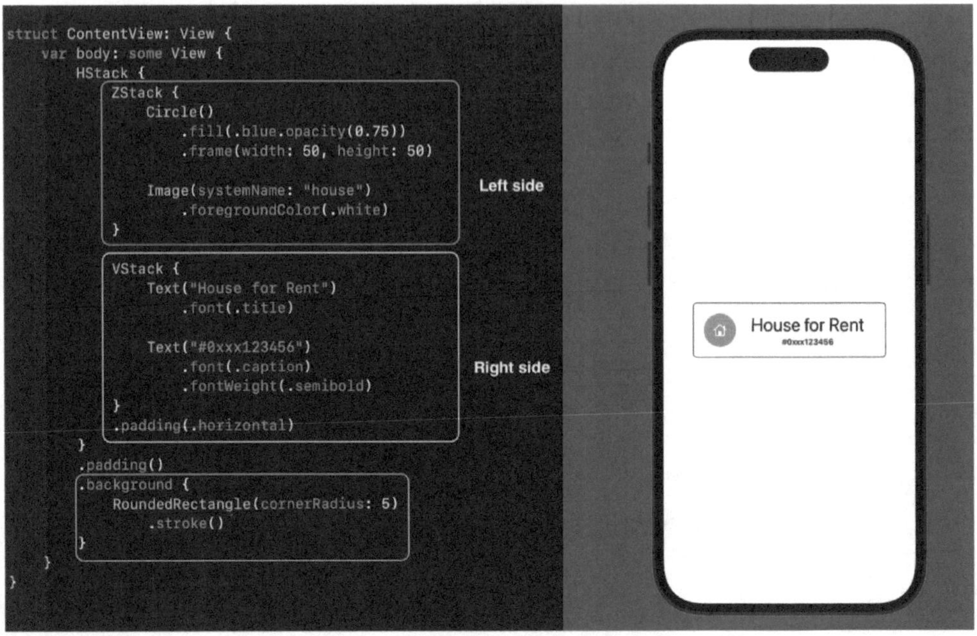

```
struct ContentView: View {
    var body: some View {
        HStack {
            ZStack {
                Circle()
                    .fill(.blue.opacity(0.75))
                    .frame(width: 50, height: 50)

                Image(systemName: "house")      Left side
                    .foregroundColor(.white)
            }

            VStack {
                Text("House for Rent")
                    .font(.title)

                Text("#0xxx123456")
                    .font(.caption)             Right side
                    .fontWeight(.semibold)
            }
            .padding(.horizontal)
        }
        .padding()
        .background {
            RoundedRectangle(cornerRadius: 5)
                .stroke()
        }
    }
}
```

Figure 2.12: *The card component's code*

Here, the `.background` modifier is added to the outside **HStack** to achieve a bounding border outside of it. We are using the **RoundedRectangle** shape with the `.stroke` modifier. You can also make another **ZStack** and place the **RoundedRectangle** behind the **HStack**, but it is unnecessary, and the `.background` modifier comes in handy in this simple case where we just need another background layer.

Remember, in the previous chapter, we mentioned that SwiftUI is functional programming. And sitting at the core of the concept is to break into small reusable components. Let's do it here.

Figure 2.13: *Making multiple instances of the card*

Here, we extract and make a **CardComponent** that represents the view of each card. Then, we can make a view with three cards vertically align easily. This is the power of SwiftUI and functional programming. However, I guess you might ask how those three renting cards have different information about different houses. We have already discussed struct and its properties. Let's exact the variable information of each card and make their properties. You can find them with the yellow arrows:

Figure 2.14: *Generalize the card*

We have extracted and made three properties that will be the input of **CardComponent: symbolName**, **title,** and **subTitle**. And with this, we have three different marketing cards for **Home**, **Cars**, and **Bikes**.

Once again, what we were doing here is the core feature of SwiftUI and functional programming. The primary goal is to make the code easier to understand, maintain, and reason about by breaking down complex problems into smaller, composable, reusable, and predictable parts. Here, **CardComponent** is such a great example of this. Inside it, you will find all the required properties and later methods. They are all wrapped into a component and ready to use anywhere in the project.

Before we continue, we find it better to pause here and try to understand more about the definition of the important concepts in SwiftUI: What is a view in SwiftUI? And what is a view modifier?

View in SwiftUI

In SwiftUI, a view is a struct that represents a visual element on the screen. It can be used to display text, images, and other content, and can be combined with other views to create more complex user interfaces. View also has the ability to handle user interactions and respond to changes in the data it displays. The View protocol is one of the core building blocks of the SwiftUI framework.

Every view in SwiftUI must conform to the View protocol. The **protocol** defines a single requirement, a body property, which returns the underlying view's content. The **body** property is a closure that returns a single view, which can be a combination of other views, arranged using various layouts and stack views.

In SwiftUI, a **protocol** is a blueprint of methods, properties, and other requirements that suit a particular task or piece of functionality. It allows you to declare what an object or struct should do, but not how it should do it, giving the implementer the flexibility to implement the protocol in their own way. SwiftUI uses protocols extensively to define the behavior and appearance of its views.

For example, **View** is a protocol in SwiftUI that defines the basic structure and behavior of all views in the framework. We can create custom views by creating a struct that conforms to the **View** protocol and implements the **body** property. You can also use various built-in views, such as **Text**, **Image**, **Button**, and many more, to create your user interface.

However, let's think about it this way in this situation: **protocol** comes with constraints and gains. By adopting a **Protocol**, there are things that we have to follow in order to gain unique functionalities.

Now, let's *Option + Right Click* on the view keyword to see more detailed information.

Remember, this is a very handy Shortcut, and you should use it whenever some keyword may look unfamiliar to you in Xcode:

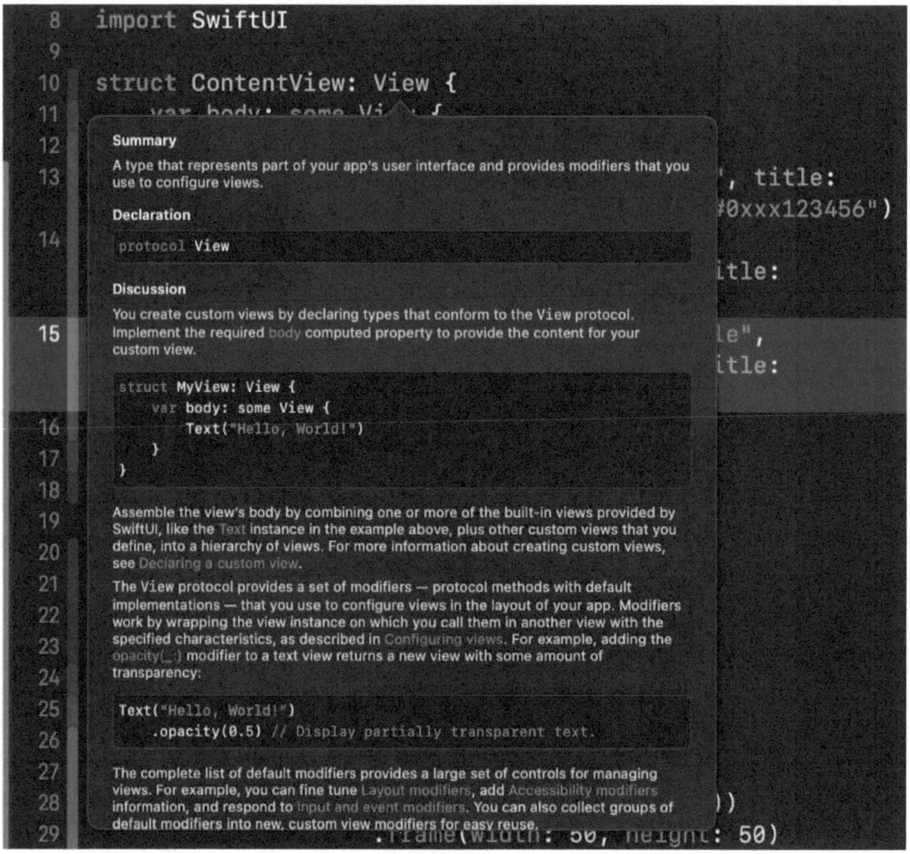

Figure 2.15: *View protocol definition*

View here is a protocol. As we have already mentioned, when something conforms to a protocol, it gains something in exchange for some constraints. Here, with view, it requires a body computed property; that's a constraint. So, what do we gain, you make ask? In the first chapter, we already discussed in detail about struct, and there is no way a struct alone can represent content layout on the screen. And this is our gain when adapting the view protocol. Believe it or not, all the heavy lifting is done behind the screen by the view protocol; all we need to do is to have a **body** property.

In Swift, the syntax of conforming to a protocol is the same as inheriting from a class. Therefore, many beginners mistake between those two.

The similarity in syntax, especially with the colon :, can cause confusion, but it's important to remember the distinction between the two concepts as follows:

- Conforming to a protocol means that a class, struct, or enumeration adopts the protocol's requirements, allowing it to provide implementations for those requirements.

- Inheriting from a class means creating a subclass that inherits properties and methods from a superclass, enabling code reuse and extension of functionality.

SwiftUI uses functional programming concepts to build user interfaces, where views are treated as functions of their state, and the UI updates automatically when the state changes. Now, state is another very important concept, and we will discuss it in detail in the next chapter. Let's look back at our renting card example to see a view as a function in SwiftUI:

Figure 2.16: *SwiftUI is functional programming*

Look at the **CardComponent** here; does it look familiar to you? It looks just like when the function is called! Now, let's look at those curly braces; they look familiar, isn't it? Remember when we talked about function and closure? A closure is a block of code wrapped inside curly braces and can be passed around or become the parameters of other function. And here it is, kind of hard to wrap your head around this concept, even for another programmer when they first encounter SwiftUI. Because of the way closure is being used here and their frequent appearance. So, I believe now you totally get it when they say that SwiftUI is a Declarative framework.

Now, to further prove it to you and anyone who may think that, well, **CardComponent** here is the **init** of a struct, so you can't say that it is a function. Let's make it become a function!

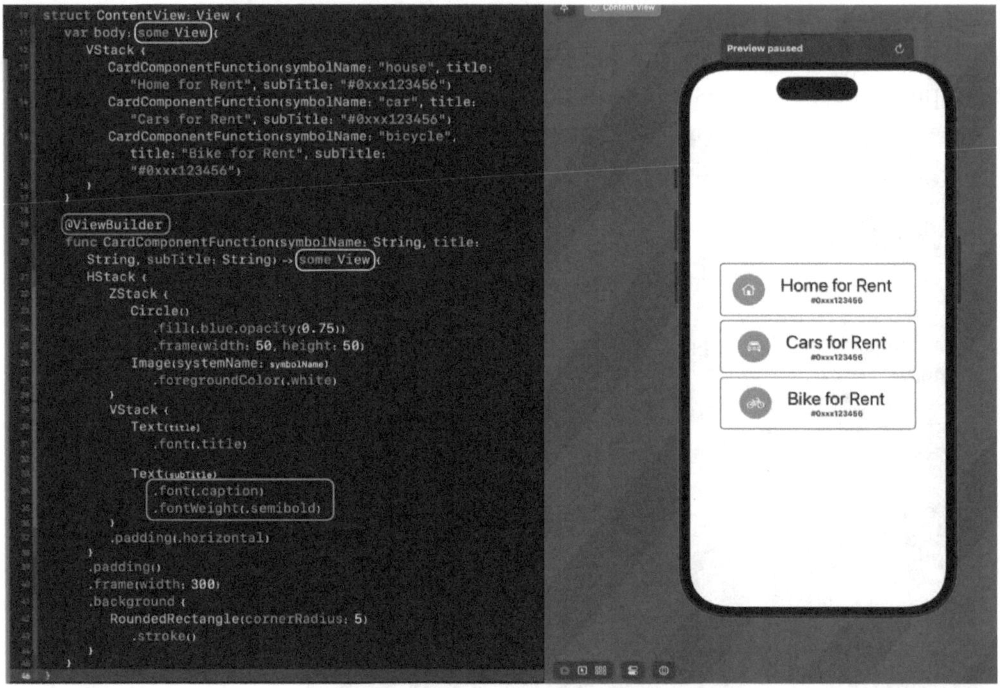

Figure 2.17: *View Builder*

It has exactly the same behavior, but this time we are using a function to make **CardComponent** View. There are two things that I want to talk about in the highlighted area above. **@ViewBuilder** is a Property Wrapper in SwiftUI. Property Wrapper is a special concept, and we will explain it in detail in the next chapter with State in SwiftUI.

Here, **@ViewBuilder** is a type of attribute that is used to annotate a closure or function that returns a view to enable it to be used as a view builder. A view builder is a mechanism for building views by composing smaller views into a larger view. By marking a closure or function with **@ViewBuilder**, you can pass it as an argument to another view and use it to build the body of the view dynamically. That is exactly what happened here with our **CardComponentFunction** function.

Next is the part **-> some View**, as we already know that after **->** specifies the return type of a function, which here is some view. It means, just like what it read here: the **CardComponentFunction** will return some kind of view. The **some** keyword allows us to return any type that conforms to view without having to specify the exact type, making the code more flexible and generic. Here, it can be any kind of View: ZStack, VStack, Text, or Image. Anything that conforms to the view protocol. Now, looking back at the body property of our struct, we also notice that its type is also some view, which means whatever is inside it has to be a View. A struct that conforms to the view protocol must return a view, which is in its body property. What kind of view? It can be any view. Next, we will talk about things inside the green area that can be added to a view: View Modifier.

View Modifier

In SwiftUI, a View Modifier is a type that defines a change to the appearance or behavior of a view. View Modifiers are used to apply styles, transformations, and other effects to a view.

They are composable, meaning that you can chain multiple modifiers together to create complex user interfaces. A modifier can also be applied to a view or another view modifier, producing a different version of the original value. This means two things: modifiers can be chained one after another like the aforementioned example of **.font()** and **.fontWeight()**. And the order matters and, depending on the circumstance, will produce different behavior with different orders.

Again, SwiftUI is a Declarative framework, and you may guess that View Modifier is also a function behind the screen. Whenever there is something unclear, let's use our shortcut on Xcode to read their documentation. Let's examine the `.frame()` modifier (*Figure 2.18*):

```
Summary
Positions this view within an invisible frame with the specified size.

Declaration
func frame(width: CGFloat? = nil, height: CGFloat? = nil,
alignment: Alignment = .center) -> some View

Discussion
Use this method to specify a fixed size for a view's width, height, or both. If you only
specify one of the dimensions, the resulting view assumes this view's sizing behavior in
the other dimension.
For example, the following code lays out an ellipse in a fixed 200 by 100 frame.
Because a shape always occupies the space offered to it by the layout system, the first
ellipse is 200x100 points. The second ellipse is laid out in a frame with only a fixed
height, so it occupies that height, and whatever width the layout system offers to its
parent.

VStack {
    Ellipse()
        .fill(Color.purple)
        .frame(width: 200, height: 100)
    Ellipse()
        .fill(Color.blue)
        .frame(height: 100)
}

The alignment parameter specifies this view's alignment within the frame.

Text("Hello world!")
    .frame(width: 200, height: 30, alignment: .topLeading)
    .border(Color.gray)
```

Figure 2.18: *Frame modifier definition*

With the *Option + Right Click* shortcut, we can view the definition of the `.frame()` modifier. As you can see, it is a function that takes three parameters: **width** and **height** are optional, and **alignment** has a default value to be center. And it returns some views.

This is exactly what every View Modifier does, and it is important to note here. The View Modifier is executed and returns a new and modified version of the view. The original view remains unchanged, and the modified view is used in place of the original view when it's rendered.

In this example, the Text view is modified using two view modifiers: **frame()** and **.border**. The frame view modifier sets the frame size of the text on the screen, and the **.border** view modifier sets the color of the border to gray:

Figure 2.19: *How view modifier works (1)*

Now, let's reverse the order of these two View Modifiers; it will result in a completely different outcome:

Figure 2.20: *How view modifier works (2)*

It is because in the first scenario, we get a text with a width of 200 and a height of 30 first. Then, we set the border of it. Now, in the second scenario, we set the border of the text first and then set the frame of the text with the border to be 200 by 30. So, now you can see why their order matters.

SwiftUI View Modifiers are very powerful tools because they can be chained together in different orders and combinations. There are many built-in ones, just like Views, so you can go and explore them yourself:

Figure 2.21: *SwiftUI documentation interface for View Modifiers*

Tap the **Plus** button and then navigate to the second tab to learn more about them and what is available for you to use.

Conclusion

In conclusion, implementing layout in SwiftUI is an essential aspect of creating visually appealing and functional user interfaces. With the wide range of layout tools and techniques provided by SwiftUI, developers have the ability to create dynamic and responsive layouts that adapt to different screen sizes and orientations.

We have learned about fundament views, including VStack, HStack, and ZStack and how views are arranged and determine their size behind the screen. Once again, we have proved that SwiftUI is functional programming. We have also learned about common view modifiers like .font and .frame, and the key thing is their order matters. We will learn more useful view modifiers in the next chapter. In the meantime, you can browse and explore all the Views and Views Modifiers that SwiftUI provides using the Xcode shortcut mentioned earlier.

Whether you are building a simple prototype or a complex application, understanding the fundamentals of layout in SwiftUI will enable you to create interfaces that are both intuitive and engaging for your users. By leveraging the power of SwiftUI's layout system, developers can focus on creating meaningful user experiences and delivering high-quality applications.

Well, that's just a lot of theory to wrap your head around. So, take some time to rest, and we will come back in the next chapter where we will talk about how layouts work in SwiftUI.

CHAPTER 3
Implementing Layout in SwiftUI

Introduction

SwiftUI is a powerful, intuitive, and declarative framework for building user interfaces in iOS, macOS, watchOS, and tvOS applications. One of the core features of SwiftUI is its layout system, which enables developers to easily define the structure and appearance of their app's user interface.

The most important aspect of building a great user interface is implementing an effective layout. SwiftUI provides a variety of layout tools and techniques that allow developers to create complex and dynamic layouts with ease. In this chapter, we will explore the fundamentals of implementing layout in SwiftUI, including the use of stacks, frames, and alignment guides. Whether you are a seasoned SwiftUI developer or just getting started, this topic will provide you with the knowledge and skills you need to create beautiful and responsive user interfaces in your applications.

Structure

In this chapter, the following topics will be covered:

- How SwiftUI chooses to layout a View

- Common Fundamental View Modifiers of SwiftUI

- The coordinate system behind every iOS App development

- Positioning vs Alignment

- Life cycle methods in iOS development

Layout in SwiftUI

In SwiftUI, the layout is performed using a declarative approach. We build our user interface by composing views and containers that define how they should be arranged on the screen.

The main layout containers in SwiftUI are as follows:

- **VStack**: A vertical stack container that arranges views vertically, one after the other, in a top-to-bottom order.

- **HStack**: A horizontal stack container that arranges views horizontally, side by side, in a left-to-right order.

- **ZStack**: A stack container that arranges views in a back-to-front order, allowing you to overlap and layer views.

- **List or ScrollView**: A container that creates a scrollable list of views, each represented by a row.

Each view in the layout can be customized to determine its size, position, and behavior. To do this, you use various layout options such as fixed sizes, flexible proportions, or manual frames. You can also apply alignment and padding to control the placement of the views within the container.

There are three steps when determining the size of a View as follows:

- A parent view proposes a size for its child

- A child then chooses its own size, and the parent must respect those choices

- The parents then place the child inside it coordinates space somehow

This allows us to create a very complicated Layout where every view decides how and when it's getting resized without the Parent having to get involved.

Let's go through some examples to get a better understanding of the preceding three steps:

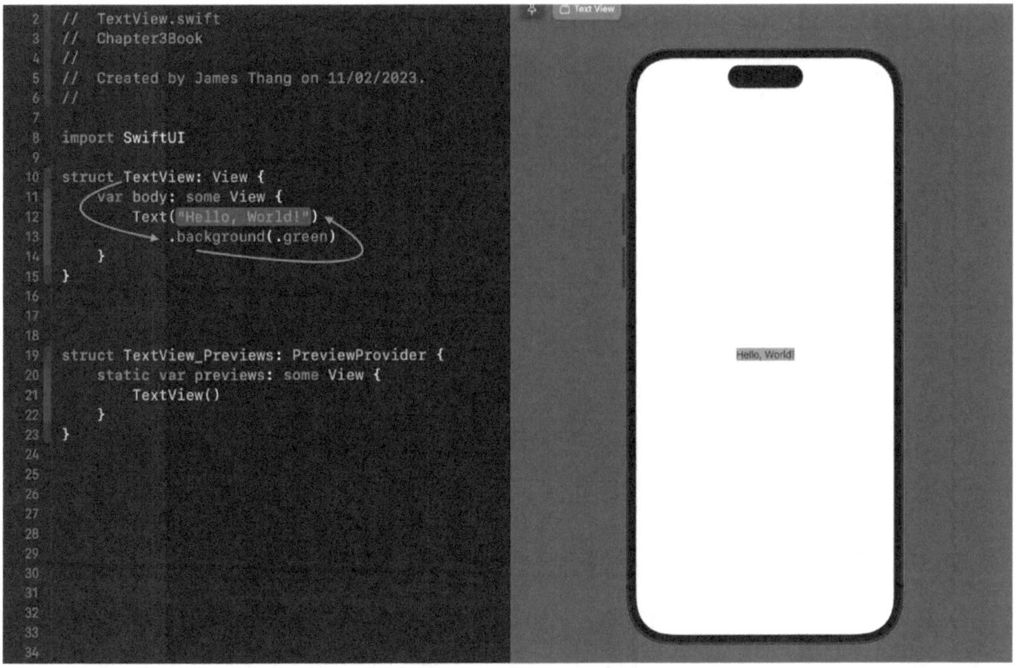

Figure 3.1: *Size of TextView*

Here, we have a text, then passing through the `.background()` modifier, which then gives us the result on the right side. The question here is how much space is in the TextView view? The answer is it is the exact space of its child. We have already learned about view modifiers and know that they transform a view passed into them into a new view because they are function.

In SwiftUI, there is a layout-neutral View that decides their size by asking its child. Here, the TextView will have the whole iPhone Screen Size available for it, but it will go and ask its children how much space it should take. Now, it will go and ask the `.background()` modifier first: How much size do you want? Again, here, the `.background()` modifier is also layout-neutral. So, it will then ask its inside child, the text, how much space it needs. The Text View in SwiftUI only needs enough space to display its content, which gives us the final result. The preceding three steps functioned as follows: the TextView had all the iPhone Screen available, and it then asked its child for the space. The Text only needs enough space for its content, so it proposes back to the Parent: the TextView. Then, the TextView layout its Contents inside the iPhone Screen, and by default, it will be center-aligned.

Now, let's add another modifier, `.padding(45)`:

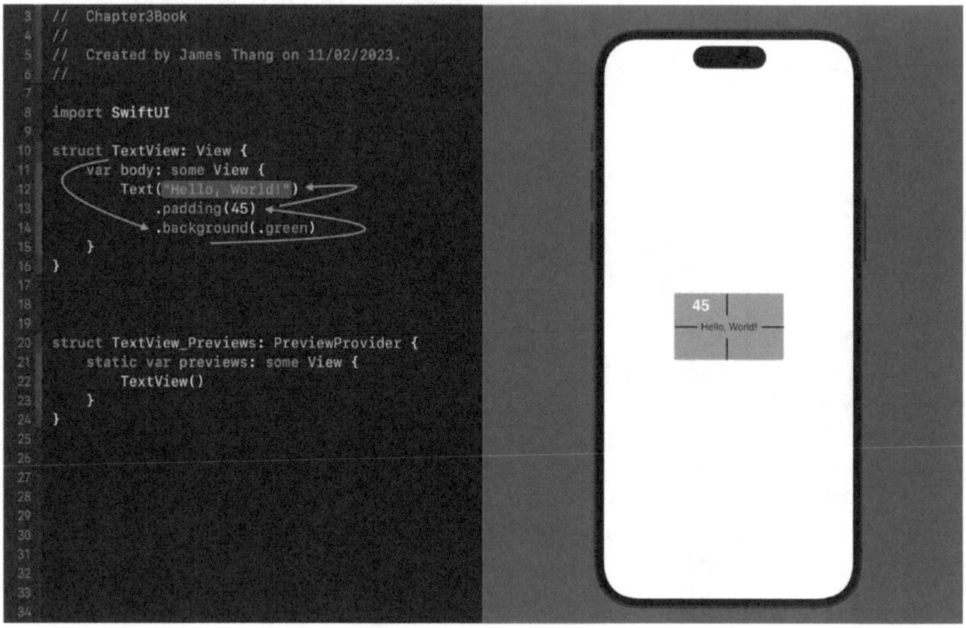

Figure 3.2: Size of TextView with padding(45)

With the same flow, the TextView asks the `.background()` modifier =>, and the `.background()` asks the `padding()` modifier. Here comes its features: whatever space its child asks for will be adding more 45 pixels in all directions => `.padding()` modifier then ask Text View. With this example, we hope it helps further prove to you that the order of View Modifiers matters. Because of this, and with many Views and View Modifiers, there is a lot of room for creativity Layout in SwiftUI.

An important thing to note here is that there are Views that will ask only for their required space, like `Text()`, but there are Views that will try to take as many spaces as possible, like `Color()` or `Spacer()`. It is their default characteristics, and it's better to know for your future usage.

Here, we wrap the above Text into a ZStack with **Color.orange** behind the Text View. As we can see, the color orange area will try to expand as much as possible. There are white spaces on top and bottom and those are safe areas. It is a layout guide for the user interface, representing the area of the screen that is not obscured by the device's notch, the home indicator, or other system-level elements that might be present on the device's screen.

The **safe area** helps developers ensure that the important content in their user interface is not covered by these elements and is always visible to the user. When designing an interface for iOS devices, it's recommended to layout your content within the safe area to ensure that it's visible and usable on all devices, including those with notches, home indicators, or other system-level elements:

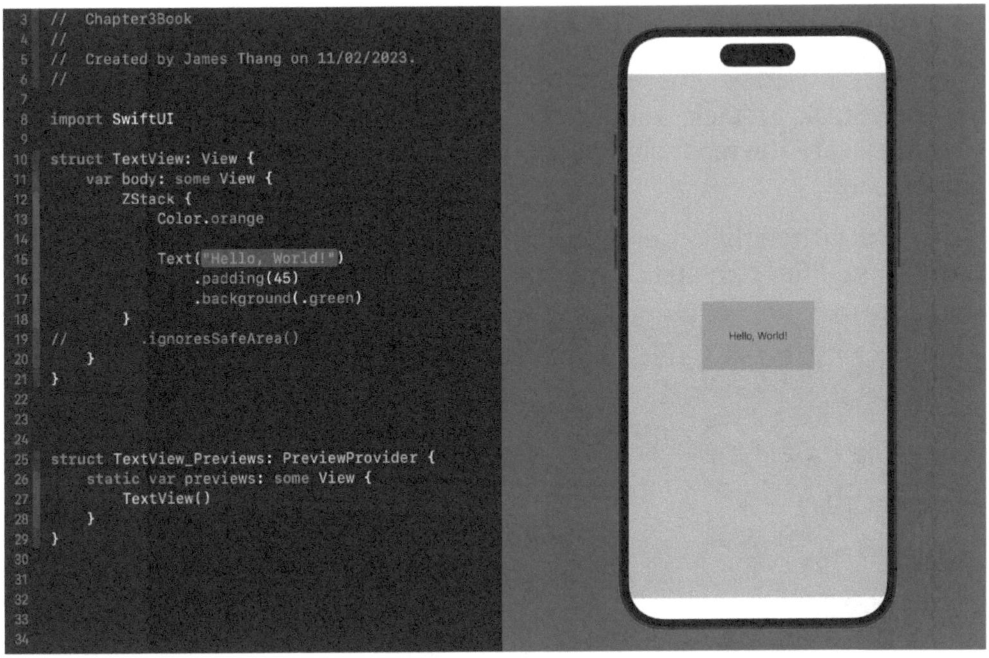

```
3    //   Chapter3Book
4    //
5    //   Created by James Thang on 11/02/2023.
6    //
7
8    import SwiftUI
9
10   struct TextView: View {
11       var body: some View {
12           ZStack {
13               Color.orange
14
15               Text("Hello, World!")
16                   .padding(45)
17                   .background(.green)
18           }
19   //        .ignoresSafeArea()
20       }
21   }
22
23
24
25   struct TextView_Previews: PreviewProvider {
26       static var previews: some View {
27           TextView()
28       }
29   }
30
31
32
33
34
```

Figure 3.3: *Safe area space*

If you want to omit the Safe Area, for example, here, if we just want the background of the App to be completely orange, then in SwiftUI, we have a modifier **.ignoreSafeArea()** to use. We can also choose to ignore the top or bottom side separately with it. Uncomment the modifier to see things change.

Of course, anyone who stops here will ask: What if I don't want that behavior? What if I want Text to have as many spaces as possible and Color to only have 100 × 100-pixel space?

No worries because SwiftUI also provides several layout modifiers that allow you to change the layout behavior of views. These include:

- **.frame**: Changes the size and position of a view by specifying its origin and size.

- **.padding**: Adds padding to a view, which creates space between the view and its container.

- **.offset**: Changes the position of a view by specifying a horizontal and/ or vertical offset.

- **.zIndex**: Specifies the front-to-back order of overlapping views in a ZStack.

- **.overlay**: Adds one or more views on top of a view, creating an overlapping effect.

Just like VStack, HStack, and ZStack are the most basic and frequently used Views, these are the most commonly used view modifiers. Let's take a look into **.frame()** first.

Now we will switch the order of the text and color inside the ZStack and use the **.frame()** modifier to help us achieve our custom behavior:

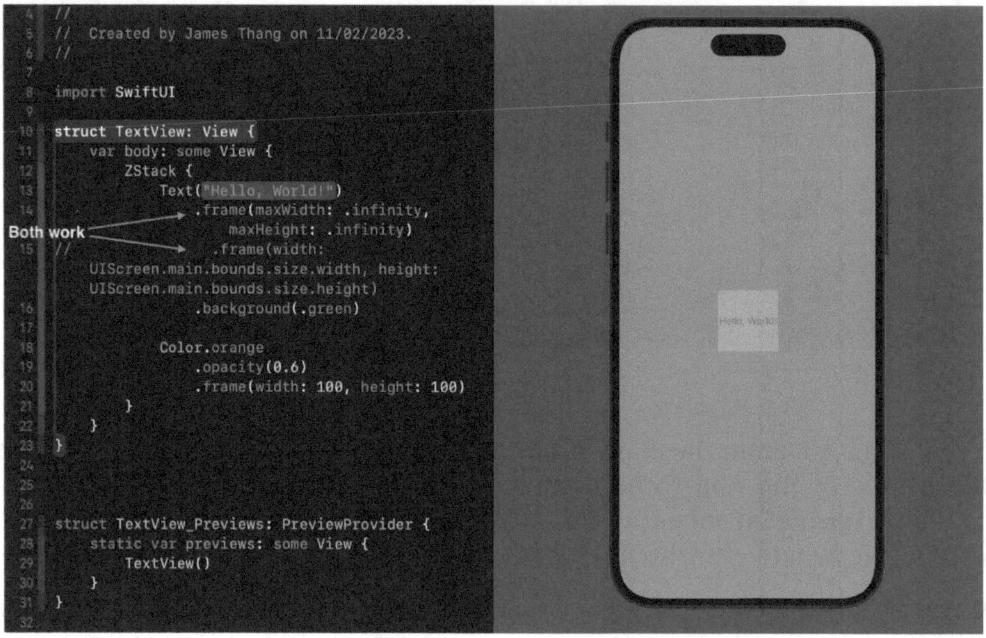

```
//
//  Created by James Thang on 11/02/2023.
//

import SwiftUI

struct TextView: View {
    var body: some View {
        ZStack {
            Text("Hello, World!")
                .frame(maxWidth: .infinity,
                       maxHeight: .infinity)
//              .frame(width:
                UIScreen.main.bounds.size.width, height:
                UIScreen.main.bounds.size.height)
                .background(.green)

            Color.orange
                .opacity(0.6)
                .frame(width: 100, height: 100)
        }
    }
}

struct TextView_Previews: PreviewProvider {
    static var previews: some View {
        TextView()
    }
}
```

Both work

Figure 3.4: *Frame Modifier*

With the help of the **.frame()** modifier, we can easily achieve what we want. There are two different **.frame()** view modifiers in SwiftUI, and both are very handy depending on what you want:

- **.frame(width: _ , height: _ , alignment: _)**: Changes the size and position of a view by specifying its origin and size.

- **.frame(minWidth: _ , idealWidth: _ , maxWidth: _, minHeight: _ , idealHeight: _ , maxHeight: _, alignment: _)**: can also guess when reading the parameters. With this modifier, you can specify the minimum, maximum and idea values for width and height. This modified is for responsive layout with different Screen sizes.

Both of them can also be used to achieve the same result as above. To have a text or a view to propose covering as much space as it can, we can specify the **maxWidth** and **maxHeight** to be infinity. Or in Swift, you can get the size of the device with: **UIScreen.main.bounds.size**.

Overall, SwiftUI's layout system provides a high level of abstraction and makes it easy to create beautiful and responsive user interfaces. You can use a combination of containers, views, and layout modifiers to create complex and dynamic designs that adapt to different screen sizes and orientations.

Positioning View in SwiftUI

As you have already seen previously, we used **.frame()** with params width and height to input numbers, which are also called pixels. But what exactly is the logic behind it? How do we know which numbers we want? Or better, what if we want our Text to be positioned at the top-left corner instead of in the center of the Screen?

In iOS development, we used the coordinate system to define the positions inside the Screen. You may find this familiar because it comes from Mathematics when we want to identify the position of a point in 2D space. The difference here is that the y-axis starts at the top and goes downward with positive values:

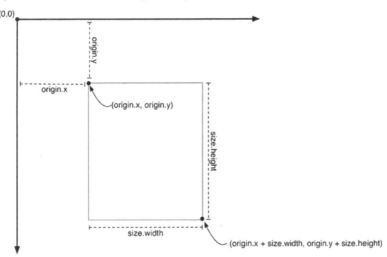

Figure 3.5: *The Coordinate system*

By definition, the top-left corner of each Screen will be point (0, 0). The X-axis goes to the right, and the Y-axis to the bottom for a positive value. Of course, the negative value is totally fine here and is usually used to achieve a beautiful custom layout like Carousel style or horizontal scroll bar.

One thing I want to point out here is that there are different iPhone models, and as you can guess, each of them has a different width and height. So, things will look and behave somewhat differently. A button that is out of reach on a small device like the iPhone SE is a common bug that almost every iOS developer has experienced. Make sure you double-check on every different device size before release. Here is one of the reference links for different iPhone device sizes: **https://yesviz.com/iphones.php**

Back to the figure, we can see that there are two sets of things we need to know in order to position a view inside a screen. First, we need the width and height of our rectangle view. Second is the position point (x, y), which will be the start location.

In iOS development, every view, no matter what shape it takes - circle, hexagon, ellipse, line, arrow, curve line, and so on - always has an outside frame for layout, which will always be a rectangle. And that outside rectangle frame will always be used to do the layout.

The **width** and **height** parameters from **.frame()** modifier are for specifying the width and height of the rectangle frame of the view. That's the first element. But how about the second? How to specify the origin point? This is where the **.position()** modifier comes into play:

Figure 3.6: *Position View Modifier (1)*

Here, with the help of **.position()** modifier, we can place the center of our Text View at point (100, 100). Now, here is a very great question you could ask: What if, instead of the center, we want it top-left or bottom-right point to be placed at position (100, 100)? It's even greater because we already know that the Text View is dynamically adjusted with its inside content.

Of course, we can set its size with **.frame()** modifier and then add half of the frame size to our **.position()** modifier:

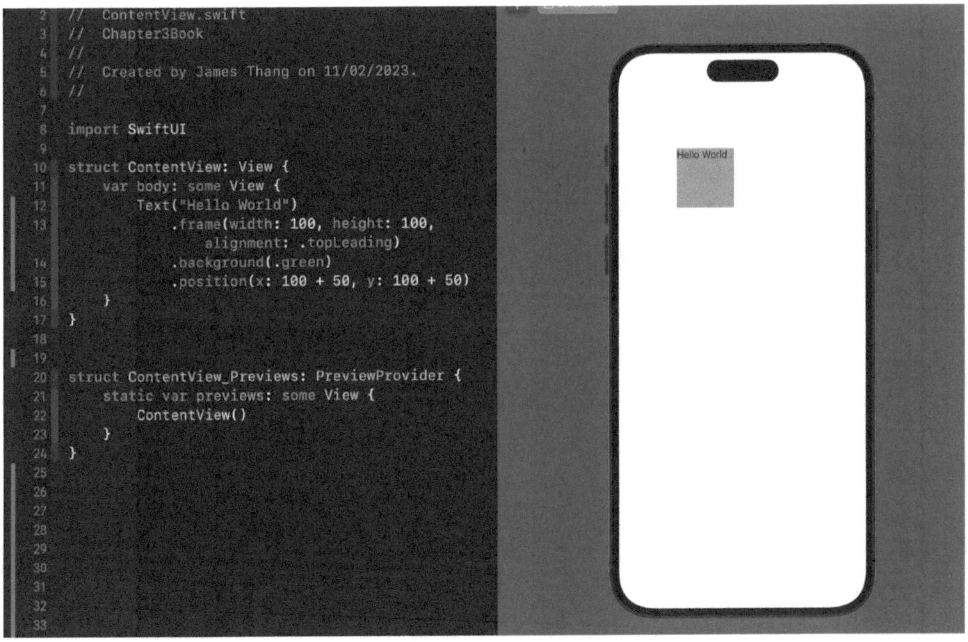

```
 2    //  ContentView.swift
 3    //  Chapter3Book
 4    //
 5    //  Created by James Thang on 11/02/2023.
 6    //
 7
 8    import SwiftUI
 9
10    struct ContentView: View {
11        var body: some View {
12            Text("Hello World")
13                .frame(width: 100, height: 100,
                       alignment: .topLeading)
14                .background(.green)
15                .position(x: 100 + 50, y: 100 + 50)
16        }
17    }
18
19
20    struct ContentView_Previews: PreviewProvider {
21        static var previews: some View {
22            ContentView()
23        }
24    }
```

Figure 3.7: *Position View Modifier (2)*

Now the top-left corner of our "**Hello World**" is exactly at point (100, 100). Here, we now see the last parameter of the **.frame()** modifier, alignment, comes into play. The default alignment state of almost every view in SwiftUI is center. However, the **alignment** parameter helps us to change the position inside its frame space. We will discuss in detail about **alignment** in the next section. However, what if we don't want to set a fixed frame to our text and let it expand freely?

The things we need here are the **width** and **height** of our text view, no matter how long its content is. There is a very powerful container View in SwiftUI that helps us to achieve this: Geometry Reader.

Geometry Reader is a container view in SwiftUI that allows you to dynamically adjust the size and position of its child views based on its own size. This means that you can use Geometry Reader to create custom layouts that are responsive to changes in the size and orientation of the device or parent view.

Here's how you can use **GeometryReader** in your SwiftUI code:

```
GeometryReader { geometry in
    // The child views you want to position using the
        geometry object
}
```

Figure 3.8: *Geometry Reader (1)*

This view will return a flexible preferred size to its parent layout:

Figure 3.9: *Geometry Reader (2)*

Here is a simple example where, with the help of Geometry Reader, we will always have a red square with a size exactly one-third of its parent, which in this case is the whole screen size.

The geometry object passed to the closure is a **GeometryProxy** object, which provides information about the size and position of the Geometry Reader in its coordinate space. You can use the properties and methods of this object to set the size and position of its child views. We then use the **.frame()** modifier to specify its frame as one-third of the width of the parent.

You can play around with it and add more padding outside, and you will see the size of the red square change responsively.

Geometry Reader is a powerful tool that allows you to create custom and flexible layouts in SwiftUI. It's especially useful when you need to create layouts that respond to changes in the size and orientation of the device or parent view.

Now, here with the help of its combination with our knowledge in SwiftUI so far, we can position our Text View at point (100, 100) without having to preset its frame.

Here is how it is done:

```swift
3   //  Chapter3Book
4   //
5   //  Created by James Thang on 11/02/2023.
6   //
7
8   import SwiftUI
9
10  struct ContentView: View {
11
12      @State var width: CGFloat = 0
13      @State var height: CGFloat = 0
14
15      var body: some View {
16          Text("Hello World")
17              .background {
18                  GeometryReader { geometry in
19                      let size = geometry.size
20
21                      Color.green
22                          .onAppear {
23                              width = size.width
24                              height = size.height
25                          }
26                  }
27              }
28              .position(x: 100 + width/2, y: 100 +
                    height/2)
29      }
30  }
31
32
33
```

Figure 3.10: *Geometry Reader* (3)

Geometry Reader will let us know the size in the parent coordinate space. Here, we use it with our `.background()`. Follow the yellow arrow direction; remember that the background is layout neutral, so it will go and ask its child how much space it needs. Here, we get our desired behavior to get the size of our text view dynamically.

We get our size here, but we can't use it to set our text view position. Why? Because of scope in the programming language. We already discussed it in *Chapter 1, Swift Language*. In case you have forgotten, scope refers to the region of code where a variable, constant, function, or other identifier is accessible. The scope of an identifier is determined by its location in the code and the curly braces that enclose it. Identifiers declared outside of any function or class have global scope and can be accessed from anywhere in the program, while identifiers declared within a function or other block of code have local scope and can only be accessed from within that block.

Here, our size is local scope; therefore, we cannot use it as input for our **.position()** modifier. To help us achieve this, two new important things that help us to position our top-left corner at point (100, 100). These are two important concepts that you will be introduced to now and will delve deeper into in the next chapter: State and lifecycle methods.

Knowing the Scope, you may have guessed that the solution here is to make global variables and then assign our needed **width** and **height** value to them. This is exactly what we do here: we declare two variables outside at global scope and then assign the value we have inside the scope of Geometry Reader to them. You may ask: Why not write the assignment actions right inside after we get the geometry proxy? Well, you can try it, but Xcode will give you this error:

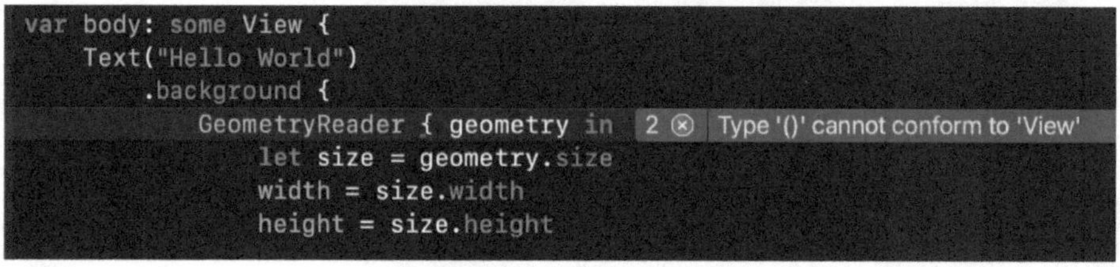

```
var body: some View {
    Text("Hello World")
        .background {
            GeometryReader { geometry in   2 ⊗  Type '()' cannot conform to 'View'
                let size = geometry.size
                width = size.width
                height = size.height
```

Figure 3.11: *SwiftUI Error*

This is a very common mistake for newcomers, one that even confuses experienced programmers when they first jump into SwiftUI. They always wonder why some code is not allowed inside the scope of views when, from their extinct through years of programming, everything seems totally fine. It's intuitive, and it is common to make variable assignments inside of the function's body. However, SwiftUI View with body requirements is special. That's because, in the body, SwiftUI builds views and only views. And the assignment actions here, or maybe the print(...), are functions that return Void (not return anything): signature is "**()**", as reported in this error alert. Once again, these are very common mistakes that I myself have made a lot because assigning values to variables and printing to see what is happening is very frequently used by us programmers.

So, we cannot assign our wanted values here this way. You already see our solution is to use the **.onAppear { }** life circle method. I will give detailed explanations about the life circle at the end of this chapter. Here, the purpose of this method is to add an action to perform before this view appears on the Screen. Let's go back to *Figure 3.10* and follow the directions of those orange arrows:

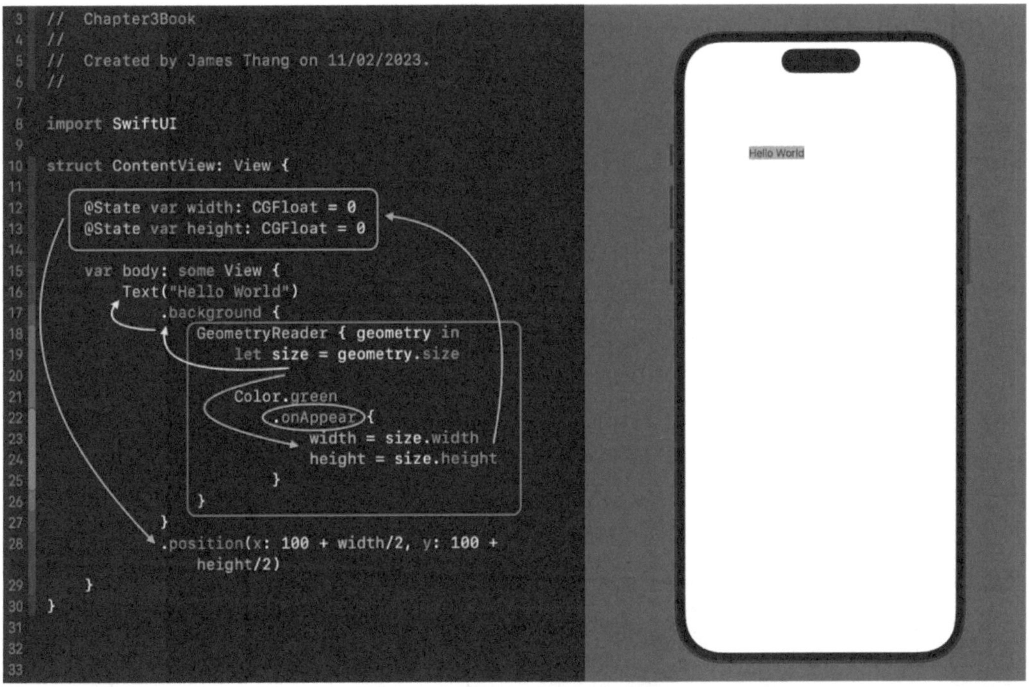

Figure 3.12: *onAppear and logic flow*

We get our wanted values and assign them back to global variables when the green background appears. Then we use those values to position our "Hello World" in the top left corner at point (100, 100).

Inside the green area, notice that our two global variables look different from the normal one because we have added the syntax **@State** before them. Try to remove it, and you will see the position of our text is different. And it is not because the width and height here are both zero; their values have already changed, but the problem is that the **.position()** modifier is called before both of the values are zero. And we already know that in Swift, Struct is Immutable. For now, the keyword **@State** here tells SwiftUI that whenever these variable's values change, destroy the old ones and make a new one with the new values. Now, our **Hello World** is positioned in the top-left corner at **point (100, 100)**. We will go deeply into State in the next chapter.

With all this, we have successfully done our custom positioning in two different ways. And through this, you have been introduced to some of the core and fundamental knowledge in SwiftUI. Feel free to reread and do some more research on these topics, as we will soon use them a lot and they are irreplaceable when developing Apps with SwiftUI.

Another point that needs to be emphasized from this is that there are many different creative ways to achieve the same result. SwiftUI provides us with a variety of toolboxes that can be mixed and matched in many ways. So, open your mind and try to think outside of the box, knowing what tools (Views, View Modifier) you can use.

There are two ways of positioning a view: absolute way with **.position()** modifier and relative way with **.offset()** modifier. We have already learned about **.position()**, now let's talk about **.offset()**.

In SwiftUI, the **.offset()** modifier is used to move a view from its original position by a specified distance in the horizontal and/or vertical direction.

The **.offset()** modifier takes a CGSize/(x, y) value, which represents the distance to move the view. Positive values move the view to the right and down, while negative values move the view to the left and up. For example, to move a view 100 points to the right and 100 points down, you can use the following code:

Figure 3.13: Offset View Modifier (1)

The important thing to note here is that when we offset some View from their original locations, the original values don't change even though the View rendering somewhere else. Let's switch the positions between our two modifiers, **background** and **offset**, to see the interesting part:

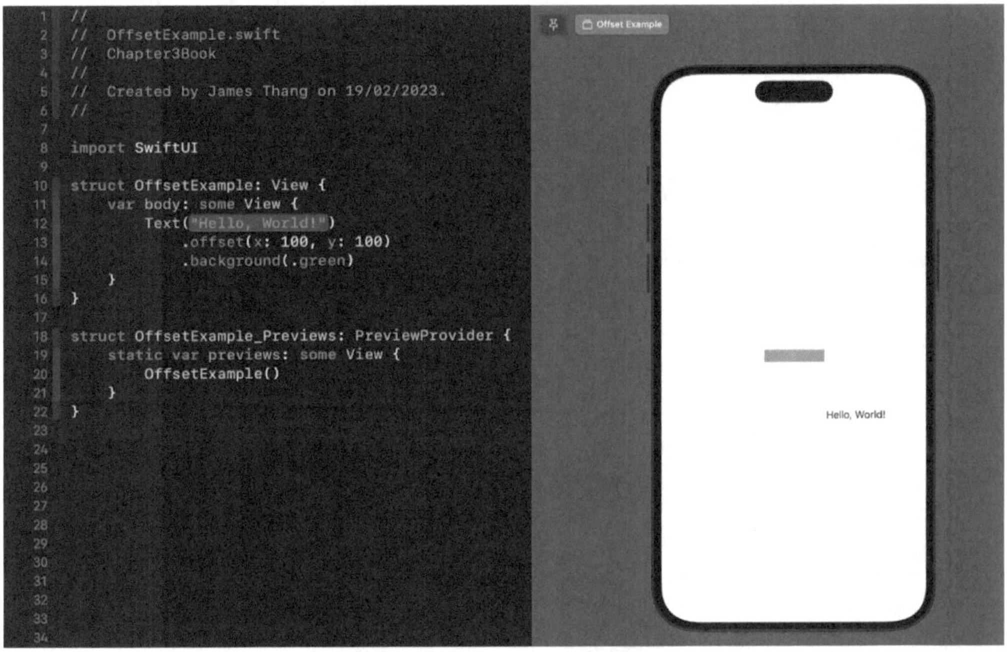

Figure 3.14: *Offset View Modifier (2)*

When we use the offset modifier like this, we are changing the location of where a View should be rendered/placed without changing its underlying original locations. That's why we see the background is applied at the center of our screen. Once again, with this example, I want to emphasize that the order of the View Modifier matters a lot.

Not only are they useful for layout and placement, but both the **.offset()** and **.position()** modifiers are also used a lot for animations, transitions, or Drag and Drop Gesture. We will soon explore them all in upcoming chapters.

Some of the others frequently used are **.padding()**, **.zIndex()**, and **.overlay()**. By default, the value input to padding will be transformed to space adding to all four directions. However, if you want, you can specify your needed, whether it is for each direction solely or for vertical/horizontal:

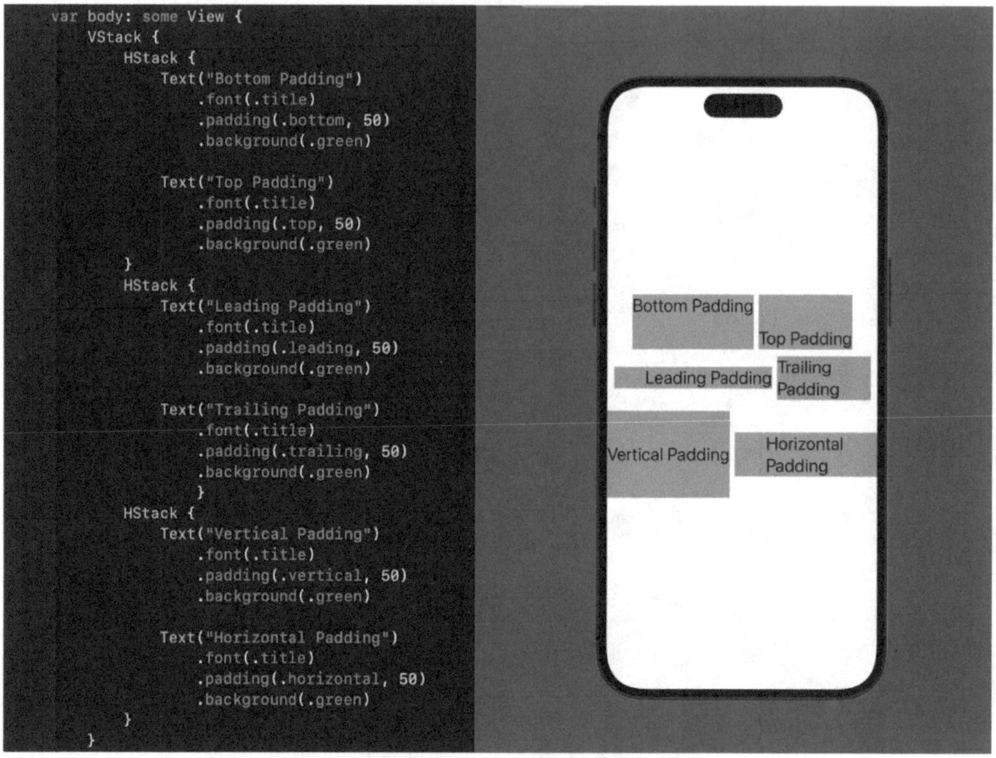

Figure 3.15: *Multiple ways of using padding*

The `.zIndex()` changes the front-to-back order of overlapping views in a ZStack. You may wonder why we need it when we can place them in order inside the ZStack. It's because when users perform actions, the order of our components will change in reactions. So, this modifier is a way to achieve it with code.

The `.overlay()` is the opposite of the `.background()`. It allows you to add additional views on top of an existing view. The overlay modifier can be used to add visual effects, additional content, or even interactive elements to a view. Of course, you can totally use ZStack, but `.overlay()` and `.background()` are much more convenient. Also, remember that you can chain them repeatedly; two or three overlay one after each other is totally fine with SwiftUI.

Now that we have known about the coordinate system and the logic behind positioning/placement Views, the last crucial topic I want to talk about in this chapter is **Alignment**.

Alignment View in SwiftUI

Alignment in SwiftUI refers to the way views are positioned and aligned within a container view or a layout.

Here is the difference between positioning and alignment: positioning is when we place our view at the place of the parent or global coordinator locations, whereas alignment is about aligning the content of the views within a frame container of itself.

There are a variety of alignment options available in SwiftUI, including:

- **Leading**: This aligns the view to the leading edge of its parent view or layout, which is typically the left edge in a left-to-right language environment.

- **Trailing**: This aligns the view to the trailing edge of its parent view or layout, which is typically the right edge in a left-to-right language environment.

- **Top**: This aligns the view to the top edge of its parent view or layout.

- **Bottom**: This aligns the view to the bottom edge of its parent view or layout.

- **Center**: This centers the view horizontally and vertically within its parent view or layout.

- **FirstTextBaseline** and **LastTextBaseline**: These are used to align text within a container view or layout.

- There also options for corners alignment with: **Top Leading**, **Top Trailing**, **Bottom Leading** and **Bottom Trailing**.

Here for a better visualization:

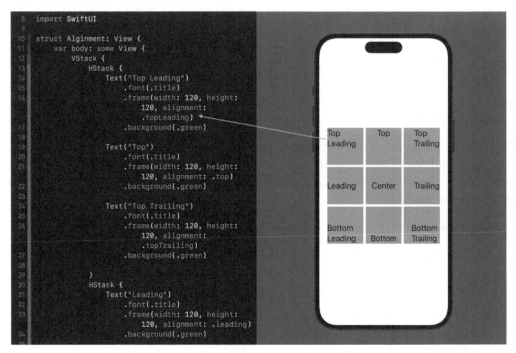

Figure 3.16: *Multiple cases of alignment*

Here, we set a constant frame for each Text and then use the last parameter of the `.frame()` modifier to align its text content inside of its frame container. And you can see the different results.

Again, this is one of the basics that is easy to miss, including me. For a very long time, I found it strange that the alignment does not work as expected. Whether I **try** to change it to leading, trailing, or bottom, nothing seems to change. It is because alignment is within itself, and for Text, if we do not set the width and height frame, it will take just exactly what it needs.

So, the alignment inside will always be the same no matter each side because it only has the space of its content. Whenever you find alignment doesn't work, try using `.background()` modifier to see how much space it has available.

In SwiftUI, there are other ways of setting an Alignment. The first one you already know is by using the **.frame()** modifier. Another one comes with SwiftUI container views like VStack, HStack, or ZStack:

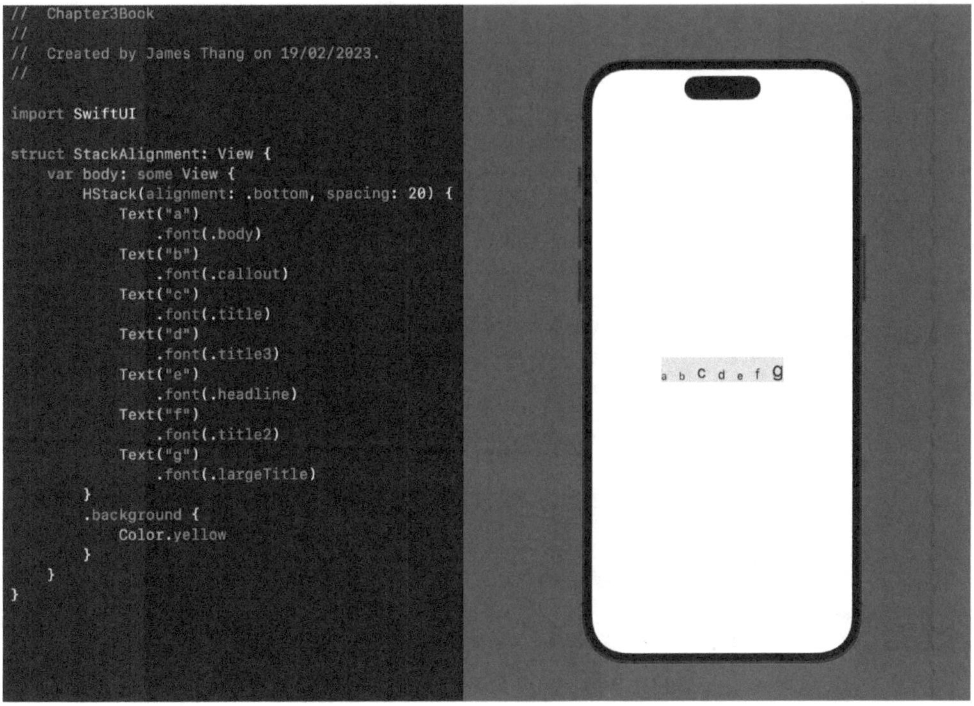

```
//  Chapter3Book
//
//  Created by James Thang on 19/02/2023.
//

import SwiftUI

struct StackAlignment: View {
    var body: some View {
        HStack(alignment: .bottom, spacing: 20) {
            Text("a")
                .font(.body)
            Text("b")
                .font(.callout)
            Text("c")
                .font(.title)
            Text("d")
                .font(.title3)
            Text("e")
                .font(.headline)
            Text("f")
                .font(.title2)
            Text("g")
                .font(.largeTitle)
        }
        .background {
            Color.yellow
        }
    }
}
```

Figure 3.17: *Alignment inside HStack (1)*

In this example, we use the alignment available with the HStack to bottom-align all of its children. You can see they are all near the bottom of the yellow area, but the overall isn't so correct. It is because they each have different font sizes. If all the text has the same font, then you will have a beautiful alignment result. I intentionally did this to introduce a very handy case alignment for this situation: **FirstTextBaseline** and **LastTextBaseline**. Both work the same, the difference is whether the baseline will follow the first or the last item among the children views.

Now everything looks correct:

```
5   //  Created by James Thang on 19/02/2023.
6   //
7
8   import SwiftUI
9
10  struct StackAlignment: View {
11      var body: some View {
12          HStack(alignment: .firstTextBaseline,
                   spacing: 20) {
13              Text("a")
14                  .font(.body)
15              Text("b")
16                  .font(.callout)
17              Text("c")
18                  .font(.title)
19              Text("d")
20                  .font(.title3)
21              Text("e")
22                  .font(.headline)
23              Text("f")
24                  .font(.title2)
25              Text("g")
26                  .font(.largeTitle)
27          }
28          .background {
29              Color.yellow
30          }
31      }
32  }
33
34
35
36
37
```

Figure 3.18: *Alignment inside HStack (2)*

That is the basics of Alignment in SwiftUI. There is also more advanced knowledge on this, where you want to align two completely separated views. In such situations, we will have to make a custom Alignment on our own. Hopefully, we will see an example in later chapters.

With this, we conclude the end of this chapter where you have learned and understood the concept behind SwiftUI layout: the coordinator system. You have also learned about frequently used view modifiers like `.frame()`, `.padding()`, `.positioning()`, `offset()`, and so on, along with the Geometry Reader container. You now know how to position a View and the difference between positioning and alignment.

Over the last two chapters, we have gained enough knowledge about SwiftUI Views and View Modifiers. We have also made a lot of basic beautiful designs. However, we are still missing one of the most important things of the app: reactive. If it is just for presentation or information, then that is the original characteristic of a Website, though things have changed a lot since then. Since the beginning, mobile Apps were not for that, they are for reactions and interactions with users. So, making the layout is the first part, and the next important part is to make it interactive. In SwiftUI, we achieve this with the help of State. It is a crucial fundamental concept for every iOS SwiftUI developer. The next chapter is very important and requires a lot of focus. So, take a deep rest, and I will see you soon.

As promised, there will be a bonus section in this chapter talking about lifecycle methods. This is also a very important concept to understand. Now, let's learn about it.

Lifecycle methods in SwiftUI

The *life cycle* of a view in SwiftUI refers to the sequence of events that occur from the moment a view is created, through its updates and layout changes, until it is eventually removed from the screen.

The SwiftUI framework provides a number of methods that allow you to respond to various stages of the view's lifecycle, and these methods are collectively referred to as the lifecycle methods.

In SwiftUI, every view has a defined lifecycle that consists of the following stages:

- **Creation**: When the view is first created, SwiftUI calls the **init()** method to create the view and set its initial state.

- **Configuration**: After the view is created, SwiftUI configures it by setting its properties and passing any necessary data.

- **Update**: If the view's state changes, SwiftUI will update the view and call the **updateUIView(_:context:)** method to apply any necessary changes.

- **Layout**: After the view has been updated, SwiftUI will layout the view by calling the **layoutSubviews()** method.

- **Display**: Finally, the view is displayed on the screen.

SwiftUI provides a number of methods that allow you to respond to various stages of the view's lifecycle, and these methods are collectively referred to as the lifecycle methods. The most commonly used lifecycle methods in SwiftUI are as follows:

- **init()**: This method is called when the view is first created, and it is used to set up the initial state of the view.

- **onAppear()**: This method is called when the view is about to be displayed on the screen. You can use this method to perform any necessary setup or data loading.

- **onDisappear()**: This method is called when the view is about to be removed from the screen. You can use this method to clean up any resources or perform any necessary teardown.

- **onReceive(_:)**: This method is used to handle changes to any observed objects or publishers. You can use this method to update the view's state or perform any necessary side effects.

By leveraging these lifecycle methods, you can create views that respond dynamically to changes in the app's state, providing a more seamless and responsive user experience:

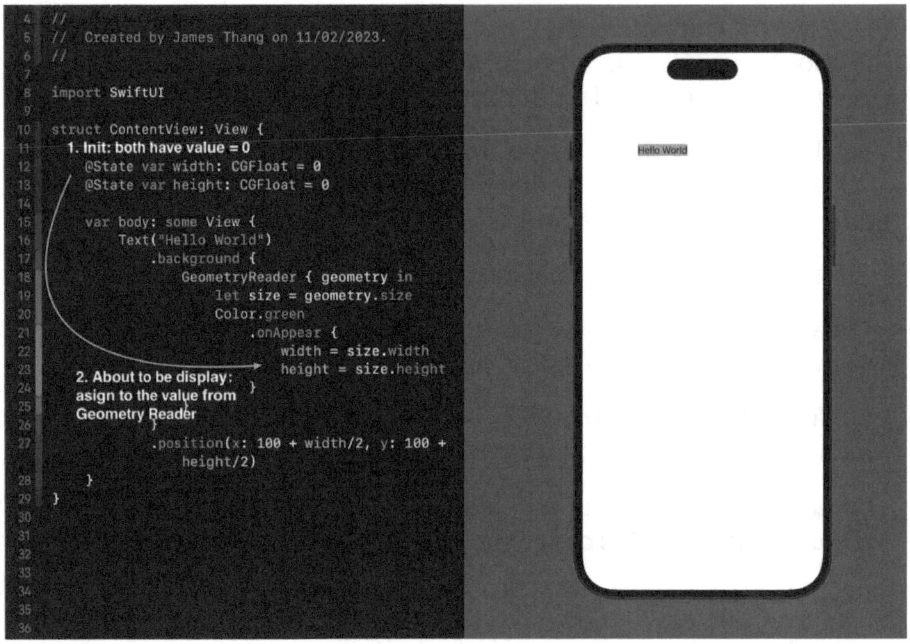

Figure 3.19: *Lifecycle in SwiftUI*

Remember this example; we leverage the power of the **.onAppear()** life circle to get the values we wanted. We have to do it this way at the Appearance State because we do not have the values at the initialization. However, it won't affect the user because **.onAppear()** gets called before the view is displayed.

Conclusion

Overall, the use of lifecycle methods in SwiftUI is an important tool for developers to create more dynamic and responsive views, improve performance, and create more modular and maintainable code. You will soon see all of these life cycle methods in later chapters.

CHAPTER 4
State, Binding, Property Wrapper, and Property Observer

Introduction

Have you ever used an app that responds quickly to your every tap, swipe, or scroll? Have you ever wondered how developers manage all of that dynamic content? It is because developers have followed proper appliances, best practices, and design principles. And it is no exception with modern UI frameworks like SwiftUI. In this chapter, we will discover how to make interactive applications in SwiftUI. And this is where the concepts of State and Property Wrapper come into play.

State and Property Wrapper are like the backbone of SwiftUI. They allow developers to manage the data that powers their app's user interface in a clean and efficient way. We will learn about these concepts in this chapter, and along the way, we will combine all of the previous knowledge to build a very familiar App from scratch: The Calculator.

We will also discuss another topic related to variables: Computed Property

Structure

In this chapter, the following topics will be covered:

- State in SwiftUI

- Binding and its differences to State
- Property Wrapper
- Property Observer
- Layout and build the Calculator App

Layout the Calculator

Let's begin by using all that we have learned and try to replicate the look of the following Calculator App. Spend some time trying to think about it before reading the next page:

Figure 4.1: *The Calculator Layout*

Remember what we emphasized on the layout in SwiftUI? Think about it like Lego bricks. Try to break it into small easy-to-make pieces. Once again, you can take a break here and try making it all by yourself. There can be many ways of doing this calculator layout. Here are our suggestions: We will break it into six columns:

Figure 4.2: *The Calculator Layout breaking down*

Great! So now we know that we will have a VStack with six columns, let's break it down further into each one:

Figure 4.3: *The Calculator Layout column breaking down*

Each column, except the first and the last one, will have four same buttons, which we will use HStack in SwiftUI. For each button, it will have a descriptive symbol and a circular background. You can guess it; that's for the ZStack or the `.background()` modifier. However, we will use ZStack this time so that we will have all three common containers in SwiftUI: ZStack, VStack, and HStack in this project. So, this will be our smallest component.

Now, without further ado, let's open up Xcode and make our own calculator. We will start by making the number 9 button:

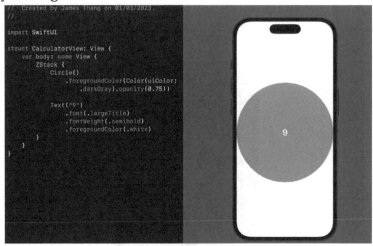

Figure 4.4: *Button Layout*

In the previous lesson, we already used a rounded rectangle for our renting card. Conveniently, in SwiftUI, a `Circle` is also one of those already-to-use shapes. Also, `ZStack` and `Circle` will automatically try to have as much space as possible. But no worries, we already know that these can be overwritten by the `.frame()` modifier.

Now, let's separate our button layout into a Struct and make our columns with `HStack,` containing four buttons:

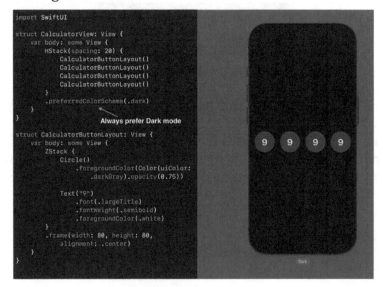

Figure 4.5: *Column layout*

And here we have our column looking beautiful just like the design. Please note that on iOS, there are light mode and dark mode. Depending on the node, the layout's color will look different; for example, the background color of the screen will be white in light mode and black in dark mode. For our Calculator App, the design looks the same for both light mode and dark mode, so we will force it to always be in dark mode using the `.preferredColorScheme()` modifier.

Next, let's make our button reusable by extracting those different inputs into properties. We can clearly see that the text and the background color will be different from button to button. The text color will also be different and so will the width of the frame. Take a look at the zero (**0**) button from the design:

```
struct CalculatorButtonLayout: View {
    let text: String
    let textColor: Color
    let backgroundColor: Color
    var width: CGFloat = 80
    var height: CGFloat = 80

    var body: some View {
        ZStack {
            Circle()
                .foregroundColor(backgroundColor)

            Text(text)
                .font(.largeTitle)
                .fontWeight(.semibold)
                .foregroundColor(textColor)
                .frame(alignment: .center)
        }
        .frame(width: width, height: height, alignment:
            .center)
    }
}
```

Figure 4.6: *Calculator button Struct*

With this on our hand, let's make our first column:

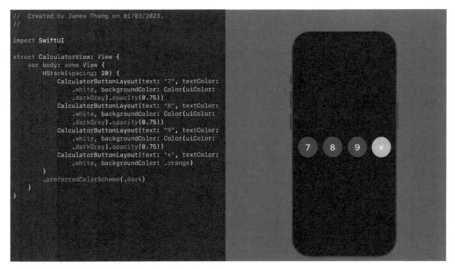

Figure 4.7: *Calculator column layout*

Now, what's next? You already know that our design has five columns that look kind of the same. So first, let's copy this five times. Everything is like Lego blocks! The power of SwiftUI really shines here:

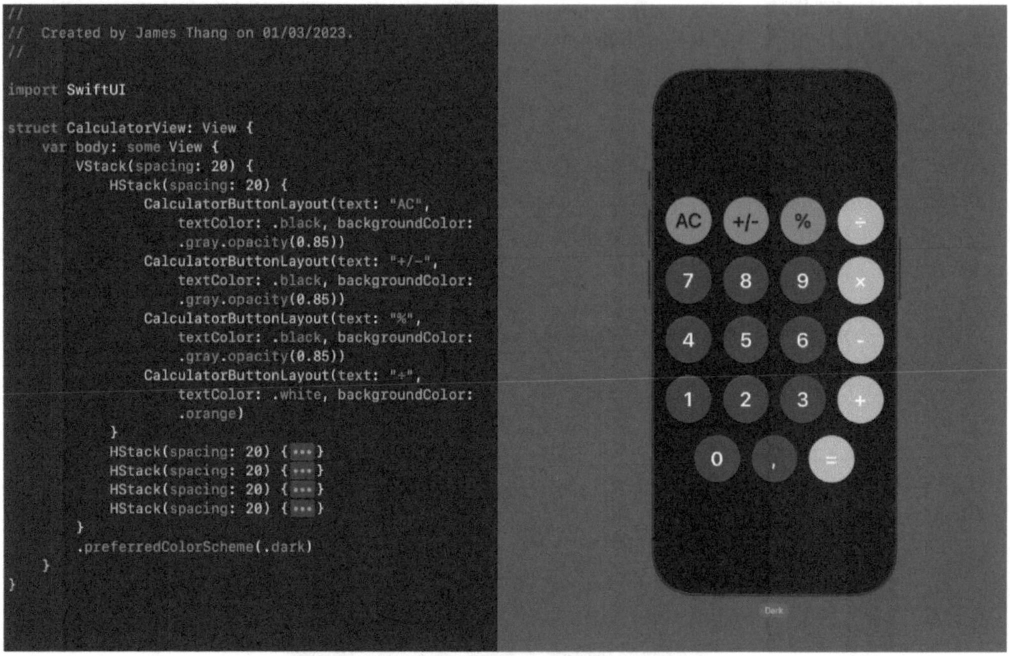

```
//
// Created by James Thang on 01/03/2023.
//

import SwiftUI

struct CalculatorView: View {
    var body: some View {
        VStack(spacing: 20) {
            HStack(spacing: 20) {
                CalculatorButtonLayout(text: "AC",
                    textColor: .black, backgroundColor:
                    .gray.opacity(0.85))
                CalculatorButtonLayout(text: "+/-",
                    textColor: .black, backgroundColor:
                    .gray.opacity(0.85))
                CalculatorButtonLayout(text: "%",
                    textColor: .black, backgroundColor:
                    .gray.opacity(0.85))
                CalculatorButtonLayout(text: "+",
                    textColor: .white, backgroundColor:
                    .orange)
            }
            HStack(spacing: 20) { ••• }
            HStack(spacing: 20) { ••• }
            HStack(spacing: 20) { ••• }
        }
        .preferredColorScheme(.dark)
    }
}
```

Figure 4.8: *Calculator design layout*

Now everything starts to look into place. There are two missing things: the zero button at the bottom to take the place of twice the other one, and the result calculation label at the top.

Let's start with the zero button first. Remember that we already created a **width** property for our button. So, now we need to modify it for our zero button. Instead of 80 by default, the correct value here will be 180 (80 * 2 + 20 for the spacing between two buttons). However, we are not finished yet because back to the design, the background shape of the zero button is not a circle. Conveniently, just like **Circle()** and **RoundedRectangle()**, SwiftUI also has this shape built in, and it is called **Capsule()**. We will use an if-else statement to check when to use a circle or capsule shape as the background based on the incoming width and height values:

```swift
struct CalculatorButtonLayout: View {
    let text: String
    let textColor: Color
    let backgroundColor: Color
    var width: CGFloat = 80
    var height: CGFloat = 80

    var body: some View {
        ZStack {
            if width == height {
                Circle()
                    .foregroundColor(backgroundColor)
            } else {
                Capsule()
                    .foregroundColor(backgroundColor)
            }

            Text(text)
                .font(.largeTitle)
                .fontWeight(.semibold)
                .foregroundColor(textColor)
                .frame(alignment: .center)

        }
        .frame(width: width, height: height, alignment:
            .center)
    }
}
```

Figure 4.9: *Capsule or Circle background*

After this, here is what our zero-button layout will look like:

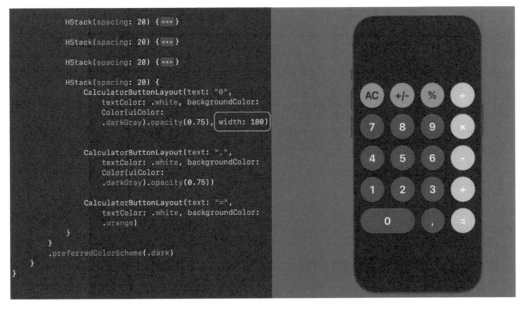

Figure 4.10: *Zero button layout*

Now, let's add the result label to finalize the design:

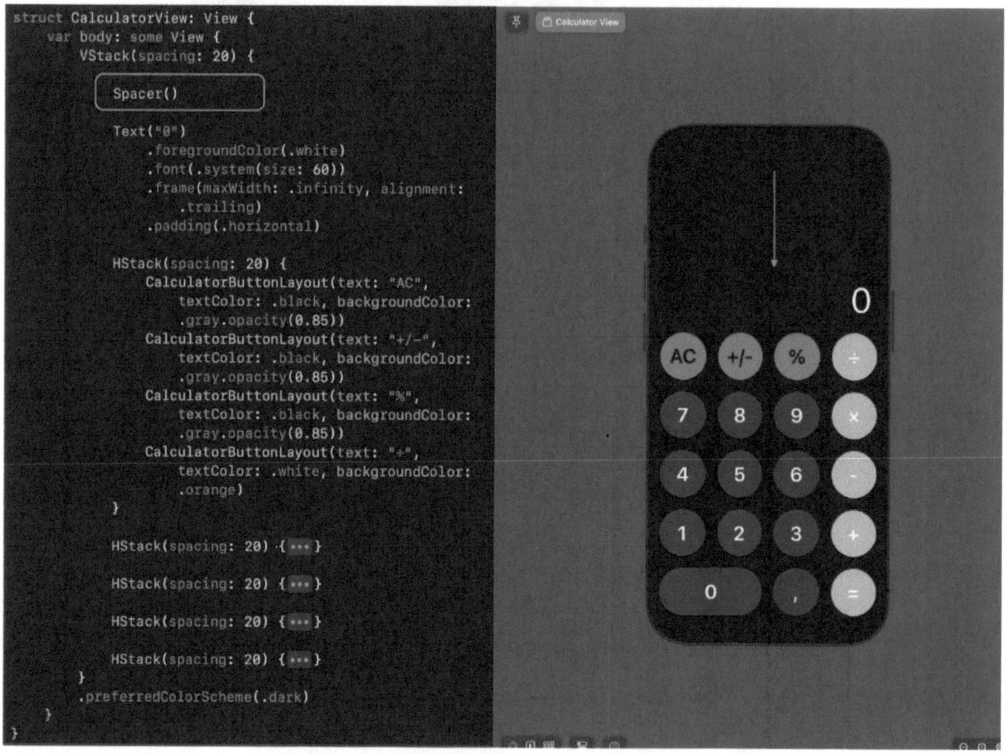

Figure 4.11: *Calculator App final layout*

It is just a simple **Text** view with a large font size. Remember to set the max **width** parameter of the frame modifier to infinity so that it covers as much space as possible, not just enough for its content. Then, align it to the left trailing side and add horizontal padding for a good look.

We can see there is a new highlighted container: the **Spacer()**. Without it, all six of our columns will be at the center of the screen. However, following the design, we want them to be bottom aligned. One of the solutions here is to add another seven columns: the **Spacer()** column at the top. You may wonder why is it working this way?

It is because, by definition, a **Spacer** is a flexible space that expands along the major axis of its containing stack layout, or on both axes if not contained in a stack. Here, because it is inside a VStack, it will try to take as much space as possible in the vertical direction, which will then push all six other columns to the bottom side.

Making it Interactive

Now that we are done with the layout, let's go to the long-awaited interesting part: making our App interactable. Right now, you can click everywhere inside our app and nothing will happen. It is because our app now is just big lifeless View with no interaction. For that, we will need a **Button** component. Remember the shortcut to find View and View Modifier in Xcode: click the plus button on the top right corner, go to the first tab, and search for button. It will be at the top of the list:

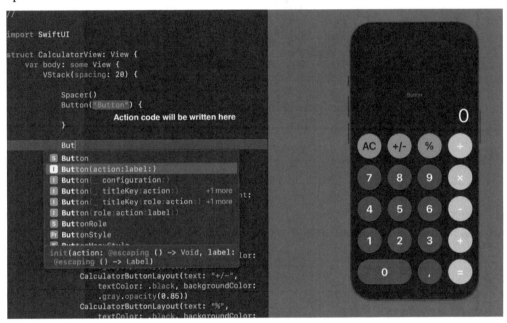

Figure 4.12: Add button

As you drag and drop it into our VStack, you will see the default style button appear on the live preview. The action code that we want to execute will be written inside the next block of the closure. However, this version of the button is not what we want because here we can only specify the text string. We want a more flexible version so that we can use our custom layout button. So, start typing **Button** in Xcode and select the **Button(action:label:)** option, and then click *Enter* two times:

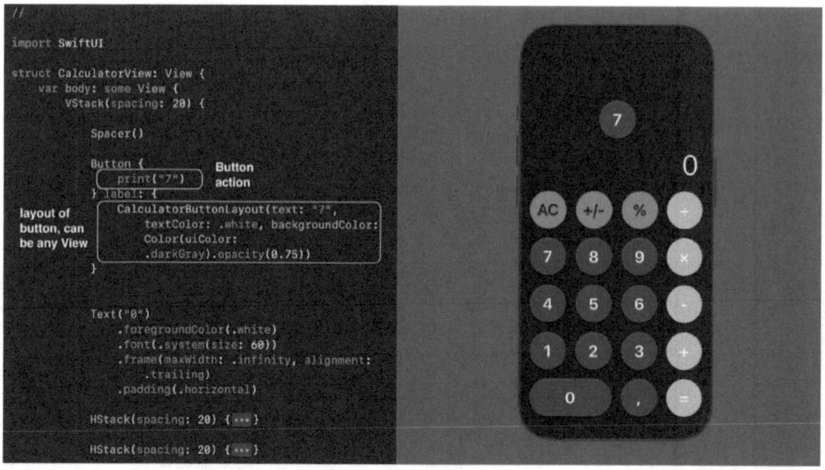

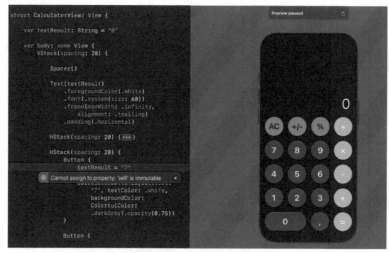

Figure 4.13: *Add our custom button*

With this version out, our button is now working. The first closure is for the action, and the second closure is for the button layout. Try running it on a simulator and open the debugger tab when clicking on the seven button. You will see the number seven being printed. Now, let's go and change all of our buttons into this format and make them clickable.

Instead of printing out value on the debugger, let's move a step closer to our final goal by changing the result text label to the button label every time each button is tapped. Well then, let's make the result label text become a global variable and reassign its value every time each button gets tapped:

Figure 4.14: *Assigning Text*

Unfortunately, it is now working as we expected. The reason Xcode gives us here is that Struct is immutable in Swift language. Recall from the first chapter, Introducing to Swift Language, you may think that the solution here is to add the keyword **mutating** before our `textResult` variable declaration. However, it still will not work because mutating is for functions only. So, what is the right solution here?

You may have already guessed, as it is in the title of this chapter. This is where we use **State** of SwiftUI. By adding the **@State** keyword before our variable declaration, everything is fixed. Now, try running the app and tapping the buttons; you will see our text result label changing. Our app is now interactive and reactive!

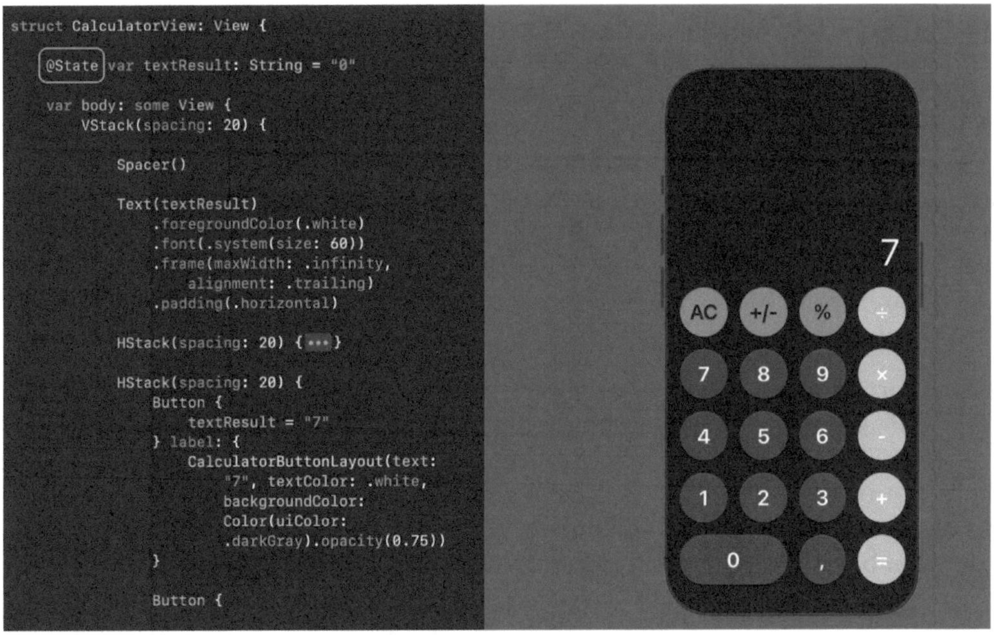

Figure 4.15: *Adding State*

Magically, isn't it? Let's pause the process of making the Calculator App here because **State** is one of the most important concepts introduced with SwiftUI. So, we will go deep dive to understand it before coming back.

State

In SwiftUI, **State** is a fundamental concept that allows us to manage and update data that drives the user interface of our app. Essentially, State is the data that defines how a particular view or UI element should look and behave at any given moment.

@State is a property wrapper in SwiftUI that allows you to store mutable values in a view. It automatically causes the view to re-render whenever the state value changes. This ensures that the view always reflects the current state of the app. **@State** is used to manage local state within a single view and should not be used to store app-level state.

In the preceding example, we marked **textResult** as **@State**, so that when its value changed, our **CalculatorView** view would be re-rendered to reflect the latest data. So, behind the scenes, it is not that the value zero gets changed to seven. Instead, the entire view, including the six columns with the zero label, gets destroyed and replaced. SwiftUI makes a new view, now knowing that the value of **textResult** is seven, but not zero.

You may stop here and wonder if this is so overkill, needing to replace everything just because a text changes from zero to seven. But believe it or not, this is the way of Declarative Programming. The compiler will layout the views based on its State properties. Whenever those properties change, a new view is created for replacement. As opposed to Imperative Programming, which will need the developers to specify the order of operations and how the program should interact with data at each step of the process. Behind the scenes, SwiftUI is doing a lot of heavy lifting to make all this happen smoothly and efficiently. Also, one thing to note is all Views in SwiftUI are Struct, and in Swift, Struct is very cheap and memory-efficient.

It is important to note that **@State** is designed for local state specific to a single view. Also, **@State** is used for simple data structures like String, Int, or Boolean. For more complicated data structures and logic related to multiple views, there are other property wrappers to solve them, such as **@ObservedObject**, **@EnvironmentObject,** and **@Binding**. We will learn about @Binding next and discover about others in the future chapters.

One mistake many newcomers make when they first know about **@State** is to use it everywhere possible. Some automatically mark every new property with **@State**. However, you should avoid using **@State** in situations where the value doesn't change over time. For instance, if you're displaying a static label that never changes, you don't need to use **@State**, as this is a bad practice and will affect performance.

You should be able to distinguish and know when to use State and when not. We want to mark a property with **@State** only when we know its value will change over time in the future, and those changes need to be reflected in the App's user interface.

In summary, use **@State** in SwiftUI when you need to manage and update data that changes over time and affects the user interface of a single view. Avoid using State for static data or when you need to share data between multiple views.

State versus Binding

Besides knowing when to mark a property as State or not, there is another commonly mismatching concept here between State and Binding.

In SwiftUI, **@Binding** is a property wrapper that allows us to create a two-way connection between a property in one view and a property in another view. By using a Binding, we can pass data between views in a way that allows both views to modify the same underlying data.

When we create a Binding, we define a getter and a setter method that allow us to read and write the value of the underlying data. The getter method returns the current value of the data, while the setter method updates the value of the data and notifies any observers of the change.

Bindings are particularly useful when we want to pass data between two views, where one view is responsible for modifying the data, and the other view is responsible for displaying the data. For example, let's go back to our Calculator App and this time separate the columns with "7, 8, 9, x" into a separate view called TestColumns. We are doing this just for this example, so you don't have to change the code if you don't want to:

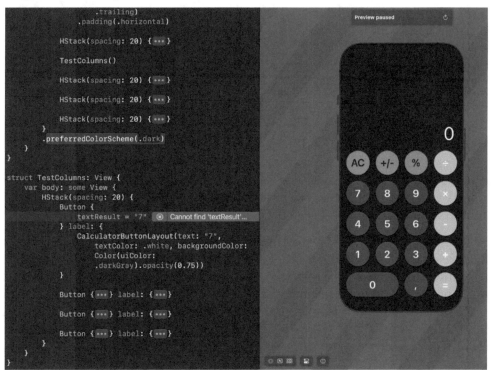

Figure 4.16: *Adding State*

Here, Xcode gives us the error because it cannot find the **textResult** property within its scope. Based on all the previous experiences, there may be something you come up with to solve this problem:

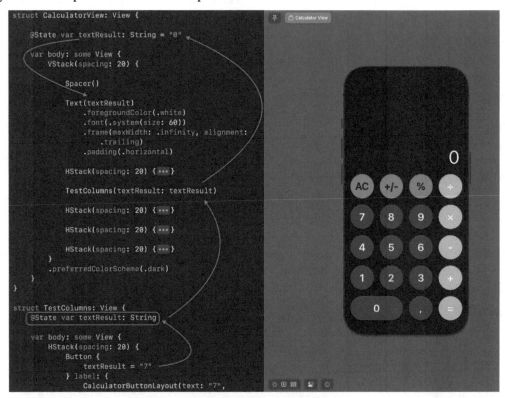

Figure 4.17: *The Binding Problem*

Because of the error, we must declare a **textResult** property as a required input to our **TestColumns** view. We just learned about **State**; in this situation, clearly, **textResult** is a changing overtime value. So, we have to mark it with the **@State** property wrapper so that SwiftUI knows to re-render all the views whenever the value gets modified.

The flow of all the red arrows is the expected way of data flowing. Everything looks great, let's build and see the result. And yeah, you may guess it, nothing is working. The text is still zero no matter how many times we pressed the seven button. Try it on the Simulator to confirm it yourself. But what is wrong here? The logic behind it is correct, and yes, **State** will re-render the view. The real problem here is that the two **textResult** properties of **TestColumns** and **CalculatorView** are not the same ones. When we use **@State** here, SwiftUI will create a copy of the input as its value:

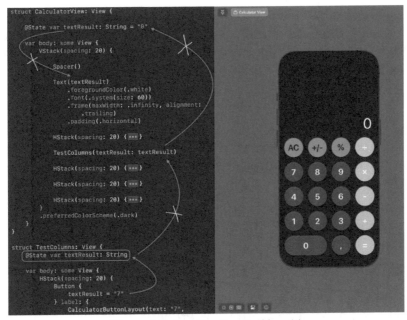

Figure 4.18: *The Binding Problem (2)*

Here is what **exactly** happened in this case. Because the two properties are not the same, only the first arrow direction was working here. To fix this problem and make SwiftUI understand that we want those two properties to be only one, our solution **here** is to use the **@Binding** property wrapper:

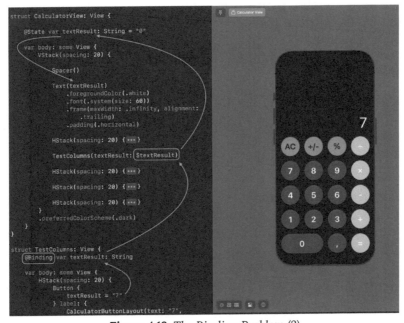

Figure 4.19: *The Binding Problem (3)*

Now, that's all the data flow is working in the directions of those green arrows as we expected. Notice there are two different changes here: we replace the **@State** with **@Binding,** and there is a prefix "**$**" symbol before the **textResult** input. This is because we can create a Binding by using the "**$**" prefix on a **State** variable, which creates a reference to the **State** variable that can be passed to another view. With this, our calculator is back to functioning again.

In summary, Binding is a powerful feature in SwiftUI that allows us to create a two-way connection between views, enabling us to pass data between them and keep them in sync. By using Binding, we can create more dynamic and interactive user interfaces and write more modular and reusable code.

Before we move on to the next section, let's discuss the concept that is used to build **@State** and **@Binding**: Property Wrapper in Swift language.

Property Wrapper

In Swift, a **property wrapper** is a way to encapsulate a piece of behavior or functionality and apply it to a property. Property wrappers are a new feature introduced in Swift 5.1. They are similar to computed properties, but they allow you to encapsulate more complex behavior and reuse it across multiple properties.

A property wrapper is defined as a struct that has a **wrappedValue** property, which is the property that will be wrapped. You can use the property wrapper by placing the "**@**" symbol before the property's name. Whenever you see the "**@**" symbol, it means there is a property wrapper in Swift. Each will bring up different functionalities to our properties, and if you want, you can totally make your own custom property wrapper. However, the scope of this is far beyond the scope of this book.

To understand more deeply about this concept and all other things related to property in Swift language, we suggest you take some time and read through the Property section in the Apple Swift Documentation. Here is the link: **https://docs.swift.org/swift-book/documentation/the-swift-programming-language/properties/**.

In summary, a property wrapper is a way to add additional functionality or behavior to a property without having to write that functionality yourself every time you use the property. This makes our code more readable, maintainable, and reusable, which explains the magical behavior we have just by adding **@State** or **@Binding** just before property declaration. These keywords add more functionality to our properties in an easier, shorter, and more convenient way.

Now, let's go back to our project and finish it by adding arithmetic computation so that we can use our app as a real calculator. During that, we will learn more about an advanced topic related to property: **Property Observer**.

Property Observer

In Swift, a property observer is a way to observe and respond to changes in a property's value. Property observers can be added to stored properties and are called every time a property's value is set.

There are two types of property observers: **willSet** and **didSet**.

The **willSet** observer is called just before a property's value is about to be set. This observer provides you with the opportunity to take some action before the new value is set. You can access the new value using the **newValue** keyword.

The **didSet** observer is called immediately after a property's value has been set. This observer provides you with the opportunity to take some action after the new value has been set. You can access the old value using the **oldValue** keyword.

Here's an example of how to use property observers:

```
class MyClass {
    var myProperty: String = "Hello" {
        willSet(newValue) {
            print("About to set myProperty to \(newValue)")
        }

        didSet(oldValue) {
            print("myProperty was changed from \(oldValue) to
                \(myProperty)")
        }
    }
}

let myInstance = MyClass()
myInstance.myProperty = "World" // About to set myProperty to
    World, myProperty was changed from Hello to World
```

```
About to set myProperty to World
myProperty was changed from Hello to World
```

Figure 4.20: Property Observer

In this example, we defined a class, **MyClass,** with a property, **myProperty,** that has both **willSet** and **didSet** observers. When we create an instance of **MyClass** and set **myProperty** to **World**, the **willSet** observer is called first, followed by the **didSet** observer. The output in the console shows the messages printed by the property observers.

In conclusion, a property observer is a way to observe and respond to changes in a property's value over time. This might sound familiar if you remember the part where we talked about **lifecycle** methods in the previous chapter. It is the same logic, but this time it is for the life of properties instead of views. In every programming language, the moment when something changes is very important. We usually try to perform or capture something at that moment, which is why **lifecycle** methods and property observers are very strong tools. Every programmer uses them frequently.

Now, let's get back to our calculator and finish the logic. Before this, you can try opening your own default calculator on your phone and play with it sometimes. When you are ready, let's analyze the problems we are facing. Take a look and dissect this mathematics operation:

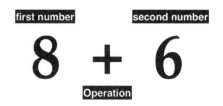

Figure 4.21: *Analyze and dissect math operation*

There is clearly a pattern here, and recognizing it is the most important part of programming. Most of the time, the hardest part is from the problem to breaking it down into small pattern. The coding parts are not a burden when you have done it quite a few times.

Here, we will have to store the first and second numbers and the mathematical operation between them. Then, that information is enough to make a calculation. Besides our **textResult** for display, we will need three more variables: **firstNumber**, **secondNumber,** and operation. Remember that we definitely know these values will change, so they must be marked with **@State**. For the operation, we will use String and later use an if-else statement to check the difference. As for **firstNumber** and **secondNumber**, we will use Double because we will perform the math on them later:

```
struct CalculatorView: View {

    @State var operation: String = ""
    @State var firstNumber: Double = 0
    @State var secondNumber: Double = 0
    @State var textResult: String = "0"
```

Figure 4.22: *Analyze and dissect math operation*

We will have ten number actions, from button 0 to button 9, and seven operations. We have highlighted them in the green area for number actions and the orange area for operation actions:

Figure 4.23: *Number actions and operation actions*

Why do we need to separate them? As you will soon see, the code logic behind those two types is similar. Let's tackle the easier part: the number of actions first. When you tap on any of those numbers, what do you expect? That the tapped number should be displayed on our **textResult** label, right? That's the first step before anything can happen. This is also the time when we want to store user input into the **firstNumber** property.

Now, the code for each numeric button will look kind of like this:

```
HStack(spacing: 20) {

    Button {
        textResult = "\(7)"
        firstNumber = 7
    } label: {
        CalculatorButtonLayout(text: "7",
            textColor: .white,
            backgroundColor: Color(uiColor:
            .darkGray).opacity(0.75))
    }
```

Figure 4.24: *Number action*

We set **textResult** and our **firstNumber** here. Let's pause here and try to apply what we just learned about Property Observer to make an improvement here. Why this is one of the best places to use Property Observer? Because there is a relationship between these two actions here. Whenever we change the value of our **firstNumber**, the **textResult** label is expected to change to reflect it. In this case, **willSet** or **didSet** is the same, but we choose to use **willSet**:

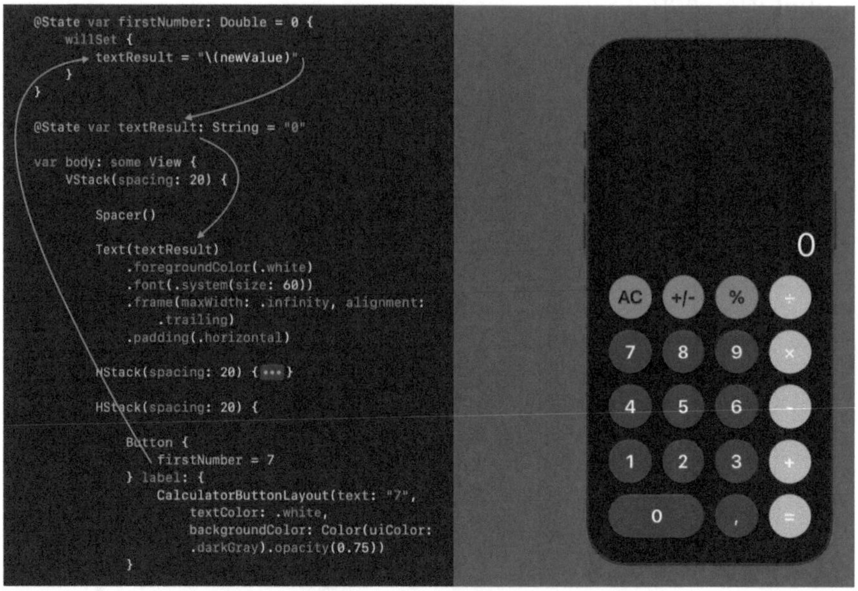

Figure 4.25: *Property observer for firstNumber*

In this stage, we have a relationship that follows the green arrow's directions. Whenever the value of our **firstNumber** changes, we will use that new value and assign it to our **textResult** text as a String. This will then automatically reflect in our app interface because **textResult** is marked with **@State**. The logic with the **secondNumber** property is the same as with **firstNumber**. However, the interesting part is with the operation, where we will use both **willSet** and **didSet** observers in a different way. Let's modify these two properties into property observers:

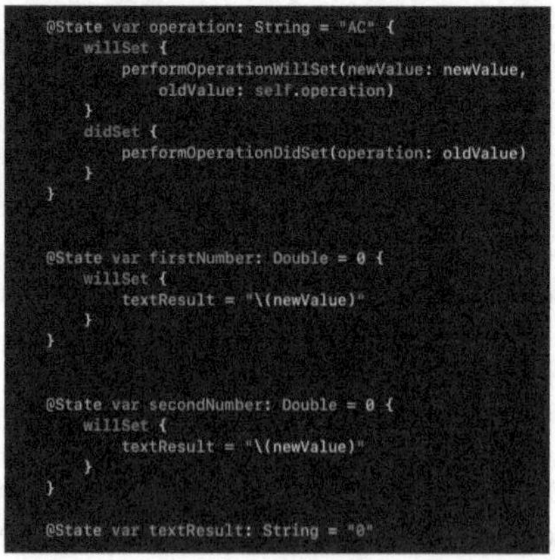

Figure 4.26: *All our calculator properties*

We will write two new functions, which will be executed when **willSet** and **didSet** of the operation occur. We will use **willSet** for "+, -, x, :" operations and **didSet** for "=, AC, +/-, %" operations. Why do we need this separation? It is because those "+, -, x, :" symbols can have the behavior of "=" too. Try this operation: "1 + 2 - 3", you will see when the second operation minus is tapped, the **textResult** label will show the result of the previous operation, "1 + 2". Because of this behavior, we will use both **didSet** and **willSet** observers. Here is the logic of them:

```
func performOperationDidSet(operation: String) {
    if operation == "+" {
        let result = firstNumber + secondNumber
        secondNumber = 0
        firstNumber = result
    } else if operation == "-" {
        let result = firstNumber - secondNumber
        secondNumber = 0
        firstNumber = result
    } else if operation == "x" {
        let result = firstNumber * secondNumber
        secondNumber = 0
        firstNumber = result
    } else if operation == "÷" {
        let result = firstNumber / secondNumber
        secondNumber = 0
        firstNumber = result
    }
}
```

Figure 4.27: *didSet operation*

Remember, with **didSet,** we are passing in the old value of it. So, like in the previously demonstrated example when we hit the minus operation, then the old value here will be the plus operation. And here, we will perform the action "1 + 2 = 3", then we set our second number to zero and save the result value to the **firstNumber**.

You may question why we assign the **secondNumber** value before the **firstNumber** value. Well, it is because these two properties also have property observers that will change the **textResult** label to their new value. So, if we set our **secondNumber** later, then our **textResult** will always be zero, which is not correct.

Before you can try chaining arithmetic operations, for example, like "((1 +2 – 3 + 5) x 6) : 4" and see the results one after another, we must change the assigning logic when tapping the numerical number. Right now, we only assign it to the **firstNumber**. Let's change it to:

```
Button {
    if operation == "AC" {
        if firstNumber == 0 {
            firstNumber = 7
        } else {
            firstNumber = firstNumber *
                10 + 7
        }
    } else {
        if secondNumber == 0 {
            secondNumber = 7
        } else {
            secondNumber = secondNumber
                * 10 + 7
        }
    }
} label: {
    CalculatorButtonLayout(text: "7",
        textColor: .white,
        backgroundColor: Color(uiColor:
        .darkGray).opacity(0.75))
}
```

Figure 4.28: *Tap button logic*

Here, we perform two logic checks. First, we check the current value of the operation to determine which property will be assigned. If it is the default state, "AC", then we know to assign it to the **firstNumber**; every other case will fall to the **secondNumber** because right now we have an operation to perform.

Secondly, we check if the assigned property's value is zero or not, if it is, we then assign it the value of the button. If not, then just like writing a whole large number, we have to multiply the old value by ten and then add to it our button's value.

With all this, everything is ready so you can now try performing some chained arithmetic operations.

Now if you are ready, then let's tackle all those left operations: "AC, +/-, %". We will use the **willSet** observer, which will use **newValue** as an input. Here, we will pass and use both the old value and the new value of the operation:

```
func performOperationWillSet(newValue: String, oldValue: String) {
    if newValue == "+/-" {
        performOperationDidSet(operation: oldValue)
        firstNumber = -firstNumber
    } else if newValue == "%" {
        performOperationDidSet(operation: oldValue)
        firstNumber = firstNumber/100
    } else if newValue == "AC" {
        firstNumber = 0
        secondNumber = 0
    }
}
```

Figure 4.29: *Operation willSet observer logic*

As you can see, we also reuse our previous function and make a call on an old value of the operation before we apply the functionality of the operation's new value. This will make sure our behavior is correct and align with user logic.

With this, now you can build and experience the Calculator App. Maybe it is your first functional App, and praise yourself for it.

Conclusion

Let's recap what we have learned in this chapter. We learned how to use **@State**. It automatically causes the view to re-render whenever the state value changes. This ensures that the view always reflects the current state of the app.

However, there is a problem when a view wants to modify data from another view. This is when we need **@Binding**. It is a property wrapper that allows us to create a two-way connection between a property in one view and a property in another view. By using a Binding, we can pass data between views in a way that allows both views to modify the same underlying data.

During this chapter, we have been able to make our first functional app: The Calculator. Through building this, we have strengthened and applied all the previous knowledge. We also learned a new concept about the life cycle but with variables: Property Observer. We can now interfere and take action in two states of a variable: **willSet** when its value is about to change, and **didSet** when the value just changed We then leveraged this characteristic to build and make our Calculator App work correctly.

In the next chapter, we will learn about design patterns on iOS, specifically the MVVM pattern, which works beautifully with SwiftUI. During that, we will go back and refactor this Calculator App to make it more refined and architecturally.

CHAPTER 5

Design Patterns with MVVM

Introduction

In history, developers saw the same problem repeatedly, and as a result, they standardized how to handle these kinds of problems and occurrences, which led to the development of the Design Patterns. They are an elegant and simple solution to repetitive problems in the software industry and generalize the ways to handle these problems. This is where Designs Pattern comes into play.

In the last chapter, we built our first app: the calculator. Though it is great, throughout your career, you will have a chance to work on a lot of projects. For a long time, there existed a critical problem because everyone is different and has their own unique coding style, and software engineering is a team-oriented job. For it to work, it is best for everyone to find a way to work effectively as a team with other people. This is also another benefit of having knowledge about design patterns.

Structure

In this chapter, the following topics will be covered:

- Design patterns introduction

- Common design patterns and architecture patterns in iOS development

- Benefit and purpose of applying Design Pattern

- Common iOS design patterns

- MVVM pattern introduction

- Applying MVVM to our Calculator

- @StateObject and @ObservedObject property wrapper

Design Pattern

In software engineering, a design pattern is a general reusable solution to a commonly occurring problem in software design. It is a proven solution to a specific problem that can be adapted and applied in different contexts.

Design patterns help to solve complex software development problems by providing tried and tested solutions. They make it easier to communicate about software design and architecture within a team, improve code readability, and simplify the maintenance and evolution of software systems.

Here are some reasons why we need design patterns in programming:

- **Reusability**: Design patterns provide reusable solutions to commonly occurring problems in software development, making it easier to solve similar problems in the future.

- **Scalability**: Design patterns enable software systems to be more scalable by providing a structured approach to software design and architecture.

- **Maintainability**: Design patterns help to improve the maintainability of software systems by making code more modular and easier to understand.

- **Testability**: Design patterns make it easier to write testable code. This means that developers can more easily test the application's functionality and catch errors before they become a problem.

- **Code quality**: Design patterns help to improve the overall quality of code by providing best practices and guidelines for software design.

- **Collaboration**: Design patterns facilitate collaboration and communication among team members by providing a common vocabulary for discussing software design and architecture.

- **Efficiency**: By using design patterns, developers can write code more efficiently. This means that they can spend less time on repetitive tasks and more time on creating new functionality.

- **Faster development time**: By using established design patterns, developers can focus on the specific needs of their application, rather than spending time designing and building new solutions from scratch.

Now all of this is not a problem if you are coding alone for your personal project or some kind of future unicorn. You can freely choose how to code just so you can understand it later. However, it is not when you have to work in a team with other people. Or even more, another person in the far future will come and work on your code base when you are long gone from the project.

Because of this fact, design pattern comes to exist. They are a set of best practices and guidelines that help software engineers solve complex problems more efficiently, improve the quality of their code, and simplify the maintenance and evolution of software systems.

They also enable software engineers to solve complex problems more efficiently and provide a common language for communication and collaboration within a team.

Design Pattern in iOS development

There are several architecture patterns and design patterns that iOS developers commonly used to build robust and scalable applications. Here are a few of the most common ones:

Architecture patterns

- **MVC (Model-View-Controller)**: This is a widely used design pattern that separates an application's data, user interface, and control logic into three distinct components. It allows developers to keep their code organized and maintainable while improving the overall user experience.

- **MVVM (Model-View-ViewModel)**: This is gaining popularity among iOS developers in recent years. It separates the user interface (View) from the business logic and data (ViewModel), allowing for better maintainability and testability. MVVM also allows for easier data binding and provides a more streamlined way to handle user input.

MVP (Model-View-Presenter) is a design pattern in iOS app development that divides the application into three components: Model, View, and Presenter. The Model handles data and business logic, the View displays the UI and captures user input, and the Presenter acts as the mediator between them. MVP promotes testability, code organization, and maintenance by separating concerns and facilitating clear interactions between components. The Model represents the data, the View handles the UI, and the Presenter orchestrates communication between them, resulting in a more modular and manageable iOS app architecture.

VIPER: This is a design pattern used in iOS development to improve code modularity, testability, and maintainability. It consists of five components: View, Interactor, Presenter, Entity, and Router. The View handles UI display and user interactions, while the Interactor manages the app's business logic and data. The Presenter acts as a bridge between the View and Interactor, handling user input and data updates. The Entity represents the app's data model, and the Router handles navigation between different screens. VIPER promotes the separation of concerns, making it easier to understand, modify, and test iOS apps.

Clean Architecture: This is a software design principle that emphasizes a clear separation of concerns and dependencies in order to create robust and maintainable systems. It consists of distinct layers, including the Domain, Application, Interface, and Infrastructure layers, each with specific responsibilities. The Domain layer contains the core business logic, the Application layer coordinates use cases, the Interface layer handles the user interface, and the Infrastructure layer manages external dependencies. By adhering to Clean Architecture, developers can achieve code that is modular, testable, and adaptable to change, resulting in more scalable and maintainable iOS applications.

Design patterns

- **Delegate**: The delegate pattern is used extensively in iOS development to enable one object to communicate with another object. It is commonly used in **UIKit** classes, such as **UITableView** and **UICollectionView**, to provide custom behavior for specific events.

- **Singleton**: The singleton pattern is used to ensure that a particular class has only one instance, allowing for centralized control over resources and data.

- **Observer**: The observer pattern is used to notify interested objects of changes to a specific object. It is commonly used in iOS development to implement event-driven programming, such as in notifications and user interface updates.

As you may guess, in this chapter, we will focus on the MVVM architecture pattern, as it is a modern one with strength and works seamlessly with SwiftUI. Let's dive deep into this pattern to see what it brings to the table. Along the way, we will be making changes to the calculator app that we built in the last chapter. We will adapt the MVVM pattern into it to see the difference it brings.

MVVM Pattern

MVVM stands for Model View and View Model. These are the three different separated functionalities that this pattern suggests us to follow.

In the MVVM pattern, each component - Model, View, and View Model - has a specific responsibility in the application as follows:

- **Model**: The Model is responsible for managing the data and business logic of the application. It is where the data is stored and manipulated, and it defines the rules and operations related to that data. In an iOS application, the Model can include classes that represent the database or network service, or it can simply be a collection of data structures and algorithms that perform operations on that data.

- **View**: The View is responsible for displaying the UI elements and user interface of the application. It contains all the visual components of the application, including buttons, text fields, labels, and other elements. The View is passive, meaning it does not contain any business logic or data manipulation. Instead, it simply displays the data provided by the View Model and forwards any user input back to the View Model for processing.

- **View Model**: The View Model is the mediator between the Model and the View. It is responsible for exposing the data from the Model to the View, and for handling any user interactions from the View and updating the Model accordingly. The ViewModel also contains the business logic of the application, such as rules for validating user input and performing calculations. It acts as a bridge between the Model and the View, allowing them to remain separate and decoupled.

Here is a better visualization of the relationship in the MVVM pattern:

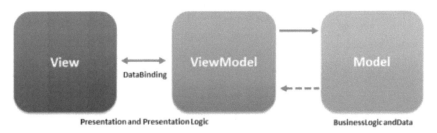

Figure 5.1: *MVVM Pattern Visualization*

The main advantage of using the MVVM pattern is that it helps to separate concerns and make the code more modular and testable. By isolating the UI logic in the view model, it becomes easier to write unit tests for the code and also to reuse the code in different parts of the application.

To use MVVM in an iOS app, developers typically create separate classes for the model, view, and view model, and then connect them using bindings or other mechanisms for communication between the components.

There are also many third-party libraries and frameworks available that provide additional support for implementing the MVVM pattern in iOS development, such as **ReactiveCocoa**, **RxSwift** for **UIKit** as a third-party library, and Combine, recently announced by Apple as a native framework solution.

In conclusion, the **Model** represents the data and business logic of the application, the View represents the UI elements, and the View Model acts as a mediator between the model and the view. The view model exposes data from the model to the view, and it also handles user interactions from the view and updates the model accordingly.

In the previous chapters, we have made some components: the renting card and the calculator app. However, all of the codes are in one place, with the UI component and its logic in the same file. In the next section, we will come back to our calculator and make some changes to it. You can see we will separate and architect our codebase into three separated layers according to the MVVM pattern.

The best way to learn anything is to get your hands dirty. Now, let's get back to the calculator app.

Implementing MVVM Pattern into the Calculator App (1)

Now, let's restructure our code base:

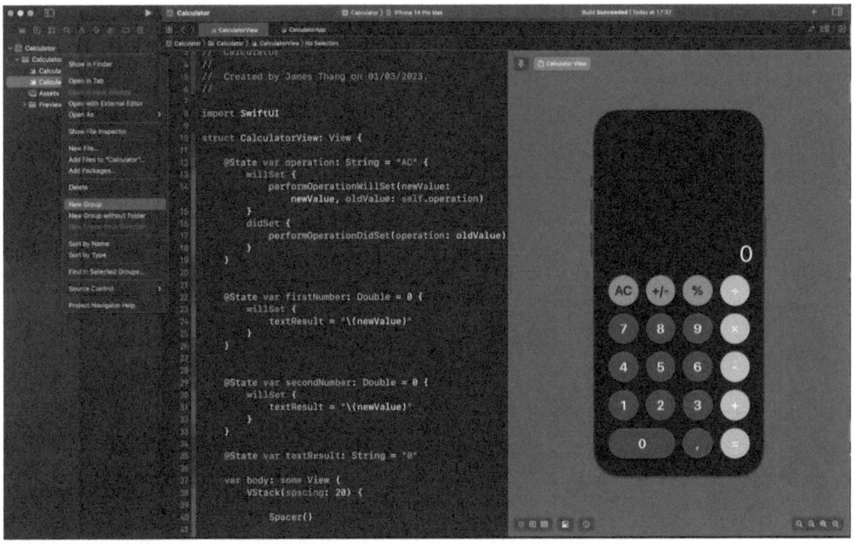

Figure 5.2: *Restructuring codebase following MVVM pattern (1)*

To start, left-click on our app folder and select Create **New Group** to make a new folder. We will create three new folders according to the three layers of MVVM: Model, View, and View Model. Then, drag all the view files into the View Folder. This is a preference of choice to separate them into three different folders. Some may combine them in the same folder for different modules, pages, or user story. For our application, structuring them into three separate folders makes it cleaner and easier to navigate:

Figure 5.3: *Restructuring codebase following MVVM pattern (2)*

Now, let's refactor our code to follow the MVVM pattern. We will work on creating and separating the Model layer first, and then the View Model layer later.

The Model is responsible for managing the data and business logic of the application. It is where the data is stored and manipulated, and it defines the rules and operations related to that data. So, where is the part of the Model in our Calculator app?

Remember when we laid out the buttons inside each HStack? Here's the code:

```
HStack(spacing: 20) {
    Button {
        if operation == "AC" {
            if firstNumber == 0 {
                firstNumber = 7
            } else {
                firstNumber = firstNumber * 10 + 7
            }
        } else {
            if secondNumber == 0 {
                secondNumber = 7
            } else {
                secondNumber = secondNumber * 10 + 7
            }
        }
    } label: {
        CalculatorButtonLayout(text: "7", textColor: .white, backgroundColor: Color(uiColor: .darkGray).opacity(0.75))
    }

    Button { ••• } label: { ••• }

    Button { ••• } label: { ••• }

    Button { ••• } label: { ••• }
}
```

Figure 5.4: *Extracting Model (1)*

Once again, we come back to our '7' button. Remember, the Model is where we store data of the View, which is the button here. What input parameters does it need?

```
HStack(spacing: 20) {
    Button {
        if operation == "AC" {
            if firstNumber == 0 {
                firstNumber = ⑦
            } else {
                firstNumber = firstNumber * 10 + ⑦
            }
        } else {
            if secondNumber == 0 {
                secondNumber = ⑦
            } else {
                secondNumber = secondNumber * 10 + ⑦
            }
        }
    } label: {
        CalculatorButtonLayout(text: ⑦, textColor: .white, backgroundColor: Color(uiColor: .darkGray).opacity(0.75))
    }

    Button { ••• } label: { ••• }

    Button { ••• } label: { ••• }

    Button { ••• } label: { ••• }
}
```

Figure 5.5: *Extracting Model (2)*

It seems that all of our buttons need three information: the text number it represents, the color of the text, and its background color. Now, let's make our model. We will call it **ButtonInfoModel**, short for information about the button:

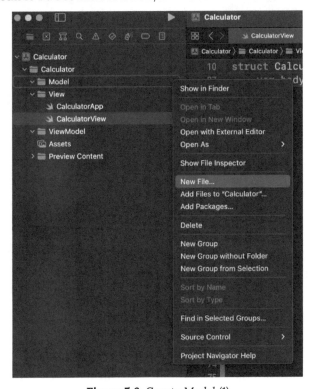

Figure 5.6: Create Model (1)

We will choose a plain Swift file for this:

Figure 5.7: Create Model (2)

Then, click **Next**, and enter our file name, which is **ButtonInforModel**. Make sure the **Targets** is checked:

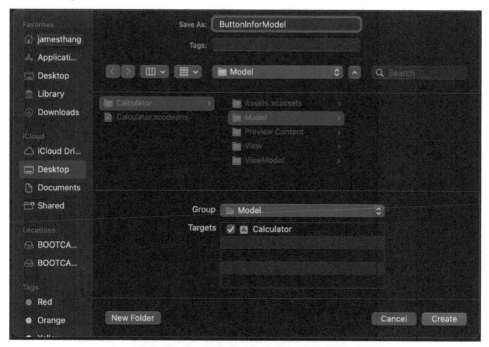

Figure 5.8: *Create Model (3)*

Let's write the code to make our model. We will use Struct for this purpose to define the sketch of each button:

```swift
import SwiftUI

struct ButtonInforModel: Identifiable {
    var id: UUID = .init()
    var textNumber: String
    var textColor: Color
    var backgroundColor: Color
    var isOperation: Bool

    var number: Double {
        return Double(textNumber) ?? 0
    }
}
```

Figure 5.9: *Button Model*

Here, we have our button model, and because we also need the value as **Double** for arithmetic calculations, we create a computed property number to automatically transform our **textNumber String** into a **Double** value that's ready to use.

We also make our button model adapt to the Identifiable protocol. Just in case you don't remember, a protocol comes with constraints and gains. Just like the View protocol requires us to have a body, this Identifiable protocol requires us to have an id property, and it has to be unique for every instance, which is why we use UUID here. In case you don't know yet, UUID stands for Universal Unique Identifier. As the name suggests, when we create a new UUID, it is guaranteed to be unique. Now, what is the gain here for Identifiable? It provides a stable notion of identity to a class or a value type that adopts it. Every button we have created from this model will be unique and can be identified from each other. But why do we need this characteristic? It is very useful in SwiftUI, as some structures require their input data to be uniquely identifiable from each other. For example, here is the **ForEach** building block that we will soon use to replace the redundant copy-paste button four times for each HStack.

Also, remember we separated all the buttons into two types: numeric and operation. So, in this model, we need a Boolean variable to clarify them.

Let's look back to see the structure of our app's button:

Figure 5.10: *Buttons structure*

Except for the first **textResult** label, we have five HStacks, four of which contain four buttons, and the last contains three buttons. So, we will need a two-dimensional array to represent the data for these buttons. It means that we will have five arrays, each representing the data for one row HStack of buttons. These five arrays will be inside one large array that represents all the button data that this calculator needs.

Here is the data for our buttons:

```
private var buttonData: [[ButtonInforModel]] = [
    [
        ButtonInforModel(textNumber: "AC", textColor: .black, backgroundColor: .gray.opacity(0.85), isOperation: true),
        ButtonInforModel(textNumber: "+/-", textColor: .black, backgroundColor: .gray.opacity(0.85), isOperation: true),
        ButtonInforModel(textNumber: "%", textColor: .black, backgroundColor: .gray.opacity(0.85), isOperation: true),
        ButtonInforModel(textNumber: "+", textColor: .white, backgroundColor: .orange, isOperation: true)
    ],
    [
        ButtonInforModel(textNumber: "7", textColor: .white, backgroundColor: Color(uiColor: .darkGray).opacity(0.75), isOperation: false),
        ButtonInforModel(textNumber: "8", textColor: .white, backgroundColor: Color(uiColor: .darkGray).opacity(0.75), isOperation: false),
        ButtonInforModel(textNumber: "9", textColor: .white, backgroundColor: Color(uiColor: .darkGray).opacity(0.75), isOperation: false),
        ButtonInforModel(textNumber: "x", textColor: .white, backgroundColor: .orange, isOperation: true)
    ],
    [
        ButtonInforModel(textNumber: "4", textColor: .white, backgroundColor: Color(uiColor: .darkGray).opacity(0.75), isOperation: false),
        ButtonInforModel(textNumber: "5", textColor: .white, backgroundColor: Color(uiColor: .darkGray).opacity(0.75), isOperation: false),
        ButtonInforModel(textNumber: "6", textColor: .white, backgroundColor: Color(uiColor: .darkGray).opacity(0.75), isOperation: false),
        ButtonInforModel(textNumber: "-", textColor: .white, backgroundColor: .orange, isOperation: true)
    ],
    [
        ButtonInforModel(textNumber: "1", textColor: .white, backgroundColor: Color(uiColor: .darkGray).opacity(0.75), isOperation: false),
        ButtonInforModel(textNumber: "2", textColor: .white, backgroundColor: Color(uiColor: .darkGray).opacity(0.75), isOperation: false),
        ButtonInforModel(textNumber: "3", textColor: .white, backgroundColor: Color(uiColor: .darkGray).opacity(0.75), isOperation: false),
        ButtonInforModel(textNumber: "+", textColor: .white, backgroundColor: .orange, isOperation: true)
    ],
    [
        ButtonInforModel(textNumber: "0", textColor: .white, backgroundColor: Color(uiColor: .darkGray).opacity(0.75), isOperation: false),
        ButtonInforModel(textNumber: ".", textColor: .white, backgroundColor: Color(uiColor: .darkGray).opacity(0.75), isOperation: false),
        ButtonInforModel(textNumber: "=", textColor: .white, backgroundColor: .orange, isOperation: true)
    ]
]
```

Figure 5.11: *Buttons data*

Take a look at this; it will be the data of our fifteen buttons. And you will be surprised by how short and simple our code will look. Previously, here is how the code for the first button's row looks :

```
HStack(spacing: 20) {
    Button {
        operation = "AC"
    } label: {
        CalculatorButtonLayout(text: "AC", textColor: .black, backgroundColor: .gray.opacity(0.85))
    }

    Button {
        operation = "+/-"
    } label: {
        CalculatorButtonLayout(text: "+/-", textColor: .black, backgroundColor: .gray.opacity(0.85))
    }

    Button {
        operation = "%"
    } label: {
        CalculatorButtonLayout(text: "%", textColor: .black, backgroundColor: .gray.opacity(0.85))
    }

    Button {
        operation = "+"
    } label: {
        CalculatorButtonLayout(text: "+", textColor: .white, backgroundColor: .orange)
    }
}
```

Figure 5.12: *First button's row before refactoring*

As you can see, the code is redundant. We copy and paste the button four times, and the differences have all been abstracted to the **buttonData** from our model. One of the principles in programming is DRY, which stands for **don't repeat**

yourself. Let's apply it now in this example. Here is the same code that leverage the characteristic of the **ForEach** container:

```
HStack(spacing: 20) {
    ForEach(buttonData[0]) { data in
        Button {
            if data.isOperation {
                operation = data.textNumber
            }
        } label: {
            CalculatorButtonLayout(text: data.textNumber, textColor: data.textColor, backgroundColor:
                                   data.backgroundColor)
        }
    }
}
```

Figure 5.13: *First button's row after refactoring*

Way shorter, right? The **ForEach** container in SwiftUI will integrate through every item of data that we pass in, and with that data, we then use it to make our button. So, we only have to write the button code once. In this example, we iterate through the first-row data, because all of them are operation buttons, so their action is to set back the operation property's value with their text String. Now imagine it will be all the data; that's just another **ForEach**. How short could it be? Let's find out:

```
ForEach(0..<buttonData.count, id: \.self) { index in
    let hStackData = buttonData[index]
    HStack(spacing: 20) {
        ForEach(hStackData) { data in
            Button {
                if data.isOperation {
                    operation = data.textNumber
                } else {
                    if operation == "AC" {
                        if firstNumber == 0 {
                            firstNumber = data.number
                        } else {
                            firstNumber = firstNumber * 10 + data.number
                        }
                    } else {
                        if secondNumber == 0 {
                            secondNumber = data.number
                        } else {
                            secondNumber = secondNumber * 10 + data.number
                        }
                    }
                }
            } label: {
                if data.textNumber == "0" {
                    CalculatorButtonLayout(text: data.textNumber, textColor: data.textColor, backgroundColor:
                        data.backgroundColor, width: 180)
                } else {
                    CalculatorButtonLayout(text: data.textNumber, textColor: data.textColor, backgroundColor:
                        data.backgroundColor)
                }
            }
        }
    }
}
```

Figure 5.14: *All buttons layout after refactoring*

Here is all the code for your calculator buttons! How short is that compared to the previous solution? The first **ForEach** will be for taking out each row's data. Then, we use that data to lay out the button. If it is a numeric button, then we either assign a new value from the number property to the **firstNumber** or **secondNumber** based on logical conditions. And finally, in the label, we add another condition for our special zero button.

And here it is. We have cut down a hundred lines of code in our View. If you are new to programming, it will take you some time to familiarize yourself with this. However, iterating through an array of data and presenting/making a layout from it is very normal for us developers.

The benefits of extracting the Model layer can be seen here: shortening the code (more than a hundred lines), applying the DRY principle, and separating the data layer from the view layer.

For this reason, our codebase will be more scalable. If you want to look at and change the data of the buttons, for example, the symbol "x" to "*", then the place to go to is the Model. But if you want to change how it looks, for example, from a circle shape to a triangle shape, then go to the View. With this separation of concern, everything is now easier because things are in order.

Before we move to the next and final layer, the ViewModel, there are some new required property wrappers and protocols you need to know. Let's get familiar with them.

ObservableObject and @StateObject

In SwiftUI, an **ObservableObject** is a protocol that defines an object that can be observed by SwiftUI Views. When an object conforms to the **ObservableObject** protocol, it can notify any views that depend on it when its state changes.

Sound familiar, isn't it? Remember when we first learned about **@State**; whenever its value changes, SwiftUI will automatically refresh to present its newest value. The main difference here is that **@State** is used inside the scope of a view, whereas the **ObservableObject** protocol makes it possible for SwiftUI views to listen for changes from an outside object. This is exactly what we want and what makes the ViewModel possible.

The ViewModel is another layer; it is the mediator between the Model and the View. It is responsible for exposing the data from the Model to the View and for handling any user interactions from the View, updating the Model accordingly. It also contains the business logic of the application, such as rules for validating user input and performing calculations. It acts as a bridge between the Model and the View, allowing them to remain separate and decoupled.

To create an observable object, you can define a class that conforms to the **ObservableObject** protocol and then use the **@Published** property wrapper to mark any properties that should trigger updates when their values change. For example:

```
class MyViewModel: ObservableObject {
    @Published var count = 0
}
```

Figure 5.15: *ViewModel example (1)*

In this example, **MyViewModel** is an observable object with a single **@Published** property called count. When the value of the count changes, any SwiftUI views dependent on **MyModel** will be notified and updated automatically.

You can then use this observable object in your SwiftUI views by declaring a property that holds an instance of the object and using the **@ObservedObject** property wrapper to indicate that the view should be updated when the observable object changes. For example:

```
struct MyView: View {
    @StateObject var model = MyViewModel()

    var body: some View {
        Text("Count: \(model.count)")
    }
}
```

Figure 5.16: *ViewModel example (2)*

In this example, **MyView** declares an **@StateObject** property called a model that holds an instance of **MyViewModel**. As the value of **model.count** changes, the view will be updated automatically to show the new value. With this, you can now have a glimpse of how the ViewModel interacts with SwiftUI views.

Just like the Model layer, completely defined and separated from the views, the ViewModel is another layer outside that acts as a bridge between the View and the Model. It contains the business logic of the application. If you don't remember, then back in our calculator app, here is how we handle the business logic:

```swift
@State var operation: String = "AC" {
    willSet {
        performOperationWillSet(newValue: newValue, oldValue: self.operation)
    }
    didSet {
        performOperationDidSet(operation: oldValue)
    }
}

@State var firstNumber: Double = 0 {
    willSet {
        textResult = "\(newValue)"
    }
}

@State var secondNumber: Double = 0 {
    willSet {
        textResult = "\(newValue)"
    }
}

@State var textResult: String = "0"
```

Figure 5.17: *Calculator business logic (1)*

Here, we have a total of four properties to store values that will be reflected in views when they are modified. Additionally, we have two helper functions for changes in the operations value:

```swift
func performOperationDidSet(operation: String) {
    if operation == "+" {
        let result = firstNumber + secondNumber
        secondNumber = 0
        firstNumber = result
    } else if operation == "-" {
        let result = firstNumber - secondNumber
        secondNumber = 0
        firstNumber = result
    } else if operation == "x" {
        let result = firstNumber * secondNumber
        secondNumber = 0
        firstNumber = result
    } else if operation == "÷" {
        let result = firstNumber / secondNumber
        secondNumber = 0
        firstNumber = result
    }
}

func performOperationWillSet(newValue: String, oldValue: String) {
    if newValue == "+/-" {
        performOperationDidSet(operation: oldValue)
        firstNumber = -firstNumber
    } else if newValue == "%" {
        performOperationDidSet(operation: oldValue)
        firstNumber = firstNumber/100
    } else if newValue == "AC" {
        firstNumber = 0
        secondNumber = 0
    }
}
```

Figure 5.18: *Calculator business logic (2)*

All of this logic will then be transferred to the ViewModel. Also, remember that ViewModel is the layer between Model and View, which means our button's model will remain inside the ViewModel, not View anymore.

With this knowledge in mind, let's come back to our app and finish implementing the MVVM pattern.

Implementing MVVM Pattern into the Calculator App (2)

Unlike View and Model, we will use a Class for ViewModel, as you have already seen in the previous example.

While it is technically possible to define a ViewModel as a struct, it is often preferable to define it as a class for a few reasons:

1. **Reference Semantics:** A class has reference semantics, which means that when you pass a reference to a class instance, you are passing a reference to the same instance in memory. This makes it easier to share and update the ViewModel state across multiple views and avoid data duplication. In contrast, a struct has value semantics, which means that when you pass a struct instance, you are passing a copy of the struct's value.

2. **Identity**: Because classes have reference semantics, they have a unique identity that can be used to track and manage ViewModel instances. This can be useful when working with frameworks that require objects to be identified by reference, such as Core Data.

3. **Mutability**: Classes can be mutated after they are created, which means that ViewModel instances can be updated and changed as needed. In contrast, structs are immutable by default, which means that any changes to a struct must be made by creating a new instance.

4. **Property observers**: Classes allow for property observers like didSet and willSet which can be used to observe changes to ViewModel properties and trigger any necessary updates to the view. We used both of them in our calculator.

5. **ObservableObject** protocol can only be used for class.

Overall, while it's technically possible to define a ViewModel as a struct, using a class can often provide more flexibility and control over the ViewModel's behavior and state management in SwiftUI.

Now, let's define our ViewModel, make a new file, and call it **CalculatorViewModel** inside the ViewModel folder:

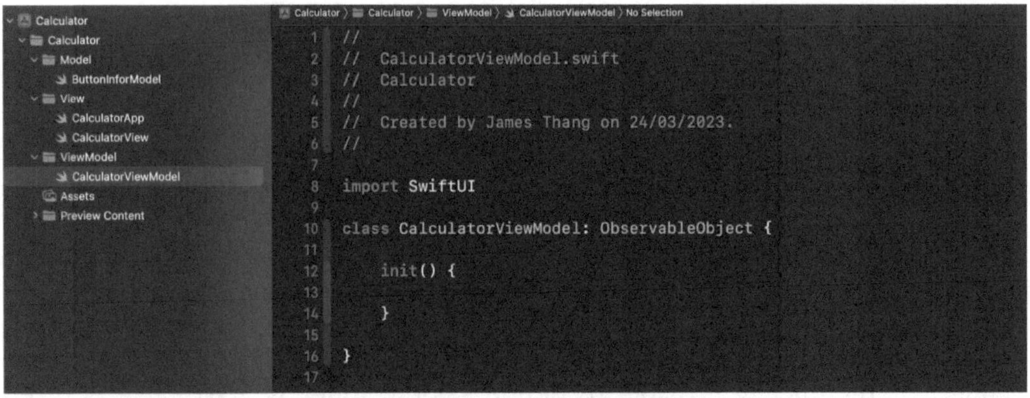

Figure 5.19: *Create Calculator View Model*

Here, we define a class **CalculatorViewModel** and conform to the **ObservableObject** protocol. To begin, let's move all of the app Model into it. In this case, it is the data of our buttons:

Figure 5.20: *Transferring Model place to ViewModel (1)*

Cut and paste it here. Notice that we have made a change to accessing level control here. Instead, if private, we now use private(set). The difference is that with private(set), this data can be read and get outside its scope, but it cannot be modified outside of its defined scope, which is the **CalculatorViewModel** here.

Xcode will give a warning error back in the **CalculatorView** because it cannot find the **buttonData** anymore. So, let's create our ViewModel inside the view:

```
private let viewModel = CalculatorViewModel()

var body: some View {
    VStack(spacing: 20) {

        Spacer()

        Text(textResult)
            .foregroundColor(.white)
            .font(.system(size: 60))
            .frame(maxWidth: .infinity, alignment: .trailing)
            .padding(.horizontal)

        ForEach(0..<viewModel.buttonData.count, id: \.self) { index in
            let hStackData = viewModel.buttonData[index]
            HStack(spacing: 20) {
                ForEach(hStackData) { buttonData in
```

Figure 5.21: Transferring Model place to ViewModel (2)

We initialize an instance of **CalculatorViewModel** here and call it **viewModel**. Then, we can get our **buttonData** from the ViewModel for use in our view here. Build and run it, and everything will work smoothly!

Next, let's tackle the business logic and move these to our view model. Similar to the button model data, let's move all of our logical properties and functions there:

```
//@State get replaced with @Published
@Published var operation: String = "AC" {
    willSet {
        performOperationWillSet(newValue: newValue, oldValue: self.operation)
    }
    didSet {
        performOperationDidSet(operation: oldValue)
    }
}

@Published var firstNumber: Double = 0 {
    willSet {
        textResult = "\(newValue)"
    }
}

@Published var secondNumber: Double = 0 {
    willSet {
        textResult = "\(newValue)"
    }
}

@Published var textResult: String = "0"
```

Figure 5.22: Transferring logic to ViewModel (1)

Instead of using the **@State,** which works only inside one view, we replaced all of it with the **@Published** property wrapper:

```swift
private func performOperationDidSet(operation: String) {
    if operation == "+" {
        let result = firstNumber + secondNumber
        secondNumber = 0
        firstNumber = result
    } else if operation == "-" {
        let result = firstNumber - secondNumber
        secondNumber = 0
        firstNumber = result
    } else if operation == "x" {
        let result = firstNumber * secondNumber
        secondNumber = 0
        firstNumber = result
    } else if operation == "÷" {
        let result = firstNumber / secondNumber
        secondNumber = 0
        firstNumber = result
    }
}

private func performOperationWillSet(newValue: String, oldValue: String) {
    if newValue == "+/-" {
        performOperationDidSet(operation: oldValue)
        firstNumber = -firstNumber
    } else if newValue == "%" {
        performOperationDidSet(operation: oldValue)
        firstNumber = firstNumber/100
    } else if newValue == "AC" {
        firstNumber = 0
        secondNumber = 0
    }
}
```

Figure 5.23: *Transferring logic to ViewModel (2)*

Similarly, with our function, we added private to make them safer because these two functions are not being used outside of our ViewModel. With this, we will have a lot of errors back in the **CalculatorView** because Xcode cannot find these properties and functions. Just like with the **buttonData**, go back and add **viewModel** reference before them, so that Xcode knows to go and get these data in the ViewModel:

```
Text(viewModel.textResult)
    .foregroundColor(.white)
    .font(.system(size: 60))
    .frame(maxWidth: .infinity, alignment: .trailing)
    .padding(.horizontal)

ForEach(0..<viewModel.buttonData.count, id: \.self) { index in
    let hStackData = viewModel.buttonData[index]
    HStack(spacing: 20) {
        ForEach(hStackData) { data in
            Button {
                if data.isOperation {
                    viewModel.operation = data.textNumber
                } else {
                    if viewModel.operation == "AC" {
                        if viewModel.firstNumber == 0 {
                            viewModel.firstNumber = data.number
                        } else {
                            viewModel.firstNumber = viewModel.firstNumber * 10 + data.number
                        }
                    } else {
                        if viewModel.secondNumber == 0 {
                            viewModel.secondNumber = data.number
                        } else {
                            viewModel.secondNumber = viewModel.secondNumber * 10 + data.number
                        }
                    }
                }
            }
```

Figure 5.24: *Transferring logic to ViewModel (3)*

Compile now, and everything will run very successfully. However, it isn't working! Our button is clicked, but the **textResult** value is not updated. What have we done wrong here? It is because we forgot to mark our view model with **@StateObject**:

```
//      private let viewModel = CalculatorViewModel()
//      View Model need to marked with @State Property Wrapper
@StateObject private var viewModel = CalculatorViewModel()
```

Figure 5.25: *@StateObject*

See if you catch this error. However, in order for **@Published** to work and notify the view model, the view model has to be marked with **@StateObject**.

Now, build it, and our calculator is back to working perfectly! And with this, we have successfully extracted the ViewModel layer. The MVVM pattern is now completed in our project. We can now see three separate layers inside the three folders of our project.

- The **Model** layer defined the required data of each button: `ButtonInforModel`.

- The **ViewModel** layer contains all of the calculation logic of the app: `CalculatorViewModel`.

- The **View** layer displays the calculation screen: `CalculatorView`.

You can also see that the ViewModel is acting as the bridge here to transfer data from the Model to the View.

Conclusion

In this chapter, we have learned about design patterns and their purposes in programming. We also have an introduction to all the common design patterns in iOS development.

Then, we dug deep into the MVVM pattern because it allows the separation of concerns that fits right in with SwiftUI.

The model represents the app's data and business logic. It is responsible for managing the data and providing it to the view model. The view is responsible for displaying the data and providing user interaction. The view model acts as an intermediary between the view and the model. It is responsible for processing user input and providing data to the view.

After learning all the behind concepts, we applied them to successfully refactor our calculator app to follow the MVVM design pattern.

In the next chapter, we will learn more complicated View building blocks of SwiftUI, which you may have seen in a lot of famous commercial Apps. The power of SwiftUI will become even better.

CHAPTER 6

Tab Bar, Navigation, and Compositional Layout

Introduction

In this chapter, we will be looking at commonly found elements and UI designs in a modern mobile application. They have multiple screens with different user stories. The tab bar and navigation bar are two important elements of modern user interface design. We will see how they work and recreate them in SwiftUI. Later, we will learn about compositional layout and how to make a modern complex layout like the Instagram or Spotify app.

Structure

In this chapter, the following topics will be covered:

- Tab bar introduction
- Making tab bar in SwiftUI
- Navigation in mobile app development
- Navigation View and Navigation Stack
- Modern application layout with the compositional layout in SwiftUI
- Load images inside our project

- LazyVGrid and LazyHGrid

Tab bar

Tab bar is a user interface component that is commonly used in mobile applications to provide navigation between different sections or views within an app. It is typically located at the bottom of the screen and consists of a horizontal bar with tabs that the user can tap to switch between different sections:

- A tab bar is a graphical user interface element that is commonly found in mobile applications and websites.

- It typically appears at the bottom of the screen and contains a series of tabs that represent different sections or views within the app or website.

- Tab bars are often used to provide quick and easy navigation between different parts of an app or website, allowing users to switch between tasks or views with just a tap.

- Each tab in a tab bar usually has a unique icon and label, which helps users to quickly identify and select the desired tab.

- Tab bars are often customizable, allowing users to rearrange the tabs, add new tabs, or remove tabs that are not frequently used.

- While tab bars are commonly used in mobile applications, they can also be found in desktop applications and websites.

- The use of tab bars can help to improve the user experience by providing a clear and consistent navigation system that is easy to use and understand.

- However, it is important to use tab bars appropriately and not overwhelm users with too many tabs or options, as this can lead to confusion and frustration.

Here's an example from the LinkedIn app:

Figure 6.1: *Tab bar*

Each tab usually represents a distinct feature or category within the app and may display a corresponding icon or text label to help the user identify the purpose of the tab. The LinkedIn app has five tab bars, each with its separate functionalities. Users can easily navigate between them with one single tap.

Tab bar is a popular layout component for mobile apps because they provide an easy-to-use and visually appealing way for users to navigate through an app. They allow users to quickly switch between different sections without having to navigate through a complex hierarchy of menus or screens, making it easier to find the information or feature they need.

Now, open up Xcode, and let's make a tab bar:

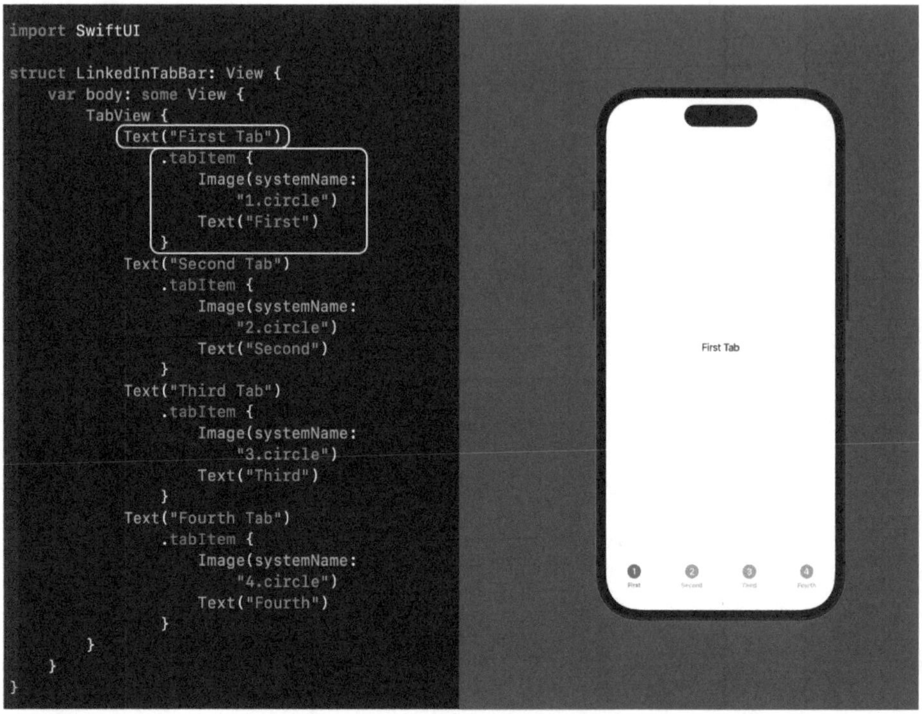

```swift
import SwiftUI

struct LinkedInTabBar: View {
    var body: some View {
        TabView {
            Text("First Tab")
                .tabItem {
                    Image(systemName:
                        "1.circle")
                    Text("First")
                }
            Text("Second Tab")
                .tabItem {
                    Image(systemName:
                        "2.circle")
                    Text("Second")
                }
            Text("Third Tab")
                .tabItem {
                    Image(systemName:
                        "3.circle")
                    Text("Third")
                }
            Text("Fourth Tab")
                .tabItem {
                    Image(systemName:
                        "4.circle")
                    Text("Fourth")
                }
        }
    }
}
```

Figure 6.2: *Layout Tab bar with SwiftUI*

How easy it is! If you have built this in UIKit, then this is incomparable. There are two conditions here as follows:

- We have the **TabView** container which is wrapping all of our tab views.

- Each view must has conformed to the **.tabItem()** modifier for that view to become a tab view. In this modifier, we can specify its displaying image and text. Try to change the Image icon and text to look just like the Linked In app.

Here, we use **Text("First tab")** just for demonstration, but it can be any SwiftUI view. In a real project, we will make a separate file for each tab view, lay them out there, and then set up the tab bar here. How convenient and clean it is!

There are two other useful things related to the tab bar:

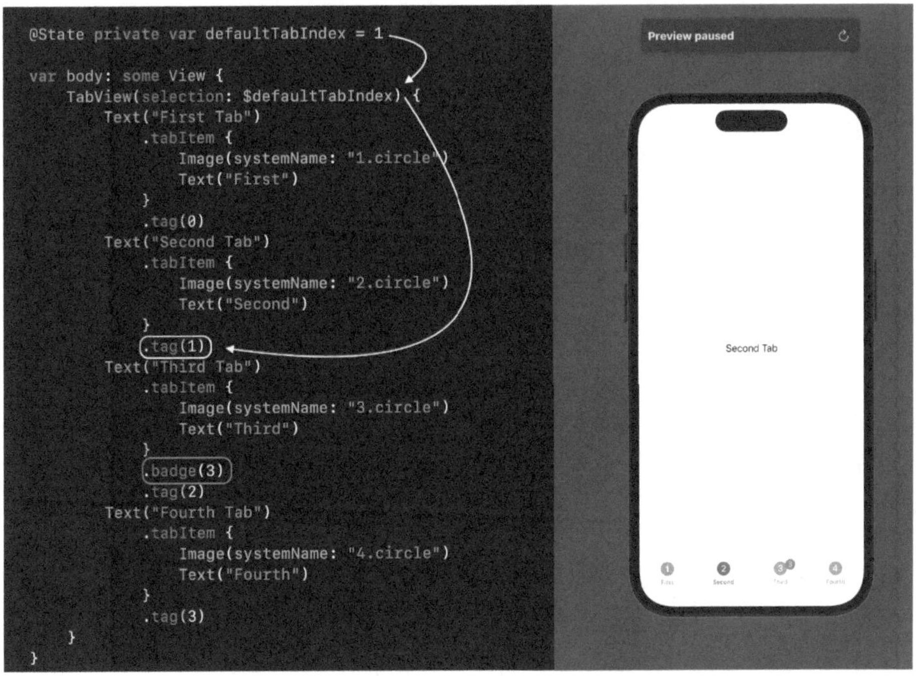

Figure 6.3: *Tab bar frequently used features*

The first thing is to select the default tab view that will appear first when the user launches the app. The **TabView** container has the selection parameter for this, which requires a binding input. For each tab view here, we use the **.tag()** modifier. It is used to differentiate among certain selectable views, like possible values of a Picker or the tabs of a **TabView**. Then, we use a **State** variable to inform SwiftUI that the first tab to be selected has the tag "1".

The second thing that is frequently seen is the badge to alert something new related to that tab view. SwiftUI has a built-in **.badge()** modifier for this functionality. Just input an Int number, and you get this out of the box.

And that's almost everything you'll ever need with the Tab bar. Very short code is needed, and everything is easy to read and grasp. This is why we iOS developers are in love with SwiftUI so much.

Tab bars are often used in conjunction with other navigation components like a navigation bar or a menu to provide a complete navigation experience. These are fundamental in almost every large app. Let's learn about navigation and how it can be implemented in SwiftUI.

Navigation in iOS development

Navigation in iOS development refers to the process of allowing users to move between different screens or views within an app. It is the core mechanism used to manage the hierarchy of views in an app and enables users to seamlessly move between different sections of an app. Here are some key aspects of iOS navigation:

- Navigation is a fundamental aspect of the iOS user experience, allowing users to move between different screens and views within an app.

- The iOS navigation system includes several key elements, including the navigation bar, tab bar, and various types of controls and gestures.

- The navigation bar is a thin strip that appears at the top of the screen and typically contains a title, or a back button.

- The navigation bar can also be customized to include additional buttons or controls, depending on the needs of the app.

- In addition to the navigation bar, iOS also includes a tab bar, which appears at the bottom of the screen and allows users to switch between different sections or views within the app.

- The tab bar is commonly used for primary navigation, while the navigation bar is used for more contextual navigation, such as moving up and down a hierarchical structure or drilling down into submenus.

- iOS navigation also includes various gestures and controls, such as swiping to go back or forward, pinching to zoom, and tapping to select.

- Effective navigation design in iOS is critical to creating a seamless user experience, and involves careful consideration of factors such as hierarchy, context, and user goals.

- Navigation in iOS should be intuitive and easy to understand, with clear labels and visual cues that guide the user through the app or website.

Here is the Storyboard visualization of it:

Figure 6.4: *Navigation in iOS development*

In UIKit, navigation is typically achieved through a navigation controller, which provides a stack-based approach to managing views. The navigation controller maintains a stack of view controllers, with the topmost view controller being the one currently displayed on the screen. Users can navigate forward and backward through the stack using buttons, gestures, or other UI elements.

The navigation controller also provides a navigation bar at the top of the screen, which typically contains a title and a back button. This bar can be customized to include additional buttons or elements, such as a search bar or a segmented control.

In SwiftUI, navigation works similarly to iOS development with UIKit. SwiftUI provides a **NavigationView** component that allows you to create a hierarchy of views and navigate between them.

NavigationView and NavigationLink

The **NavigationView** is a container view provided by SwiftUI that allows you to create a hierarchical navigation interface. It provides a navigation bar at the top of the view hierarchy that displays a title and, optionally, buttons for navigating back to the previous view or performing other actions.

In SwiftUI, the **NavigationView** component creates a navigation stack to manage the navigation flow between views. Each view pushed onto the navigation stack is displayed with a navigation bar at the top, and a back button is automatically added to allow the user to navigate back to the previous view.

Here's an example of how to use the **NavigationView** in SwiftUI:

Figure 6.5: *Navigation View in SwiftUI*

In this example, we create a **NavigationView** that contains a List view with four items. The **NavigationView** automatically adds a navigation bar with the title **My List** at the top of the screen. If we push another view on the stack, a back button will be automatically added to the navigation bar to allow the user to return to this view.

You can customize the navigation bar by adding buttons or other view elements to it. You can also customize the appearance of the navigation bar using the **.navigationBarColor()** and **.navigationBarTitleDisplayMode()** modifiers.

To navigate to a new view, you can use the **NavigationLink** component. This component creates a clickable button that will push the destination view onto the navigation stack when tapped. You can also use the **NavigationLink(destination: , label:)** initializer to create programmatic navigation.

Let's make our list link and navigate to other views:

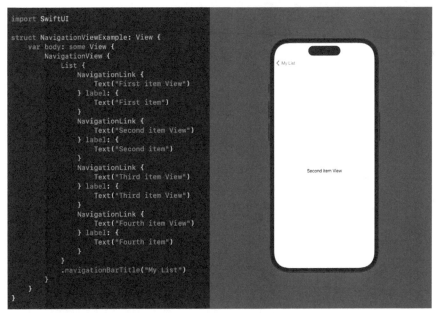

```
import SwiftUI

struct NavigationViewExample: View {
    var body: some View {
        NavigationView {
            List {
                NavigationLink {
                    Text("First item View")
                } label: {
                    Text("First item")
                }
                NavigationLink {
                    Text("Second item View")
                } label: {
                    Text("Second item")
                }
                NavigationLink {
                    Text("Third item View")
                } label: {
                    Text("Third item")
                }
                NavigationLink {
                    Text("Fourth item View")
                } label: {
                    Text("Fourth item")
                }
            }
            .navigationBarTitle("My List")
        }
    }
}
```

Figure 6.6: *Embed Navigation Link (1)*

In this example, we use a **NavigationView** to define possible paths from this view forward. When the user taps the highlighted text, a new view is pushed onto the stack using the **NavigationLink** component. The next view displays a simple text view with a custom navigation bar title:

```
import SwiftUI

struct NavigationViewExample: View {
    var body: some View {
        NavigationView {
            List {
                NavigationLink {
                    Text("First item View")
                } label: {
                    Text("First item")
                }
                NavigationLink {
                    Text("Second item View")
                } label: {
                    Text("Second item")
                }
                NavigationLink {
                    Text("Third item View")
                } label: {
                    Text("Third item View")
                }
                NavigationLink {
                    Text("Fourth item View")
                } label: {
                    Text("Fourth item")
                }
            }
            .navigationBarTitle("My List")
        }
    }
}
```

Figure 6.7: *Embed Navigation Link (2)*

We have the back button right out of the box. Clicking it will return you to our list view.

Another common feature we often see with the NavigationView is the navigation bar button. To add a button to the navigation bar in SwiftUI, you can use the `.navigationBarItems()` modifier on the **NavigationView**. This modifier allows you to add one or more navigation bar items to either the left or right side of the navigation bar.

Here's an example of how to add **Settings** and **Remove** buttons to the left and right sides of the navigation bar:

```swift
import SwiftUI

struct NavigationViewExample: View {
    var body: some View {
        NavigationView {
            List { ... }
            .navigationBarTitle("My List")
            .toolbar {
                ToolbarItem(placement:
                    .navigationBarLeading) {
                    Button {
                        print("Setting tapped!")
                    } label: {
                        Image(systemName: "gear")
                    }
                }
                ToolbarItem(placement:
                    .navigationBarTrailing) {
                    Button {
                        print("Trash tapped!")
                    } label: {
                        Image(systemName: "trash")
                    }
                }
            }
        }
    }
}
```

Figure 6.8: *Navigation Bar Button (1)*

In this example, we add two buttons as the leading and trailing navigation bar items using the **navigationBarItems** modifier. The action closure is called when the button is tapped. We also use the **systemName** property to specify the system image for the button.

You can also add multiple navigation bar items by passing an array of views to the **navigationBarItems** modifier. For example, you can add a **Trash** button and an **Add** button to the right side of the navigation bar as follows:

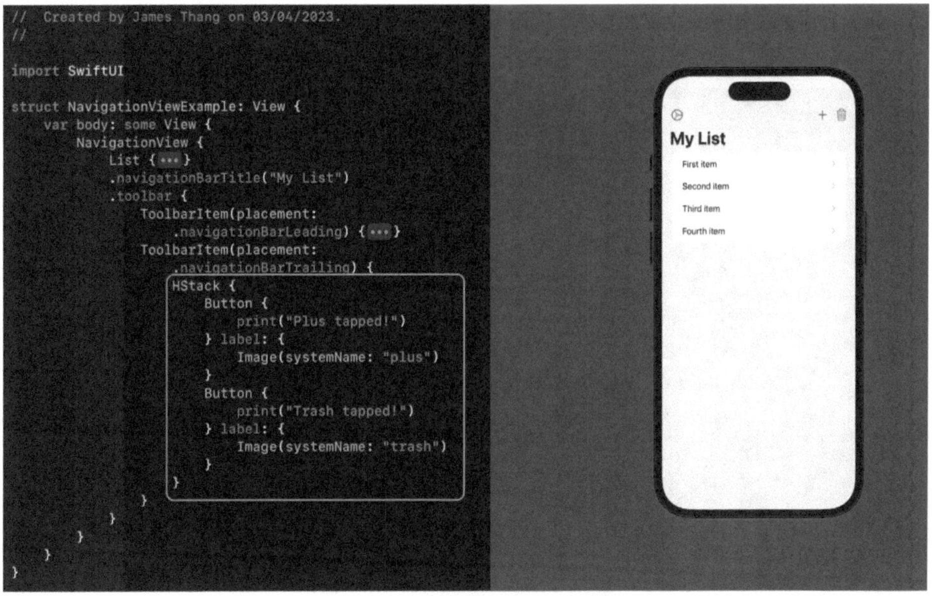

Figure 6.9: *Navigation Bar Button (2)*

In this case, we use an **HStack** to display the two buttons side by side in the navigation bar. Although **NavigationView** and **NavigationLink** are great together, they still have some flaws. Because of this, iOS 16 introduced a better solution for managing navigation in SwiftUI: Navigation Stack.

Navigation stack

NavigationView is a widely used component in iOS development. When SwiftUI was initially introduced, it included a view called **NavigationView** that allowed developers to create navigation-based user interfaces. However, with the release of iOS 16, Apple has deprecated the old **NavigationView** and introduced a new view called **NavigationStack** that can present a stack of views. This new view enables developers to build data-driven navigation.

In our example, replace **NavigationView** with **NavigationStack,** and everything will work fine:

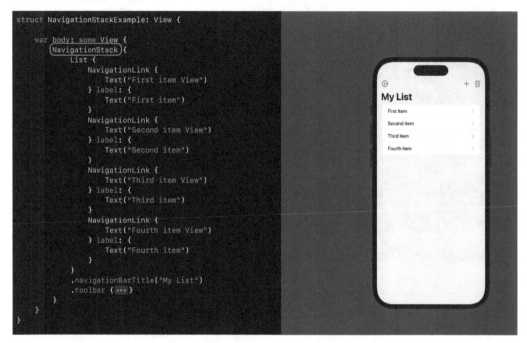

Figure 6.10: *Introduce NavigationStack (1)*

Let's do some cleaning on this code:

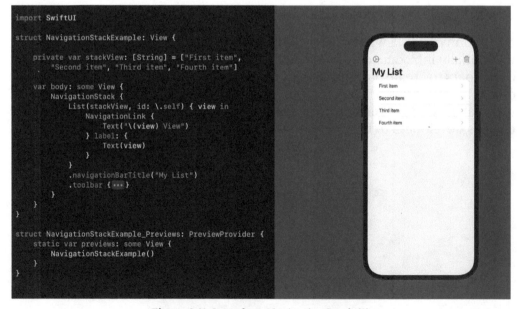

Figure 6.11: *Introduce NavigationStack (2)*

But for now, everything is still the same. With iOS 16, **NavigationStack** introduces a new modifier called **.navigationDestination()** that associates a destination view with a presented data type. The same piece of code in our example can be rewritten as follows:

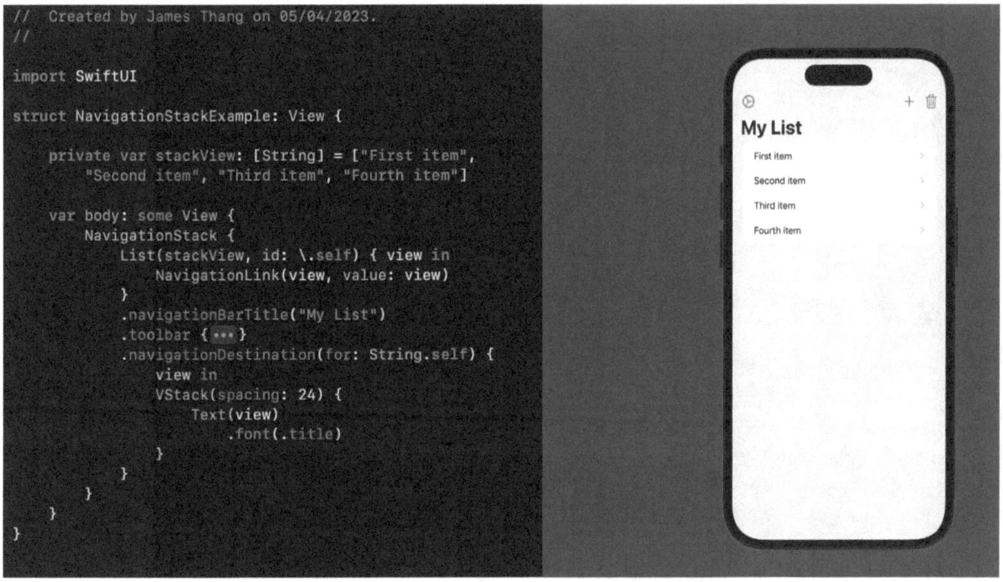

```
// Created by James Thang on 05/04/2023.
//

import SwiftUI

struct NavigationStackExample: View {

    private var stackView: [String] = ["First item",
        "Second item", "Third item", "Fourth item"]

    var body: some View {
        NavigationStack {
            List(stackView, id: \.self) { view in
                NavigationLink(view, value: view)
            }
            .navigationBarTitle("My List")
            .toolbar { ... }
            .navigationDestination(for: String.self) {
                view in
                VStack(spacing: 24) {
                    Text(view)
                        .font(.title)
                }
            }
        }
    }
}
```

Figure 6.12: *NavigationStack navigate views*

NavigationLinks are still used to present a list of data and implement navigation in SwiftUI. The difference is that each **NavigationLink** is now associated with a value. Additionally, we use the new **.navigationDestination()** modifier to capture the value change. When a user selects a specific link, the **.navigationDestination()** modifier presents the corresponding destination view for navigation links that present data of type **Color**.

When testing the app in the preview, it will function just as it did before. However, the internal implementation now utilizes the new **.navigationDestination()** modifier.

An important thing to note is that you are allowed to define more than one **.navigationDestination()** modifier for handling different types of navigation links.

Unlike the previous **NavigationView**, the new **NavigationStack** makes it simple to keep track of the navigation state. The **NavigationStack** view has an alternative initialization method that accepts a path parameter, which is bound to the navigation state for the stack.

If you want to store or manage the navigation state, you can create a state variable. Here is an example:

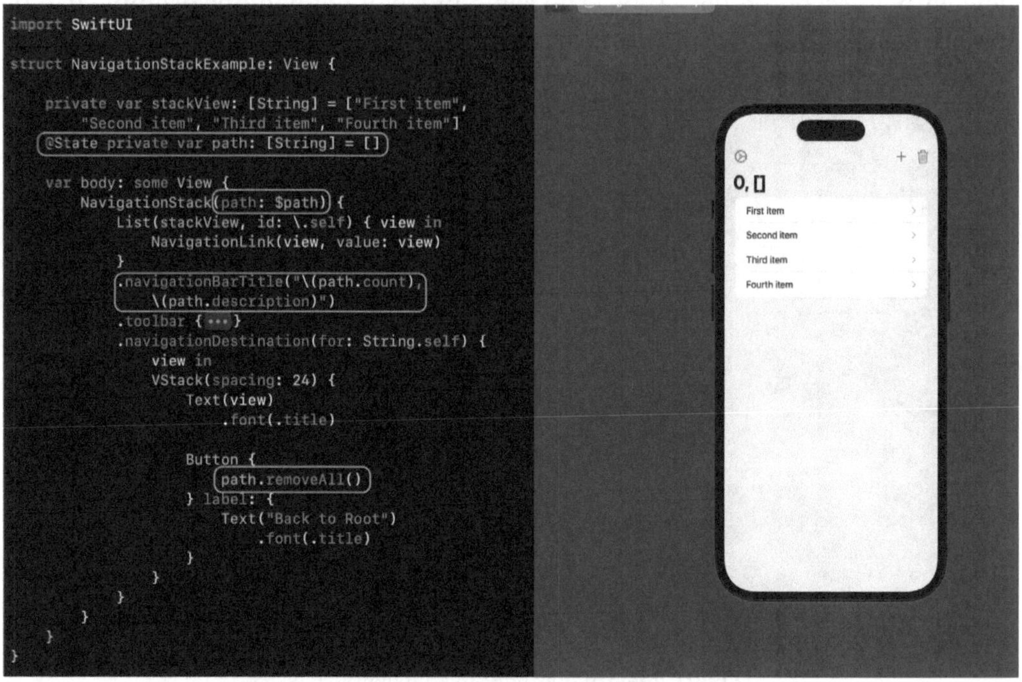
import SwiftUI
struct NavigationStackExample: View {
private var stackView: [String] = ["First item",
"Second item", "Third item", "Fourth item"]
@State private var path: [String] = []
var body: some View {
NavigationStack(path: $path) {
List(stackView, id: \.self) { view in
NavigationLink(view, value: view)
}
.navigationBarTitle("\(path.count),
\(path.description)")
.toolbar { ••• }
.navigationDestination(for: String.self) {
view in
VStack(spacing: 24) {
Text(view)
.font(.title)
Button {
path.removeAll()
} label: {
Text("Back to Root")
.font(.title)
}
}
}
}
}
}
0, []
First item
Second item
Third item
Fourth item

***Figure 6.13**: NavigationStack manages view hierarchy*

We introduced a state variable called **`path`**, which is an array of String used to store the navigation state. When initializing **`NavigationStack`**, we pass its binding for managing the stack. The value of the **`path`** variable is automatically updated when the navigation stack's state changes.

We also change our **`navigationBarTitle`** to see what's inside our path. As you can see, at the root here, our path is empty, so its count is equal to zero, and it is an empty string. This always happens when you are at the root view. So, we add a **Back to Root** button here that, when tapped, will remove and empty our path.

Now, navigate to the First Item and see how our path information changes:

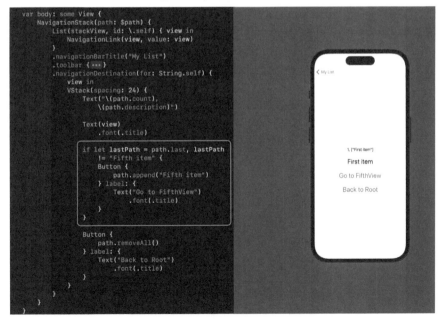

```swift
struct NavigationStackExample: View {

    private var stackView: [String] = ["First item",
        "Second item", "Third item", "Fourth item"]
    @State private var path: [String] = []

    var body: some View {
        NavigationStack(path: $path) {
            List(stackView, id: \.self) { view in
                NavigationLink(view, value: view)
            }
            .navigationBarTitle("My List")
            .toolbar { ••• }
            .navigationDestination(for: String.self) {
                view in
                VStack(spacing: 24) {
                    Text("\(path.count),
                        \(path.description)")

                    Text(view)
                        .font(.title)

                    Button {
                        path.removeAll()
                    } label: {
                        Text("Back to Root")
                            .font(.title)
                    }
                }
            }
        }
    }
}
```

Figure 6.14: Inside NavigationStack's path

As you can see, our path now has one item, which is our first item being added in. Now both the back button and **Back to Root** will work the same. We will change our path information to one text view here. We will now add another button inside each item's view to navigate to the fifth view:

```swift
var body: some View {
    NavigationStack(path: $path) {
        List(stackView, id: \.self) { view in
            NavigationLink(view, value: view)
        }
        .navigationBarTitle("My List")
        .toolbar { ••• }
        .navigationDestination(for: String.self) {
            view in
            VStack(spacing: 24) {
                Text("\(path.count),
                    \(path.description)")

                Text(view)
                    .font(.title)

                if let lastPath = path.last, lastPath
                    != "Fifth item" {
                    Button {
                        path.append("Fifth item")
                    } label: {
                        Text("Go to FifthView")
                            .font(.title)
                    }
                }

                Button {
                    path.removeAll()
                } label: {
                    Text("Back to Root")
                        .font(.title)
                }
            }
        }
    }
}
```

Figure 6.15: Adding the Fifth View

We will check the condition to add the fifth view button. Let's hit it and see what is inside our path now:

```
var body: some View {
    NavigationStack(path: $path) {
        List(stackView, id: \.self) { view in
            NavigationLink(view, value: view)
        }
        .navigationBarTitle("My List")
        .toolbar { ••• }
        .navigationDestination(for: String.self) {
            view in
            VStack(spacing: 24) {
                Text("\(path.count),
                    \(path.description)")

                Text(view)
                    .font(.title)

                if let lastPath = path.last, lastPath
                    != "Fifth item" {
                    Button {
                        path.append("Fifth item")
                    } label: {
                        Text("Go to FifthView")
                            .font(.title)
                    }
                }

                Button {
                    path.removeAll()
                } label: {
                    Text("Back to Root")
                        .font(.title)
                }
            }
        }
    }
}
```

Figure 6.16: *Path information at the Fifth View*

As you can see, our path now has two values: **"First item"** and **"Fifth item"**. Now, if you hit back, then you will be at the first item view. However, if you hit **Back to Root**, then you will return to the main list with four items.

We can direct the navigation stack to return to the root level by resetting the value of the **path** variable.

The new **NavigationStack**, introduced in iOS 16, makes it simple for developers to construct data-driven navigation user interfaces. If your app doesn't require support for older versions of iOS, you can utilize this new component to manage deep linking and intricate user flows.

Compositional layout

- Compositional layout is a powerful layout system that can be used in app development to create highly customized, dynamic layouts for iOS apps, including those built using SwiftUI.

- In SwiftUI, compositional layout can be implemented using the new `LazyVGrid` and `LazyHGrid` views, which allow developers to define layouts using a declarative, data-driven approach.

- These views can be configured with a wide range of properties and behaviors, including size, spacing, alignment, scrolling direction, and more.

- Compositional layout in SwiftUI also supports a variety of different layout types, including grids, lists, and custom layouts that can be tailored to specific use cases.

- With compositional layout in SwiftUI, developers have more control over the look and feel of their app and can create layouts that adapt to different device sizes and orientations.

- Compositional layout in SwiftUI also includes powerful features such as section headers and footers, supplementary views, and decoration views, which allow developers to add additional content and visual elements to their layouts.

- SwiftUI's declarative syntax makes it easy to build complex, nested layouts using compositional layout, with changes to the underlying data automatically reflected in the layout.

- While compositional layout in SwiftUI can be more complex and require more setup than simpler layout systems, it offers a high degree of flexibility and customization that can lead to more engaging and dynamic app experiences.

- Compositional layout is just one of many powerful tools available to app developers for creating rich, interactive user interfaces in SwiftUI, and can be used in conjunction with other SwiftUI features and technologies to create truly unique and innovative apps.

Here's an example from the Instagram app:

Figure 6.17: *Compositional layout in the Instagram app*

Now, let's return to Xcode and make this compositional layout. As you can see in this design, there will be three columns of infinity-scrolling images.

Load image

For this example, we will load a sample image from inside our project. In the next chapter, when learning about Networking, we will learn how to load images online from a URL:

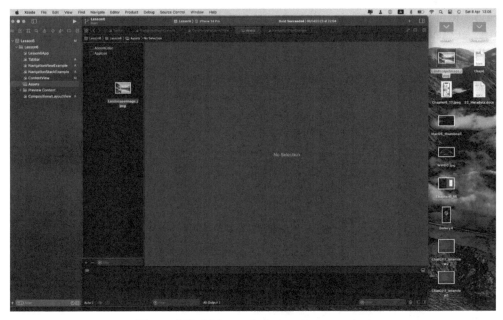

Figure 6.18: *Add sample Image to our project*

Navigate to **Assets** in our project hierarchy, and then drag and drop your sample image here. With this, we are ready to use the **LandscapeImage** inside our project. To display an Image inside the project, we will be using the Image container view:

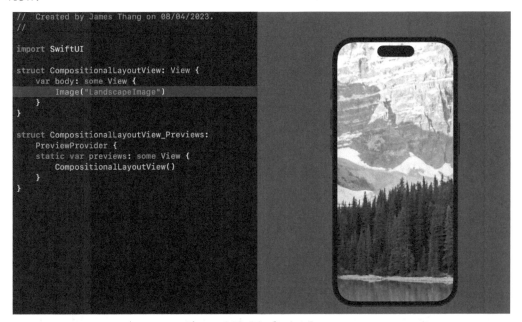

Figure 6.19: *Displaying Image*

Here, the landscape image fully covers our screen. This is because in SwiftUI, with the **Image()** container alone, it will render the original size of the input image on the screen.

To deal with this issue, there are two view modifiers always being used with the Image container: **.resizable()** and **.aspectRatio()**:

Figure 6.20: *Resizing Image*

With this, our image looks great and preserves its original appearance. Now, you may look back at the way we were doing the Calculator app layout in the previous chapter to recreate Instagram's layout. Although it will work by combining **VStack**, **HStack,** and **ForEach** containers, there is a better solution for this modern design: **LazyVGrid** or **LazyHGrid**.

LazyVGrid and LazyHGrid

LazyVGrid and **LazyHGrid** are views in iOS development that allow you to arrange views in a grid layout vertically and horizontally. It is a part of the SwiftUI framework and was introduced in iOS 14.

LazyVGrid and **LazyHGrid** both allow you to arrange views in a grid layout, but they differ in their orientation.

The main difference between these two views is their axis of arrangement. While **LazyVGrid** arranges views in vertical columns, **LazyHGrid** arranges views in horizontal rows. This means that the **columns** parameter in **LazyVGrid** corresponds to the number of columns in the grid, while the **rows** parameter in **LazyHGrid** corresponds to the number of rows.

Both can be used to replace each other, so it depends on each developer's preference. In this Instagram example, we will be using **LazyVGrid**.

The **LazyVGrid** view is similar to the VGrid view, but with one key difference: **LazyVGrid** is designed to handle large amounts of data more efficiently. Instead of creating all the views at once, it creates them on-demand as the user scrolls through the grid. This helps to conserve memory and improve performance.

To use **LazyVGrid**:

- Firstly, we need to define the layout of the grid by specifying the number of columns and the spacing between them.

- After that, we can then provide a collection of data to the view, which will be used to create the individual views in the grid.

For the Instagram layout, we will need three equal columns of images. Let's do this:

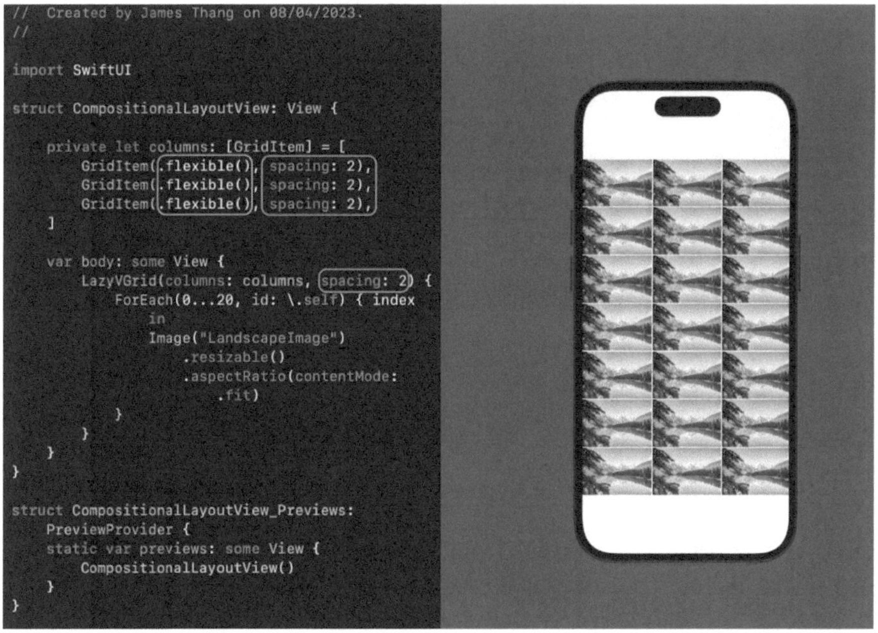

Figure 6.21: *LazyVGrid*

We create a columns property, which will be our view columns data. It is an array of **GridItem**. Because we want three equal columns, which is why we have three GridItems here.

In SwiftUI, a **GridItem** is a view that represents a single item in a grid layout. It's used in conjunction with the **LazyVGrid** or **LazyHGrid** container views to arrange views in a grid-like fashion.

A **GridItem** can be configured with properties such as spacing, alignment, and size. In this example, we use **.flexible()** to create a grid item that can expand to fill the available space, giving us three equal columns.

The spacing parameter is for the space between each column, and later, we can specify the space between each row with the spacing parameter that comes from the **LazyVGrid** itself. Thus, we have our Instagram compositional layout.

Furthermore, you can specify the **width** and **height** of a grid item by using the **.fixed()** parameter. For example, here we will set the first columns to be fixed at 100 pixels:

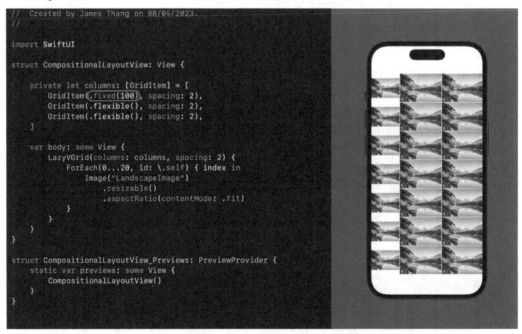

Figure 6.22: *Fixed size column in LazyVGrid*

In addition to **.fixed()** and **.flexible()**, you can also use **.adaptive()** to create a grid item that adjusts its size based on the available space. Try playing around with these different cases to see how they are used.

Let's revert back and do a final add-on to make our example look like Instagram. We are adding **ScrollView** for vertical scroll if there are more pictures and using **NavigationStack** to add navigation title:

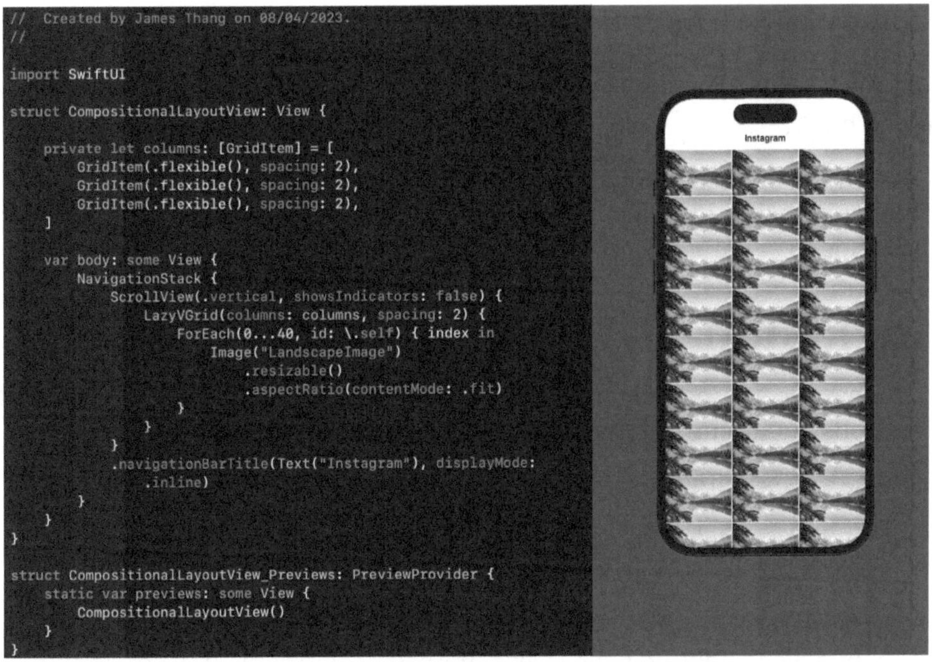

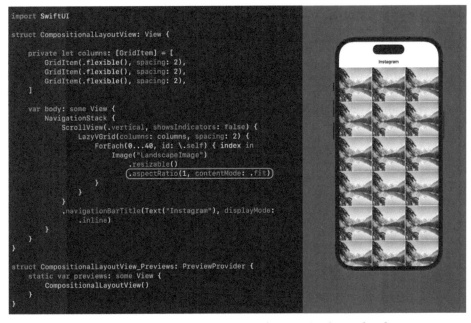

Figure 6.23: *Instagram layout with LazyVGrid*

Now, you may look back and argue that the image in our prototype is square. No worries, because we can easily achieve this on the **.aspectRatio()** modifier:

Figure 6.24: *Instagram layout with LazyVGrid completed*

The first option parameter of the `.aspectRatio()` modifier allows us to specify the width-to-height ratio of our image. If not specified, then the original ratio will be preserved. Here, because we want a square image, the width-to-height ratio will be "1".

In summary, both `LazyVGrid` and `LazyHGrid` are powerful tools for creating efficient and flexible grid layouts in SwiftUI, which are commonly seen in modern applications.

Conclusion

In this chapter, we have learned about commonly used elements in modern applications, including Tab bar, Navigation, and Compositional layout.

All of these are essential components for building great user interfaces in SwiftUI:

- Tab bar provides an easy-to-use and intuitive way for users to navigate between different sections of an app.

- Navigation helps users to move between different screens and contexts, while also enabling a clear and hierarchical organization of content.

- Compositional layout provides a powerful and flexible way to arrange and display complex collections of views in a way that is optimized for performance and adaptability.

By leveraging these tools in SwiftUI, developers can create highly customizable and engaging user experiences that are tailored to the unique needs of their app and its users.

In the next chapter, we will learn about networking to connect and retrieve data online. Then, we will learn how to implement it in iOS development with SwiftUI. Get some rest and stay excited for the next chapter.

CHAPTER 7

Networking with SwiftUI - Part 1

Introduction

Networking is a critical aspect of iOS app development as it allows apps to communicate with remote servers, retrieve data, and provide users with up-to-date information. Whether you're building a social media app, an e-commerce platform, or a news aggregator, networking is an essential tool that enables your app to interact with the world.

In today's fast-paced and interconnected world, users expect apps to work seamlessly and deliver content quickly. This is where networking comes into play, allowing apps to communicate with servers in the background, retrieve data on demand, and provide users with a smooth and responsive experience.

In this context, understanding how to implement networking in your iOS app is a key skill for any iOS developer. We will be exploring this topic in both this and the next chapter.

Structure

In this chapter, the following topics will be covered:

- Networking in programming

- RESTful API and JSON format

- URLSession and Decodable in Swift

- Building an app to get the latest price of Bitcoin

- Enumeration in Swift language

- Difference between main thread and background thread

- Asynchronous programming and its importance in iOS app development

- Completion block vs async/await

Networking

Networking in programming is the process of allowing computer programs to communicate with each other over a network. Networking enables programs to **exchange** data, messages, or commands between different devices, such as computers, smartphones, and servers. Networking is a vital component of modern software applications, enabling features such as online multiplayer games, real-time collaboration tools, and social media platforms.

Here are some important key points:

- **APIs and protocols**: Developers use **application programming interfaces (APIs)** and protocols to define the rules for how information should be exchanged between programs. Some common networking protocols include HTTP, TCP/IP, and FTP.

- **Built-in libraries and frameworks**: Programming languages provide built-in networking libraries or frameworks that simplify the process of implementing networking functionality in a program. In Swift and iOS programming, we will be using `URLSession`.

- **Socket programming**: Socket programming is a low-level networking technique that allows for direct communication between two computers or devices. Socket programming is commonly used for building networked games, real-time collaboration tools, and other applications that require fast and efficient communication.

- **Network security**: Network security is a critical consideration in networking programming, as programs must be able to exchange information securely and protect against unauthorized access. Developers may use encryption, authentication, and other techniques to ensure the security of networked applications. The most common one is HTTPS. **HTTPS**, short for **Hypertext Transfer Protocol Secure**, is a secure communication protocol widely used on the internet. It ensures that data exchanged between a web browser and a website is encrypted, safeguarding sensitive information such as passwords, financial transactions, and personal data from unauthorized access.

Networking is a fundamental aspect of programming that enables programs to connect and communicate with other systems. This can be a whole subject and a special domain inside programming.

For the scope of this book, we will only focus on the first two key points: using native iOS framework to communicate with servers through APIs.

Socket programming is very interesting and can be used to build live chat apps, live tracking stock, or crypto apps. So, if you have the time, we highly recommend you do some deep research on this topic.

RESTful APIs

API calls, or Application Programming Interface calls, are a way for iOS applications to interact with web services and retrieve data. The most commonly observed in mobile development is **RESTful APIs**.

RESTful API is an architectural style for building web-based APIs, where REST stands for Representational State Transfer. It is a standard that defines a set of constraints for creating web services that are scalable, flexible, and maintainable:

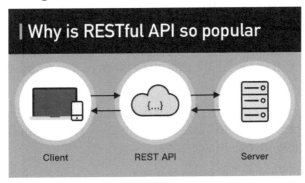

Figure 7.1: REST API

Think about RESTful or any format of API like a standardized rule of communication between two systems. Commonly, we divide them as client and server. The client is the user interface who will use the information, for example, a mobile app or website. On the other hand, the server is a place of secure storage, for example, a cloud server.

Mobile app developers often use RESTful APIs to build web-based services that can be accessed by their mobile apps. RESTful APIs provide a standardized and scalable way to exchange data between the app and the server. Some key benefits of using RESTful APIs in mobile app development include:

- **Scalability**: RESTful APIs are designed to be scalable, allowing them to handle large numbers of requests from multiple clients. This is especially important in mobile app development, where apps can be used by millions of users at the same time.

- **Flexibility**: RESTful APIs allow developers to exchange data in a wide range of formats, including JSON, XML, and plain text. This flexibility allows developers to choose the best format for their app's requirements.

- **Simplified Development**: Using RESTful APIs can simplify the development process for mobile apps, as developers can use pre-built APIs instead of building their own data storage and retrieval mechanisms.

- **Consistency**: RESTful APIs provide a standardized way to communicate between the client and server, ensuring consistency across different platforms and devices.

- **Security**: RESTful APIs provide built-in security features, such as authentication and encryption, ensuring that the data exchanged between the client and server is secure.

When building a mobile app that uses RESTful APIs, developers typically use libraries such as **Alamofire** or **URLSession** to make HTTP requests and manage network connections.

URLSession is a built-in library provided by Apple, whereas **Alamofire** is a third-party library developed by the open-source community, built on top of **URLSession**.

Both provide a simplified interface for working with RESTful APIs, making it easier for developers to build fast, efficient, and secure mobile apps that can communicate with web-based services.

Here are some differences between the two:

- **Complexity**: **URLSession** is a low-level library that provides a lot of control over the network request process. This can make it more complex to use than **Alamofire**, which is designed to provide a simplified interface for making network requests.

- **Customization**: Because **URLSession** is a low-level library, it provides a lot of customization options for things like caching, authentication, and background tasks. This makes it more flexible than **Alamofire**, which provides a simpler interface with fewer customization options.

- **Learning curve**: Because **URLSession** is a built-in library, it can be easier for developers to learn since it is already included in the iOS SDK. **Alamofire**, on the other hand, has a steeper learning curve since it is a third-party library.

- **Support**: Because **URLSession** is a built-in library, it is more likely to receive updates and bug fixes from Apple. **Alamofire**, on the other hand, relies on the open-source community for support and maintenance.

- **Application size**: **Alamofire** is a third-party library means that importing it will increase the size of the application compared to already existed native solutions like **URLSession**.

Overall, both **URLSession** and **Alamofire** have their strengths and weaknesses, and which one to use will depend on the specific needs of your project. If you need a lot of customization and control over the network request process, **URLSession** may be a better choice. On the other hand, if you need a simpler interface and faster development, **Alamofire** may be a better choice.

In this book for networking, we will be using **URLSession** as it is a native built-in solution provided by Apple. However, first, let's take a look at the most frequently seen format of data in networking: JSON.

JSON

JavaScript Object Notation (JSON) is a lightweight data-interchange format that is commonly used for transmitting data between a server and a web or mobile client.

JSON is a text-based format that consists of key-value pairs, where keys are strings and values can be strings, numbers, objects, arrays, or Boolean values. JSON is often used to represent complex data structures, such as lists of objects or nested objects.

Here is an example of a simple JSON object:

```
{
    "name": "John",
    "age": 30,
    "city": "New York"
}
```

Figure 7.2: JSON format

In this example, the object has three key-value pairs: "**name**", "**age**", and "**city**". The "**name**" key has a string value of "**John**", the "**age**" key has a numeric value of 30, and the "**city**" key has a string value of "**New York**".

JSON is widely used in web and mobile development because it is easy to read and write, can be parsed by most programming languages, and is supported by most modern web and mobile APIs. It is also a more lightweight and efficient alternative to other data interchange formats, such as XML.

URLSession

URLSession is a class in the Foundation framework of iOS, macOS, tvOS, and watchOS, which provides an interface for making network requests.

The name **URLSession** comes from the fact that it is used to manage sessions for loading data from URLs. This includes **downloading** data, **uploading** data, and even **streaming** media.

The **URLSession** class is designed to be a powerful and flexible tool for making network requests. It supports many different types of requests, including HTTP and HTTPS, and provides features like caching, authentication, and background tasks.

Three types of **URLSession** tasks that can be used to make network requests are as follows:

- **URLSessionDataTask**: This task retrieves data from the server as a Data object. We will be using this to call APIs.

- **URLSessionUploadTask**: This task uploads data to the server, such as a file or binary data.

- **URLSessionDownloadTask**: This task downloads data from the server and saves it to a file.

In addition to these tasks, **URLSession** also supports background tasks, which allow apps to continue downloading or uploading data even when the app is not actively running.

Overall, **URLSession** is a powerful and flexible tool for making network requests in iOS apps. Whether you're building a simple app that retrieves data from a web API, or a complex app that handles large file uploads, URLSession provides the necessary features to get the job done.

Now, let's make our first API call to retrieve the latest price of Bitcoin.

Making our first API call

We will create a simple app with a button to request the live price of Bitcoin, one of the hottest assets currently:

Figure 7.3: Bitcoin live price app

For this demo app, we will use the free, open-to-public API by **https://coindesk. com** to get the latest price of Bitcoin. Here is the URL link: **https://api.coindesk. com/v1/bpi/currentprice.json**.

We will make a get request to this URL and get the live price of Bitcoin. Now, copy this link, paste it to your browser, and press *Enter*:

Figure 7.4: API response as JSON (1)

As you can see, with this URL link, we will get back Bitcoin data. A close look and you will be able to find its price. The data is in a JSON format, which can be hard to look at, so we will use a Chrome Extension **JSONVue** for better visualization:

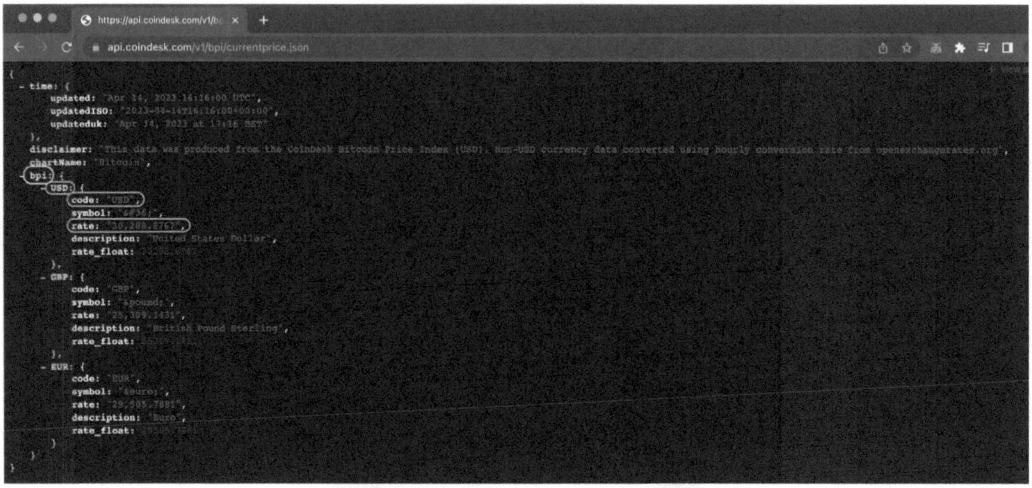

Figure 7.5: *API response as JSON (2)*

Everything now looks organized, which will help us a lot later when we write this API's model.

However, this is on the web. Now, let's open Xcode and make a call to this URL to get back this Bitcoin information within our app. Here is how we are doing it with **URLSession**:

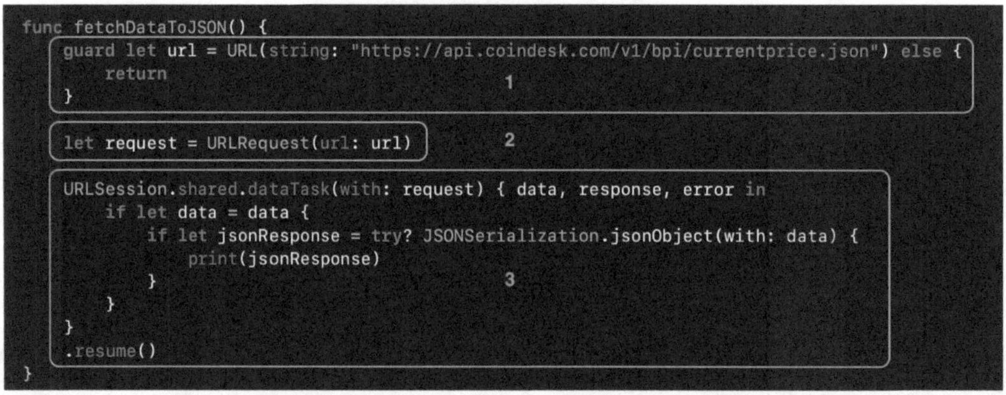

```
func fetchDataToJSON() {
    guard let url = URL(string: "https://api.coindesk.com/v1/bpi/currentprice.json") else {
        return                                                 1
    }

    let request = URLRequest(url: url)                          2

    URLSession.shared.dataTask(with: request) { data, response, error in
        if let data = data {
            if let jsonResponse = try? JSONSerialization.jsonObject(with: data) {
                print(jsonResponse)
            }                                                   3
        }
    }
    .resume()
}
```

Figure 7.6: *Fetch API to JSON with URLSession*

First, we use the URL class to create a URL object from the URL string. Next, we use this URL object to create a **URLRequest** object. We then use URLSession's **dataTask** method to make the GET request, passing in the **URLRequest** object.

Inside the **.dataTask** closure, we check if there is data returned from the server. Then, we use the built-in method from **JSONSerialization** to decode the returned data into JSON format. If it is successful, then we will print out the JSON object:

```swift
import SwiftUI

struct BitcoinPriceView: View {

    @State private var responseData = ""

    var body: some View {
        VStack {
            Text(responseData)
                .font(.title)
                .fontWeight(.medium)
                .padding()

            Button("Make Request") {
                fetchDataToJSON()
            }
        }
    }

    func fetchDataToJSON() {
        guard let url = URL(string:
            "https://api.coindesk.com/v1/bpi/currentprice.json") else {
            return
        }

        let request = URLRequest(url: url)

        URLSession.shared.dataTask(with: request) { data, response, error in
            if let data = data {
                if let jsonResponse = try? JSONSerialization.jsonObject(with:
                    data) {
                    print(jsonResponse)
                }
            }
        }
        .resume()
    }
}
```

Figure 7.7: *Bitcoin price app layout*

Here, we just have a simple VStack with a Text display of our return information and a button to fetch data. Let's press that button to make an API call:

Figure 7.8: *Successful get data from the app*

Open up the debugger and you will see the previous data has successfully fetched into our project as a JSON object. However, iOS developers don't use JSON directly inside our app. Instead, we will create a Model from Struct to represent its data and then access and use its information.

JSONDecoder and Decodable

Creating a model and decoding the JSON response into that model instead of using the raw JSON data directly provides several benefits as follows:

- **Type safety**: By defining a model, we can ensure that the JSON response is mapped to a structured, typed object that we can work with in our code. This helps us avoid errors that might occur if we were working directly with unstructured JSON data.

- **Readability and maintainability**: Having a structured model makes the code more readable and easier to understand. If we were working with raw JSON data directly, the code could quickly become difficult to follow, especially with more complex responses.

- **Ease of use**: Once we have decoded the JSON response into a model, we can use it easily in our code, without having to worry about parsing the JSON data ourselves. This can save us time and effort, especially for larger or more complex responses.

In summary, creating a **Model** and decoding the JSON response into that model provides a more structured, type-safe, readable, maintainable, and compatible way of working with the response data.

Now to write our Bitcoin data model correctly, let's come back to our browser:

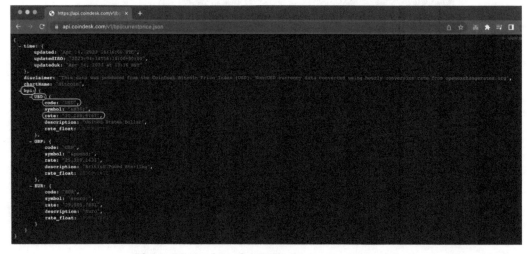

Figure 7.9: *Analyze the JSON object to write model*

Here, the extension becomes very handy. If you look closely, you will notice that the two pieces of data we need are highlighted in green: the price and the main currency, which is USD. These two pieces of information are stored as key-value pair with **code** and **rate** as the two keys. They are then nested inside an object with key **USD**. It then is one of the nested values of the **bpi** key.

Let's rewrite them into our model using Struct:

```swift
import Foundation

struct BitcoinData: Decodable {
    let bpi: BPI
}

struct BPI: Decodable {
    let USD: USDRate
}

struct USDRate: Decodable {
    let rate: String
    let code: String
}
```

Figure 7.10: *Our Bitcoin data models*

We will create three models, each representing a layer of the JSON data object. The **BitcoinData** model has the **bpi** key to the **BPI** model, which then has the **USD** key. Its value is the **USDRate** model, which has two pieces of information attached to **rate** and **code** keys. One common mistake here is a typo error in the key; for example, instead of **rate,** we might mistakenly type **rates,** which will cause all of the decoding processes to fail.

It is important to note that now all of our models must adopt the **Decodable** protocol.

Decodable is a protocol in Swift that enables us to decode data from a serialized format, such as JSON or XML, into a structured object. It is a part of the Swift Standard Library and is often used to parse data returned from a web API.

The **Decodable** protocol provides a set of requirements that must be implemented by a type for it to be decoded from a serialized format. Specifically, the type must be able to decode itself from a **Decoder** object, which provides the decoding context for the type.

To use **Decodable**, we define a struct or a class that conforms to the protocol, and we specify the properties of the type that we want to decode from the serialized format. We can then use the **JSONDecoder** class in Swift to decode the serialized data into our type.

Now, let's use this knowledge to fetch data, decode it to our models, and use it to display the current Bitcoin price in our app whenever the user taps the button.

There are two ways of doing this: the old way using a completion block and the new way using Swift Concurrency (async – await). We will be going through both of them in this example.

Completion block, Enumeration, and threads

Firstly, here is how we rewrite our **fetchData** function using the completion block:

```swift
enum NetworkError: Error {
    case invalidURL
    case requestFailed(String)                          2
}

func fetchData(completion: @escaping (Result<BitcoinData, Error>) -> Void) {
    guard let url = URL(string: "https://api.coindesk.com/v1/bpi/currentprice.json") else {
        completion(.failure(NetworkError.invalidURL))
        return
    }

    let request = URLRequest(url: url)

    URLSession.shared.dataTask(with: request) { data, response, error in       1
        if let data = data, let decodedResponse = try? JSONDecoder().decode(BitcoinData.self, from: data) {
            DispatchQueue.main.async {
                completion(.success(decodedResponse))           3
            }
            return
        }

        DispatchQueue.main.async {
            completion(.failure(NetworkError.requestFailed(error?.localizedDescription ?? "Unknown error")))
        }
    }
    .resume()
}
```

Figure 7.11: Fetch data using completion block (1)

We have replaced **JSONSerialization** with **JSONDecoder**. Instead of decoding the received data to JSON format, we now try to decode it as our **BitcoinData** model.

The second thing we have highlighted here is the use of another collection data in Swift: **Enumeration**.

In Swift, an **enum** (short for "enumeration") is a custom data type that defines a group of related values. Enumeration provides a way to define a finite set of possible values, each of which is a separate member of the enumeration.

In this example, we define an **enum** called **NetworkError** that represents the different errors that can occur during a network call. Each error is defined as a separate member of the enumeration using the **case** keyword.

Our **enum** conforms to the Error protocol. The **NetworkError** enum defines a set of error cases that could occur when making a network request, including invalid URL and request failure. We can add other cases in the future, such as authentication error, server error, and unknown error.

This can make it easier to handle errors in a more structured and organized way in our code. We are using a different type of error in our function with the help of the **completion block**.

Finally, the last thing you see here is that we have wrapped all of our completions inside the **DispatchQueue.main.asycn** closure. This block will make sure that our data will be received on the main thread. Why is that? It is because, by default, **URLSession** will be executed in a background thread. So, what are the differences between these two?

In iOS development, there are two primary types of threads: the main thread (also known as the UI thread or the main queue) and the background threads (also referred to as concurrent queues). These threads serve different purposes and have specific characteristics. Let's explore the differences between them.

Main Thread

- The main thread is the primary thread in an iOS application and is responsible for handling user interface (UI) updates, event handling, and user interactions.

- It executes the app's main run loop, which processes UI events like touch events, animations, and user input.

- All UI-related operations, such as updating views, handling touch events, and performing animations, should be executed on the main thread.

- It is crucial to keep the main thread responsive and free from heavy or time-consuming tasks to provide a smooth user experience.

- Blocking the main thread with long-running operations can result in an unresponsive UI, leading to a poor user experience and potentially triggering watchdog timers that terminate the app.

Background Thread

- Background threads are used to perform time-consuming or resource-intensive tasks without blocking the main thread.

- They can be created explicitly using **Grand Central Dispatch (GCD)** or by utilizing operation queues.

- Background threads are typically used for tasks such as network requests, file I/O, complex calculations, or any operation that might take a significant amount of time.

- By offloading these tasks to background threads, the main thread remains free to handle user interactions and keep the UI responsive.

- Background threads can execute concurrently, enabling multiple tasks to be performed simultaneously.

- It's important to note that UI-related operations should not be performed directly on background threads. If UI updates are required after completing a background task, they should be dispatched back to the main thread to ensure thread-safety and proper UI handling.

In summary, the main thread is responsible for handling UI updates and user interactions, while background threads are used for executing time-consuming tasks off the main thread to keep the UI responsive. Here, you may have guessed it; **URLSession**, by default, runs on a background thread because who knows how long it might take. So, when our tasks are finished, we need to bring those data to the main thread to update the UI to display the Bitcoin price. That's the job of the **DispatchQueue.main.asycn** closure.

By properly managing thread usage, you can ensure a smooth user experience and prevent the UI from becoming unresponsive:

```swift
func fetchData(completion: @escaping (Result<BitcoinData, Error>) -> Void) {
    guard let url = URL(string: "https://api.coindesk.com/v1/bpi/currentprice.json") else {
        completion(.failure(NetworkError.invalidURL))
        return
    }

    let request = URLRequest(url: url)

    URLSession.shared.dataTask(with: request) { data, response, error in
        if let data = data, let decodedResponse = try? JSONDecoder().decode(BitcoinData.self, from: data) {
            DispatchQueue.main.async {
                completion(.success(decodedResponse))
            }
            return
        }

        DispatchQueue.main.async {
            completion(.failure(NetworkError.requestFailed(error?.localizedDescription ?? "Unknown error")))
        }
    }
    .resume()
}
```

Figure 7.12: Fetch data using completion block (2)

This function differs from the other functions we have written.

In this line of code, we define the completion block that will be called once the **fetchData** function completes its work. Let's break it down:

- **completion**: is the name of the parameter that we're defining. We're using the name completion here, but you can choose any valid parameter name you like.

- **@escaping** is a keyword that tells the compiler that this parameter is an escaping closure. An escaping closure is one that's called after the function that defines it has returned. In this case, we're passing a closure as a parameter to **fetchData**, and we want to be able to call that closure later on, after **fetchData** has finished its work. If we are doing a network request, the response can take some time and the operation becomes asynchronous, that's why we need an escaping closure here.

- **(Result<BitcoinData, Error>) -> Void** is the closure type that we're defining. This closure takes one parameter of type **Result< BitcoinData, Error>**, which is a Swift type that represents either a success case (containing a value of type **BitcoinData** which is our data model) or a failure case (containing an error of type Error). The closure doesn't return anything, so its return type is Void.

Overall, this line of code defines a **completion block** parameter for the **fetchData** function that takes a result value (either a success case containing Bitcoin price data or a failure case containing an error) and doesn't return anything:

```swift
enum NetworkError: Error {
    case invalidURL
    case requestFailed(String)
}

func fetchData(completion: @escaping (Result<BitcoinData, Error>) -> Void) {
    guard let url = URL(string: "https://api.coindesk.com/v1/bpi/currentprice.json") else {
        completion(.failure(NetworkError.invalidURL))
        return
    }

    let request = URLRequest(url: url)

    URLSession.shared.dataTask(with: request) { data, response, error in
        if let data = data, let decodedResponse = try? JSONDecoder().decode(BitcoinData.self, from: data) {
            DispatchQueue.main.async {
                completion(.success(decodedResponse))
            }
            return
        }

        DispatchQueue.main.async {
            completion(.failure(NetworkError.requestFailed(error?.localizedDescription ?? "Unknown error")))
        }
    }
    .resume()
}
```

***Figure 7.13**: Fetch data using completion block (3)*

Now, inside our function, we will use the **completion(.success())** and **completion(.failure())** to pass the data received from this **fetchData** function. In this example, if data is successfully decoded into **BitcoinData,** then it will be a success. Otherwise, depending on the cases with the help of the **NetworkError** enum, we will return different error cases.

The **@escaping** keyword indicates that this closure will be called later, after the **fetchData** function has returned. All of this means that when we are successful (the yellow area), we will call a function here using our just-decoded data model **BitcoinData**. If there's a failure (the orange area), another function will also be called having the specific error.

Now, let's make a call to this new function:

Figure 7.14: *Fetch data using completion block (4)*

In our view, we call the **fetchData** function when the button is pressed, passing in a closure that updates the **responseData** state variable with the two values we need: the bitcoin price and its mark currency, which is USD, if the request succeeds, or prints an error message if it fails.

This approach helps to keep the networking logic separate from the view logic and makes it easier to reuse the **fetchData** function in other parts of the app.

Now, hit the button, and you should see the live price of Bitcoin in USD. At this point, it just climbed back above 27,000 USD. Install it on your device, and you will have an app just to check the live price of Bitcoin.

In summary:

- **Enumeration** is a powerful feature of Swift and can be used to represent a wide range of data types, from simple value types to more complex objects with associated values and methods. They are often used to define a fixed set of values for a specific purpose, such as days of the week or error codes.

- A **completion block** (or closure) is a way to pass a block of code as a parameter to a method or function. The block of code is executed once the method or function has completed its task. Completion blocks are often used in asynchronous operations to notify the caller when the operation has finished and provide the result or any errors that occurred during the operation.

In iOS development, completion blocks are commonly used in networking and data retrieval operations. For example, when making a network request, you can pass a completion block to the request method to be executed when the request is completed. The completion block might take parameters, such as the response data or an error, depending on the outcome of the request.

Looking great, right? But it is just when things are simple. When things get complicated, a problem that arises with completion blocks is known as "callback hell" or "pyramid of doom". This occurs when you have multiple asynchronous tasks that depend on each other, and you end up with a series of nested completion blocks that can be difficult to read and maintain.

Here's an example of what callback hell can look like:

```
fetchDataFromServer { (result1) in
    if let data1 = result1 {
        parseData(data1) { (result2) in
            if let data2 = result2 {
                processData(data2) { (result3) in
                    if let data3 = result3 {
                        displayData(data3)
                    }
                }
            }
        }
    }
}
```

Figure 7.15: Callback hell problem

We have four completion functions, each waiting for the previous one to execute. As you can see, this code is difficult to read and understand, and it can be hard to debug and maintain. Too many "{ }" blocks here; hence, it has another name called the pyramid of doom. With large and complicated apps, it is common to have multiple actions line up like this.

One solution to this problem is to use the async/await pattern, which was introduced in Swift 5.5.

Asynchronous Programming with Async Await

Async/await is a new feature introduced in Swift 5.5 that allows for writing asynchronous code in a more declarative, synchronous, readable, and intuitive way.

Here are some key points of it:

- A declarative way to write asynchronous code that is more readable, maintainable, and less error-prone than traditional completion block patterns.

- Allows you to write asynchronous code in a synchronous style by using **async** and **await** keywords.

- **async** marks a function as asynchronous, meaning that it may have to wait for some other tasks to complete before continuing.

- **await** is used to wait for the completion of a long-running task, such as a network request or a database query, without blocking the thread.

- Makes use of Swift's Result type, which allows you to handle errors more straightforwardly.

- Compared to completion blocks, **async/await** makes code easier to read, understand, and maintain by reducing nesting and eliminating the need for a lot of boilerplate code.

- Easier to reason about concurrency and parallelism in your code, by making it clear which tasks are running concurrently and which tasks are dependent on other tasks.

- Backward compatibility: – iOS 13, Xcode 13.2, macOS 10.15, watchOS 6, and tvOS 13. This backward compatibility applies only to Swift language features; you cannot use any APIs built using those language features, like the new **URLSession** APIs that use async - await (for that, you still require iOS 15.0).

Using **async/await** will help us eliminate the need for nested blocks, and we can read them line by line just like a normal block of code.

Here is how the code from the preceding example looks like with **async/await**:

```
async {
    guard let data1 = await fetchDataFromServer() else { return }
    guard let data2 = await parseData(data1) else { return }
    guard let data3 = await processData(data2) else { return }
    displayData(data3)
}
```

Figure 7.16: *Async await solution for callback hell*

As you can see, this code is much easier to read and understand than the completion block version, and it is less error-prone and easier to maintain.

The **await** keyword is used to wait for each asynchronous task to complete, and the guard statement is used to handle errors and exit early if necessary.

Now, let's come back to our Bitcoin live price app and use this knowledge to rewrite the **fetchData** function into **async/await** version:

```
func fetchDataAsync() async throws -> BitcoinData {
    guard let url = URL(string: "https://api.coindesk.com/v1/bpi/currentprice.json") else {
        throw NetworkError.invalidURL
    }

    let request = URLRequest(url: url)
    let (data, response) = try await URLSession.shared.data(for: request)

    guard let httpResponse = response as? HTTPURLResponse,
        httpResponse.statusCode == 200 else {
        throw NetworkError.requestFailed("Invalid response")
    }

    return try JSONDecoder().decode(BitcoinData.self, from: data)
}

func fetchData(completion: @escaping (Result<BitcoinData, Error>) -> Void) {
    guard let url = URL(string: "https://api.coindesk.com/v1/bpi/currentprice.json") else {
        completion(.failure(NetworkError.invalidURL))
        return
    }

    let request = URLRequest(url: url)

    URLSession.shared.dataTask(with: request) { data, response, error in
        if let data = data {
            if let decodedResponse = try? JSONDecoder().decode(BitcoinData.self, from: data) {
                completion(.success(decodedResponse))
                return
            }
        }

        completion(.failure(NetworkError.requestFailed(error?.localizedDescription ?? "Unknown error")))
    }
    .resume()
}
```

Figure 7.17: *Async/await vs. Completion block function definition*

In this version, we're using the new **async/await** syntax to make the API call. We've defined the **fetchDataAsync** function as an async function that returns a **BitcoinData** object or throws an error.

Inside the **fetchDataAsync** function, we use await to wait for the data to be fetched from the server, and then we decode the JSON response into a **BitcoinData** object.

If there is an error, we will use the **throw** keyword to return it. Side by side you can compare the difference between the two functions.

In the **BitcoinPriceView**, we call the **fetchDataAsync** function inside a **Task** block, which allows us to use **await** to wait for the function to complete. If the function succeeds, we update the **responseData** state variable with the current Bitcoin's price. If it fails, we print an error message:

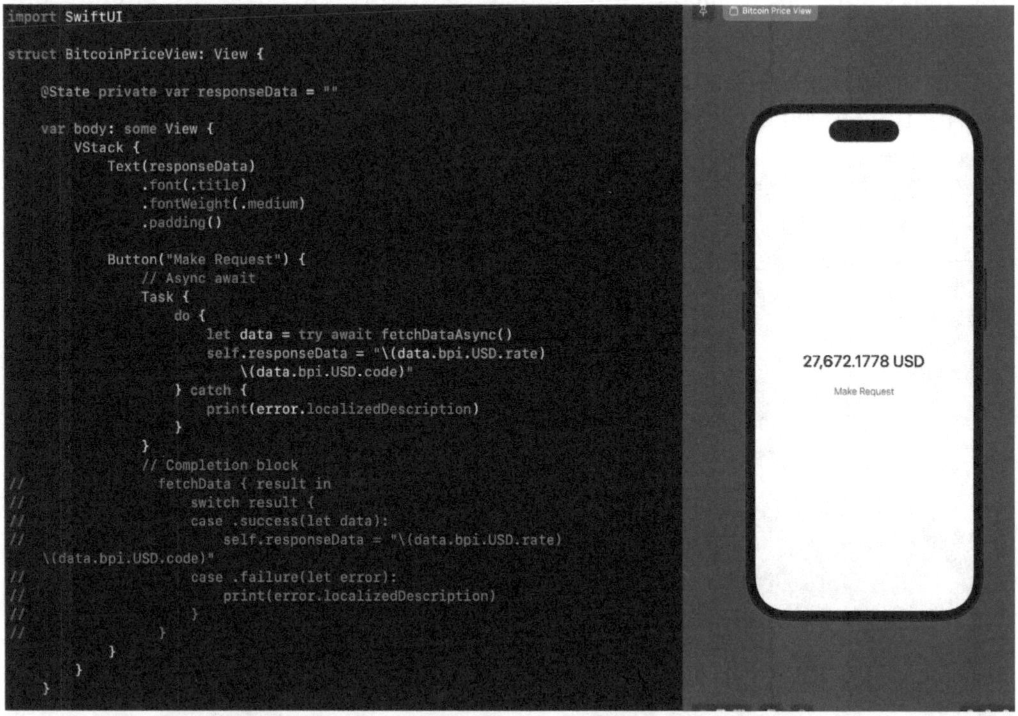

```swift
import SwiftUI

struct BitcoinPriceView: View {

    @State private var responseData = ""

    var body: some View {
        VStack {
            Text(responseData)
                .font(.title)
                .fontWeight(.medium)
                .padding()

            Button("Make Request") {
                // Async await
                Task {
                    do {
                        let data = try await fetchDataAsync()
                        self.responseData = "\(data.bpi.USD.rate)
                            \(data.bpi.USD.code)"
                    } catch {
                        print(error.localizedDescription)
                    }
                }
                // Completion block
//              fetchData { result in
//                  switch result {
//                  case .success(let data):
//                      self.responseData = "\(data.bpi.USD.rate)
//  \(data.bpi.USD.code)"
//                  case .failure(let error):
//                      print(error.localizedDescription)
//                  }
//              }
            }
        }
    }
}
```

27,672.1778 USD

Make Request

Figure 7.18: *Async await vs. Completion block execution*

Using **async/await** can make asynchronous programming in Swift more concise and easier to read, as it eliminates the need for completion handlers and makes the code look more like synchronous code. However, it's important to note that async - await for making API calls in URLSession is only available in iOS 15 and later, so it may not be available on all devices.

Until now, you have heard about asynchronous a lot of time, and you just learned about two different ways to implement it in iOS development: `async/await` and completion block. But what exactly is asynchronous programming?

Asynchronous programming allows certain tasks to be executed on a separate thread or queue, while the main thread continues to execute other tasks or update the user interface.

It is because in iOS app development, all the UI-related elements are on the main thread. And if there are long-awaited tasks, it will cause the app to become unresponsive and freeze. This is the worst outcome in App development.

Asynchronous programming is essential for iOS development because it allows applications to continue responding to user input and updating the user interface while certain tasks, such as loading data from a remote server, are being executed in the background.

Completion blocks or delegate methods are commonly used in iOS development to implement asynchronous programming. Recent technologies like `async/await` in Swift 5.5 provide a more readable and intuitive way to write asynchronous code.

In conclusion, properly handling asynchronous code is an essential skill for iOS developers to ensure their applications are responsive and user-friendly.

Conclusion

Networking is a crucial part of iOS app development. It allows apps to connect with remote servers, retrieve data, and provide users with real-time information.

In this chapter, we learned about **RESTful API** and the **JSON** format, which are essential concepts that developers must understand when implementing networking in iOS app development. Then, we implement our first API call using the URLSession framework. During this, we got to know about Decodable and Enumeration in Swift.

Next, we built an app to get the latest price of Bitcoin that demonstrates how these concepts can be applied in practice.

Finally, we learned about **Asynchronous programming**. It is critical to ensure that apps remain responsive while network requests are being processed. **Completion blocks** and **async/await** are two common approaches for handling asynchronous code, each with its benefits and drawbacks.

Overall, mastering networking and asynchronous programming is essential for developing high-quality, responsive, and user-friendly iOS apps.

In the next chapter, we will deep dive into more complicated topics in Networking, including Authentication and different types of HTTP requests. Along the way, we will build another real-world application integrated with a public API service.

CHAPTER 8
Networking with SwiftUI - Part 2

Introduction

In the previous chapter, we have learned that Networking is a critical aspect of iOS app development.

In today's fast-paced and interconnected world, users expect apps to work seamlessly and deliver content quickly. This is where networking comes in, allowing apps to communicate with servers in the background, retrieve data on demand, and provide users with a smooth and responsive experience.

In this chapter, we will continue exploring deeper in this topic with the newest used technologies to build a real-world application.

Structure

In this chapter, the following topics will be covered:

- Build a real-world application with provided APIs
- Setting up real-world API service with Unsplash
- Modern application authorization process with OAuth 2.0
- Using WebKit to present a website inside the app

- Using UIKit views in SwiftUI

- GET request vs. POST request

- Singleton design pattern

- Download and load i-mages from a URL using URLSession

Laying out the project

We will be making a simple application that displays photos, similar to Instagram. Users can interact with the like or unlike actions:

Figure 8.1: *Gallery App*

Here is the final layout of the app. Let's break it down into Lego bricks. Before continuing with the solution, try it for yourself and see if you can do it:

Figure 8.2: *Gallery App breaking down*

In this app, we will have a list of vertically scrollable items. Each item will include:

- An image

- A title for this image

- A like/unlike button, depending on whether the current user has liked this image or not

- A label displaying the total likes this image has received

Now, let's open up Xcode and do some coding.

Remember from *Chapter 6, Tab Bar, Navigation, and Compositional Layout*, we learned how to add an outside image to our project. Let's see if you can remember how to do it by adding a "landscape" image to our project and displaying it on the home screen:

Figure 8.3: *Making the Item View (1)*

If you forgot how to do this, take a look back at *Chapter* 6. Now, we will resize it, set the width-to-height ratio to 4:3, and with a corner radius of 16:

Figure 8.4: *Making the Item View (2)*

Great, now let's finish this view by adding the title, the like button, and the number of likes label. We will hardcode all of the values at this stage:

```swift
//  Created by James Thang on 11/05/2023.
//

import SwiftUI

struct ItemView: View {
    var body: some View {
        VStack(alignment: .leading, spacing: 12) {
            Image("landscape")
                .resizable()
                .aspectRatio(4/3, contentMode: .fit)
                .clipShape(RoundedRectangle
                    (cornerRadius: 16))

            Text("Image Title")
                .foregroundColor(.primary)
                .fontWeight(.medium)

            HStack {
                Button("Like") {

                }

                Spacer()

                Text("50 likes")
                    .font(.callout)
                    .foregroundColor(.secondary)
            }
        }
    }
}
```

Figure 8.5: *Making the Item View (3)*

Awesome, now let's finish this layout by adding it to a vertical scroll view with a navigation title:

```swift
//  Created by James Thang on 11/05/2023.
//

import SwiftUI

struct HomeView: View {
    var body: some View {
        NavigationStack {
            ScrollView(.vertical) {
                LazyVGrid(columns: [GridItem(.flexible())]) {
                    ForEach(0...20, id: \.self) { _ in
                        ItemView()
                    }
                }
                .padding(.horizontal)
            }
            .navigationTitle("Galerry").navigationBarTitleDisplayMode(.inline)
        }
    }
}

struct HomeView_Previews: PreviewProvider {
    static var previews: some View {
        HomeView()
    }
}
```

Figure 8.6: *Making the Home View*

All of this you have already learned from previous chapters. We are using a **NavigationStack** to display the navigation title. Then, a vertical scroll view with a **LazyVGrid** layout. Inside it is a **ForEach** block; for now, we will be looping and creating 21 rows, each will be our just-created **ItemView**. If any of this seems confusing to you, make sure to go back and check the previous chapters when we talked about them in detail.

We are finishing the layout of the app. Next, we will integrate this layout with real APIs. For this project, we are going to use the APIs provided by **https:// unsplash.com/**. If you didn't know about them, Unsplash is a photo discovery platform for free-to-use, high-definition photos. They also provide API services for developers making applications: **https://unsplash.com/documentation**.

But before jumping into it, let's first learn about OAuth 2.0, which is commonly adopted by many modern services APIs in the industry for authentication and authorization, including Unsplash.

OAuth 2.0

OAuth 2.0 (Open Authorization 2.0) is an open standard protocol that allows users to grant limited access to their resources on one website or application to another website or application, without sharing their credentials (such as passwords) directly. It is widely used for authentication and authorization in modern web and mobile applications.

It provides a framework for secure third-party access to user data stored on different services, such as social media platforms, online banking systems, or cloud storage providers. It enables users to grant permission to third-party applications to access their resources on these services on their behalf. This delegation of access is typically referred to as **OAuth authorization**.

The basic flow of OAuth 2.0 involves three primary entities: the user (resource owner), the application or service requesting access (client), and the service that hosts the user's resources (resource server). There is also an optional component called the authorization server, which handles the authentication and authorization process.

Here's a step-by-step high-level overview of the OAuth 2.0 flow:

1. The client application requests authorization from the user to access specific resources on the resource server.

2. The user is redirected to the authorization server, where they are prompted to authenticate and authorize the client's request.

3. If the user grants authorization, the authorization server issues an access token to the client.

4. The client uses the access token to make authenticated requests to the resource server on behalf of the user.

5. The resource server validates the access token and grants access to the requested resources if the token is valid.

OAuth 2.0 provides a flexible and secure framework for enabling delegated access to resources. It has become a popular standard for authentication and authorization in various scenarios, promoting interoperability and security in modern web and mobile applications.

Here are additional resources for further reading on OAuth 2.0:

https://auth0.com/docs/authenticate/protocols/oauth

https://auth0.com/intro-to-iam/what-is-oauth-2

Setting up Unsplash APIs

Unlike the Coindesk public API that we have used in *Chapter 7, Networking with SwiftUI – Part 1*, most API services will require us to sign up for a developer account to use them. Usually, there will be a free quota for developers to test and develop applications. When these applications are shipped to production, there will be a monthly payment depending on the service providers.

For our project, we need to create a developer account and will be using the free quota option to develop this project. On your browser, head on to **https://**

unsplash.com/documentation. Click register to a new account if you haven't created an Unsplash account before:

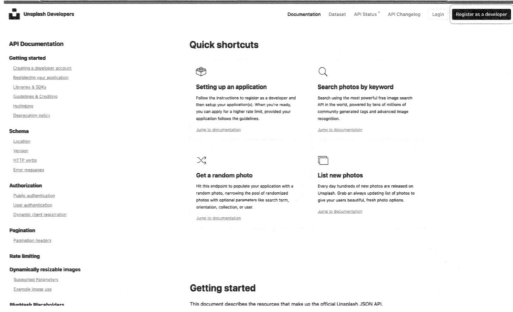

Figure 8.7: *Register Unsplash developer account*

You will now be redirected to a form for sign-up. Fill in all the required information. After successfully creating a new account, head to **https://unsplash.com/oauth/applications**:

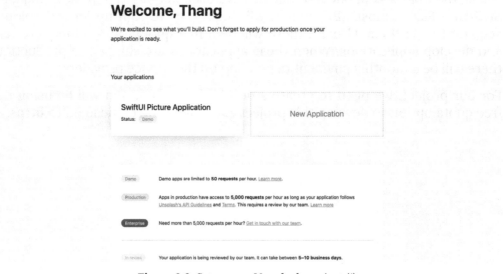

Figure 8.8: *Set up our Unsplash project (1)*

Here is the dashboard where you will manage all your Unsplash projects. We have already created a demo project here with a quota limited to 50 requests per hour. Click **New Application** to create your own:

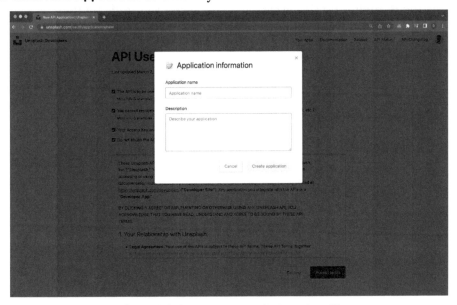

Figure 8.9: *Set up our Unsplash project (2)*

Choose your name and create your application. When you are finished, it will redirect you to the project's home page:

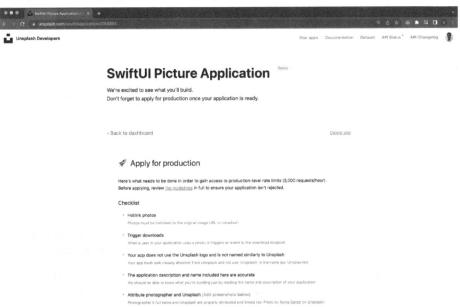

Figure 8.10: *Set up our Unsplash project (3)*

Take some time and read through all this if you want, as we have already gone through all the necessary documentation at **https://unsplash.com/ documentation**. Scroll to the bottom, and you will find all the required information for our project, including the **Access key**, the **Secret key,** and the Redirect URI:

Figure 8.11: *Set up our Unsplash project (4)*

Save all this information because soon we will make use of them for our project:

Figure 8.12: *Set up our Unsplash project (5)*

Make sure to check everything and then click **Save**. Once the setup is complete, we are ready to make API calls following the Unsplash documentation.

Now, let's get back to our project and get started with authorization following OAuth 2.0. Meanwhile, we will learn how to present a website within our app.

Authorization with OAuth 2.0

As we have discussed OAuth 2.0 earlier, our project is the client and Unsplash is the resource owner. We need to redirect the users of our project to the authorization server for them to do the authorization. If our users grant authorization, the authorization server will issue an access token to the client, which is our application/project here.

Now, with the right access token, our app can truly interact with the Unsplash resource server through its APIs to retrieve data or perform actions, such as like or unlike an image.

Once again, let's recall our Coindesk public API example from Chapter 7. Unfortunately, the majority of modern production API isn't working in this manner because of security issues and server spamming. They need some kind of authorization and verification, and OAuth 2.0 is the widely adopted modern solution.

Here is the authorization workflow for Unsplash: **https://unsplash.com/documentation/user-authentication-workflow**.

Take some time and read carefully through this well-written documentation. There are a total of four steps, and for the first task, which is the exchange for the access token, we will be looking into the first three steps. We will use the last step note when we making API calls with the Unsplash server:

Figure 8.13: *Exchange access token steps*

The access token is the final thing we want to get, and if we do this process correctly, we will obtain it by the end of *Step* 3, highlighted in the green area. Another important point to note here is that access tokens usually have an expiration time. When that time has passed, the access token will be useless, and as an application, we need to validate it and consider whether or not to request a new one. In this case for Unsplash, the access token does not expire, so we are good to go.

Starting with *Step* 1, let's analyze its requirements:

1. Direct the user to `https://unsplash.com/oauth/authorize` with the following query parameters:

param	Description
`client_id`	Your application's access key.
`redirect_uri`	A URI you control that handles successful user authorization.
`response_type`	The access response type you are requesting. The authorization workflow Unsplash supports requires the value "code" here.
`scope`	A + -separated list of requested scopes. e.g. `public+read_user`

If necessary the user will be asked to log in. They will be presented with the list of permission scopes being requested and asked to authorize.

Figure 8.14: *Exchange access token step 1*

Basically, this step requires us to form a URL and present it to the users for them to authorize through a login screen. We will use WebView to present this URL inside our app.

Usually, a URL can be divided into two parts: the base URL and its following query parameters. A base URL is an unchanged/constant part.

A query parameter, also known as a query string parameter, is a component of a URL that is used to pass specific information to a web server. It consists of a key-value pair appended to the end of a URL after a question mark (**?**) and separated by an ampersand (**&**) if multiple parameters are presented.

Here's an example URL with query parameters:

```bash
https://example.com/search?query=oauth&limit=10
```

Figure 8.15: *Example of URL with query parameters*

In this example, the URL points to a search page on the base URL **https:// example.com/search**, and it includes two query parameters: **query** and **limit**. The values of the parameters are **oauth** and **10**, respectively.

So, the requirement of *Step 1* is clear now. The final URL that we need to match will look like this:

```
let signInURL =
    "https://unsplash.com/oauth/authorize?client_id=\(Access_Key)&redirect_uri=\(Redirect_URI)&response_type=code&scope=public+write_likes"
```

Figure 8.16: *Final URL format from step 1*

The base URL is **https://unsplash.com/oauth/authorize**. Next, before adding the query parameters, we must add a **?**. Then, we have four query parameters with the following key-value pairs:

- **client_id,** which is our project Access key – we have saved it

- **redirect_uri**", which is our project Redirect URI – we have saved it

- **response_type,** which must have the related value **code** according to step 1

- **scope**", which you can further read detail for all of them. In our project, we will be using the value **public+write_like** because remember we have the feature for like/unlike the photo

Let's come back to our project on Xcode and write the code to form this first authorization URL.

We have learned about the MVVM design pattern in *Chapter 5, Design Pattern and MVVM Model*. The code will be divided into Model, View Model, and View. Each has its own responsibility. Now, you may think the code for making API calls should be inside the View Model, which is correct for small apps. However, in medium or large apps, one API can be called and reused from multiple different screens. Hence, if we put it into a View Model, then we would have to rewrite it every time a new screen needs it.

Because of this problem, we created a new type of class to handle the API calls. Whenever a screen needs to make an API call, we will initialize that class inside the View Model of it. We will classify this type of class as **Manager** inside our folder system, although some developers might call it "Service":

Figure 8.17: *Create APIs Manager to manage APIs call*

Here, we have created a new class, **APIsManager,** to control all the logic of API calls. For better control of data, we have made a Constant struct to store all the necessary data. Replace **accessKey**, **secretKey,** and **redirect_uri** with your app's data. The **baseURL** and **grant_type** will be used later. For now, let's finish *Step 1* by matching the authorization URL correctly; the function **returnAuthorizationURL** will do this job here.

An important thing to note here is that, as a general rule of security, tokens and keys should not be embedded into the code, they should be either encrypted or retrieved from a server at launch time. Otherwise, if you attach a debugger or have a jailbroken phone, you can snip all these values and then make requests on behalf of the client. However, this is a more advanced talk and goes beyond the scope of app development. Therefore, for the sake of the book and simplicity, we will store them here.

With this authorization URL, the next step is to present it as a Web View inside our app for our users performing authorization. We will use WebKit to do this.

Presenting a website inside our app with WebKit

There are many situations when we want to present a WebView that loads a website inside an app, whether it is to present additional information or make some interactions. Luckily for us iOS developers, Apple has provided not one, but two convenient built-in ways.

In iOS app development, both the **WebKit** and **SafariServices** frameworks provide functionalities related to web browsing and displaying web content. However, they serve different purposes and have distinct use cases.

WebKit:

- The **WebKit** framework is a powerful and flexible framework that allows you to embed web content within your app's user interface. It provides the **WKWebView** class, which is a modern, high-performance web view for displaying web content.

- With **WebKit**, you have more control over the web view's behavior, appearance, and interaction. You can customize various aspects such as navigation, error handling, cookies, JavaScript interaction, and more.

- **WebKit** is suitable for scenarios where you need fine-grained control over web content, such as displaying complex web applications, implementing custom browser functionality, or integrating web content seamlessly with your app's UI.

SafariServices:

- The **SafariServices** framework provides a pre-built UI component called **SFSafariViewController**. It's a full-screen web view that provides a consistent and familiar browsing experience, similar to Safari.

- **SFSafariViewController** is designed to quickly present web content without the need for extensive customization or control. It offers features like URL navigation, back/forward navigation, sharing options, and support for Safari features such as Reader Mode and Safari AutoFill.

- **SafariServices** is suitable for scenarios where you want to provide a standard, Safari-like browsing experience within your app, such as displaying web pages for reading articles, accessing external resources, or allowing users to authenticate with a web service.

In summary, if you require a high level of customization and control over web content, you should choose **WebKit** and use the **WKWebView** class. On the other hand, if you want a quick and consistent web browsing experience within your app, you can opt for **SafariServices** and use the **SFSafariViewController** class. The choice depends on the specific requirements and desired user experience for your app.

For our project, we will be using **WebKit** for more customization because later we will have to listen to callback data returned to us through the **redirect_uri** in *Step 3*.

Now at this point in time, both solutions using **WebKit** and **SafariServices** are still not natively for SwiftUI. Both of them come from the UIKit world, and we will use **UIViewRepresentable** to bridge them to a SwiftUI View:

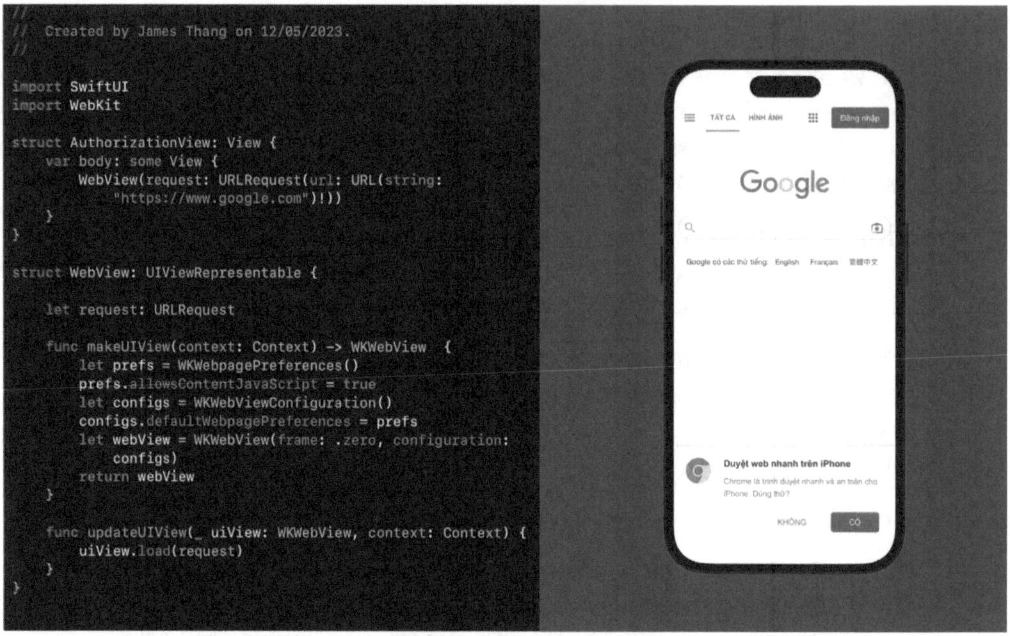

```swift
//
//  Created by James Thang on 12/05/2023.
//

import SwiftUI
import WebKit

struct AuthorizationView: View {
    var body: some View {
        WebView(request: URLRequest(url: URL(string:
            "https://www.google.com")!))
    }
}

struct WebView: UIViewRepresentable {

    let request: URLRequest

    func makeUIView(context: Context) -> WKWebView {
        let prefs = WKWebpagePreferences()
        prefs.allowsContentJavaScript = true
        let configs = WKWebViewConfiguration()
        configs.defaultWebpagePreferences = prefs
        let webView = WKWebView(frame: .zero, configuration:
            configs)
        return webView
    }

    func updateUIView(_ uiView: WKWebView, context: Context) {
        uiView.load(request)
    }

}
```

Figure 8.18: *Present a website in the app with WebKit*

With **WebKit**, we will use **WKWebView** to present a website. It's pretty straightforward: we initialize a **WKWebView** with configuration. Then, from the URL, we create a **URLRequest** and call the **.load()** function, passing the request to the **WKWebView**. That's all the code does here.

You may have some confusion here because of **UIViewRepresentable**. Learn more about how to present a custom view here:

https://www.hackingwithswift.com/quick-start/swiftui/how-to-wrap-a-custom-uiview-for-swiftui

https://www.appcoda.com/swiftui-wkwebview/

We have now successfully presented a Google search page inside our app, and it is totally interactive. You can do some Google searched here, just like in the browser.

Now, replace the Google domain with our authorization URL:

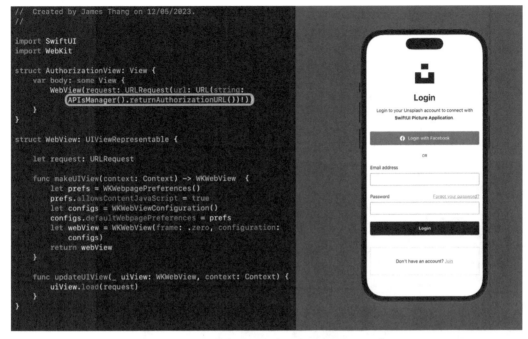

Figure 8.19: *Finish step 1 of exchange access token*

And wow, we now have a free authentication screen for users to log in or sign up.

Let's read through the next two steps to clearly understand the requirements:

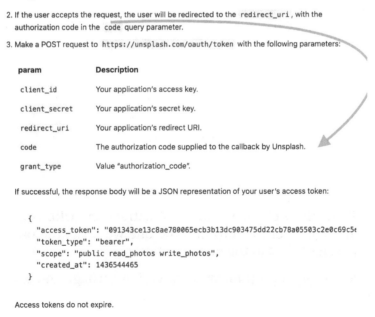

Figure 8.20: *Exchange access token steps 2 and 3*

What this means in *Step 2* is that after the user has successfully logged in, there will be an authorization code: **code** sent back to us through the **redirect_uri**. This **code** is what we want and is the only information currently missing from *Step 3* to make a final API call and retrieve the access token.

Remember we mentioned earlier that the reason we chose to use **WebKit** is because **WKWebView** has a built-in delegate function to capture the redirect URL. By conforming to the **WKNavigationDelegate**, we can listen to the return URL and extract the return **code** in *Step 2*. Here is how it works:

Figure 8.21: *Exchange access token step 2 (1)*

Here we are using the coordinator pattern to replicate the delegate pattern in UIKit. You can read more about this in this article: **https://www. hackingwithswift.com/books/ios-swiftui/using-coordinators-to-manage-swiftui-view-controllers**.

So basically, the **.didFinish()** delegate function of **WKWebView** here allows us to enter the state when the **URLRequest** is finished. We then look to the current presented URL of the web view. Then, we extract the URL components from it and filter through all of them to find the one we need, the one with the key named **code,** as described in the documentation.

Now, try to log in or sign up for authentication through the simulator to see what happens behind the screen:

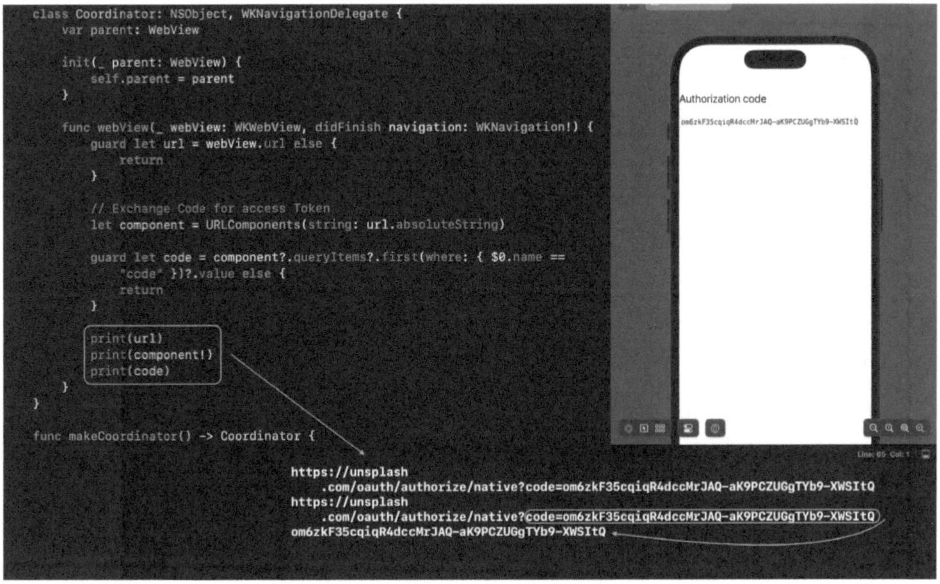

Figure 8.22: *Exchange access token step 2 (2)*

We print all three variables: **url**, **component**, and **code** here. This is a URL, and it has its query parameters. In *Step* 2, after successful authorization, we will be redirected to this URL inside our app. The thing we need is the **code** that is missing for *Step* 3, which is returned inside this URL as a query parameter with the key named **code**.

With this code in hand, step 2 is completed. Next, in *Step* 3, we will be making a POST request to the Unsplash server.

POST request and GET request

In *Chapter 7, Networking with SwiftUI – Part 1*, we were introduced to RESTful APIs. In the context of RESTful APIs, there are many HTTP methods used to interact with resources, with **POST** and **GET** being the most common among them. They have different purposes and behaviors as follows:

GET request:

- The **GET** request is used to retrieve or fetch data from a server. It is a safe and idempotent operation, meaning it should not have any side effects on the server and can be repeated multiple times without changing the state of the server or the resource.

- In a **GET** request, the parameters or data are appended to the URL as query parameters, typically separated by the **?** character. For example, **GET /users?id=123**.

- **GET** requests are commonly used for fetching data, searching resources, or accessing specific endpoints that provide read-only operations.

POST request:

- The **POST** request is used to submit or send data to the server to create a new resource or trigger a non-idempotent action. It may modify the server's state or trigger some server-side operations based on the submitted data.

- In a **POST** request, the data is sent in the body of the request, typically formatted as JSON or form data. The data is not visible in the URL.

- **POST** requests are commonly used for creating new resources, submitting forms, uploading files, or triggering actions that cause changes on the server.

There are other methods that you may have come across, such as **PUT**, **PATCH,** or **DELETE**, but **GET** and **POST** are the most frequently used.

In summary, the main difference between **GET** and **POST** requests in a RESTful API is their purpose and the way data are transmitted. **GET** requests are used for **retrieving data**, while **POST** requests are used for **submitting data** and **triggering actions**. **GET** requests have their parameters in the URL, while **POST** requests have their data in the request body. It's important to use the appropriate **HTTP** method based on the intended operation to ensure adherence to RESTful principles and best practices.

Up to this point, all of the API calls that we have made are all **GET** requests. Now with *Step 3* and the final step to exchange for the access token, we will make a **POST** request with the help of **URLSession**. The syntax will look a little bit different than before.

Back to our **APIsManager**, let's write the code to make our **POST** request:

```swift
func exchangeToken(code: String, completion: @escaping (Bool) -> Void) {
    // Get Token
    guard let url = URL(string: Constant.baseURL) else {
        return
    }

    var components = URLComponents()
    components.queryItems = [
        URLQueryItem(name: "client_id", value: Constant.acccessKey),
        URLQueryItem(name: "client_secret", value: Constant.secretKey),
        URLQueryItem(name: "redirect_uri", value: Constant.redirect_uri),
        URLQueryItem(name: "code", value: code),
        URLQueryItem(name: "grant_type", value: "authorization_code"),
    ]

    var request = URLRequest(url: url)
    request.httpMethod = "POST"
    request.httpBody = components.query?.data(using: .utf8)

    let task = URLSession.shared.dataTask(with: request) { data, _, error in
        guard let data = data, error == nil else {
            completion(false)
            return
        }

        do {
            let result = try JSONDecoder().decode(AuthResponse.self, from: data)
            print(result)
            completion(true)
        } catch {
            print(error.localizedDescription)
            completion(false)
        }

    }
    task.resume()
}
```

Figure 8.23: POST request for step 3

Just as we discussed, there is a difference between the query parameters of a **GET** and a **POST** request. For a **GET** request, we can straightforward match a string with the base URL. However, for a **POST** request, its query parameters are passed in the request body. This is what the codes in the two new green areas are doing. By default, every time you create a new **URLRequest**, it is a **GET** request. So, to change this to a **POST** request, we reset it with the **request.httpMethod** to **POST**. If you want to perform other **HTTP** methods, such as **DELETE,** then you will have to change it here.

Now we will decode the response with **JSONDecoder**. Here is another challenge to see if you remember what we have learned. Go back to the documentation and try to write the **AuthResponse** model to decode it:

```
struct AuthResponse: Codable {
    let access_token: String
    let token_type: String
    let scope: String
    let created_at: Int
}
```

Figure 8.24: *AuthResponse solution*

You have learned about Decodable in the last chapter. In Swift, the Decodable protocol is used for decoding (parsing) JSON or other data representations into native Swift objects. There is also a counterpart way when you want to encode (serialize) native Swift objects into an external representation, such as JSON or binary data. That's when you need the Encodable protocol. Because they are relatable, Swift comes up with a convenient Codable protocol that is a combination of both Decodable and Encodable. So that developers can just adopt one instead of remembering when to use which of the two.

Here, we will adopt the Codable protocol, although you can just use Decodable.

Now, let's go back to the **AuthorizationView** and call the just written **exchangeToken** function:

Figure 8.25: *Successfully exchange access token*

Now, we have successfully exchanged the access token. With this token, we can now use it to call all the APIs of Unsplash and complete our project.

However, there is a problem occurring at this point with this code where we save our token. Naturally, you may think that we can create a variable name **accessToken** inside the **APIsManager** and save it there like this:

```swift
var accessToken = ""

func exchangeToken(code: String, completion: @escaping (Bool) -> Void) {
    // Get Token
    guard let url = URL(string: Constant.baseURL) else {
        return
    }

    var components = URLComponents()
    components.queryItems = [
        URLQueryItem(name: "client_id", value: Constant.acccessKey),
        URLQueryItem(name: "client_secret", value: Constant.secretKey),
        URLQueryItem(name: "redirect_uri", value: Constant.redirect_uri),
        URLQueryItem(name: "code", value: code),
        URLQueryItem(name: "grant_type", value: "authorization_code"),
    ]

    var request = URLRequest(url: url)
    request.httpMethod = "POST"
    request.httpBody = components.query?.data(using: .utf8)

    let task = URLSession.shared.dataTask(with: request) { [weak self] data, _, error in
        guard let data = data, error == nil else {
            completion(false)
            return
        }

        do {
            let result = try JSONDecoder().decode(AuthResponse.self, from: data)
            self?.accessToken = result.access_token
            completion(true)
        } catch {
            print(error.localizedDescription)
            completion(false)
        }

    }
    task.resume()
```

Figure 8.26: Saving data problem (1)

Often, newcomers make this mistake because they forget the difference between a Class and an Object. We have discussed this in *Chapter 1* about Swift programming language. In summary, a class is like a blueprint or a template, while an object is a concrete instance created based on that blueprint. The class defines the structure and behavior, and the object represents a specific realization of that structure with its data and behavior.

Now, take a look back at our code from the **AuthorizationView**:

```
struct AuthorizationView: View {
    var body: some View {
        WebView(request: URLRequest(url: URL(string:
            APIsManager().returnAuthorizationURL())!))
    }
}

struct WebView: UIViewRepresentable {

    let request: URLRequest

    class Coordinator: NSObject, WKNavigationDelegate {
        var parent: WebView

        init(_ parent: WebView) {
            self.parent = parent
        }

        func webView(_ webView: WKWebView, didFinish navigation: WKNavigation!)
        {
            guard let url = webView.url else {
                return
            }

            // Exchange Code for access Token
            let component = URLComponents(string: url.absoluteString)

            guard let code = component?.queryItems?.first(where: { $0.name ==
                "code" })?.value else {
                return
            }

            APIsManager().exchangeToken(code: code) { success in

            }
        }
    }
}
```

Figure 8.27: Saving data problem (2)

We have created two different objects from the class **APIsManager**. Now, if we try to save the access token, then which one of the two objects will have the right access token? You may have guessed it based on the color, but only the green object will hold our recently retrieved access token. The red object doesn't have it, and any future object will not too.

Now this is a problem because later we will write more functions to call different APIs inside the **APIsManager,** and this will be used in other screens. Based on your knowledge about class, then you might think about creating a global class, and since a class is a reference type when pass assign them, they will be the same one. This will work here, but what if someone doesn't know about it and accidentally makes a new instance?

Again, this is a very common problem, and one of the solutions to this is to use the **Singleton design pattern**.

Singleton design pattern

The Singleton pattern is a creational design pattern that restricts the instantiation of a class to a single object. It ensures that there is only one instance of a class created and provides a global point of access to that instance.

In software development, the Singleton pattern is commonly used when we want to have a single, shared instance of a class that can be accessed from different parts of an application. This can be useful in scenarios where having multiple instances of a class could cause issues, such as when managing resources, controlling access to a shared database, or coordinating actions in a system.

To implement the Singleton pattern, the class typically provides a static method or property to access the instance, and the constructor of the class is made private or protected to prevent direct instantiation. The class also keeps track of whether an instance has already been created and returns the existing instance if it exists or creates a new one if it doesn't.

Here's how we will implement Singleton to our **APIsManager**:

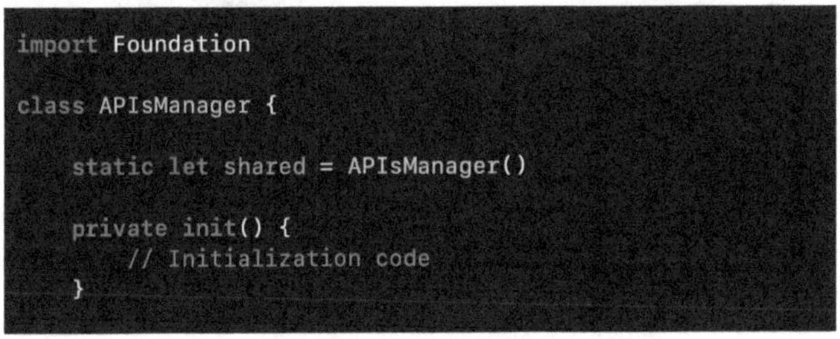

```
import Foundation

class APIsManager {

    static let shared = APIsManager()

    private init() {
        // Initialization code
    }
```

Figure 8.28: Singleton implementation

Now, the **APIsManager** class has a static property shared, which represents the single and only instance of the class. The shared property is declared as **static let**, which means it's lazily initialized and guarantees a single instance throughout the app.

The **private init()** method ensures that the class cannot be directly instantiated from outside the class, preventing the creation of multiple instances. Other methods and properties can be added to the class as needed.

To use the Singleton in your iOS app, you can access it using **APIsManager. shared**:

```
struct AuthorizationView: View {
    var body: some View {
        WebView(request: URLRequest(url: URL(string:
            APIsManager.shared.returnAuthorizationURL())!))
    }
}

struct WebView: UIViewRepresentable {

    let request: URLRequest

    class Coordinator: NSObject, WKNavigationDelegate {
        var parent: WebView

        init(_ parent: WebView) {
            self.parent = parent
        }

        func webView(_ webView: WKWebView, didFinish navigation: WKNavigation!)
        {
            guard let url = webView.url else {
                return
            }

            // Exchange Code for access Token
            let component = URLComponents(string: url.absoluteString)

            guard let code = component?.queryItems?.first(where: { $0.name ==
                "code" })?.value else {
                return
            }

            APIsManager.shared.exchangeToken(code: code) { success in

            }
        }
    }
}
```

Figure 8.29: *Access properties and methods from Singleton*

By using **APIsManager.shared**, you can access the shared instance of the class from anywhere in your app. Both of these now refer to one instance: the shared instance, so both of them now will have the same access token.

It's important to note that the Singleton pattern is not without controversy, as it can introduce a global state and make code harder to test and maintain. Therefore, it should be used judiciously and only when it provides a clear benefit for the specific use case.

Completing the project

After successfully exchanging for the access token, we can now show the **HomeView** that we made at the beginning:

Figure 8.30: *Present the HomeView after successful authorization and have access token*

Remember we use the completion handler here and return a Boolean value indicating whether we have successfully exchanged the access token or not. If it is a success, then we can confidently present the **HomeView**.

Inside our WebView, we defined a **@Binding** value **isSuccessAuthorized,** which binds with the value from the **AuthorizationView**. If we successfully receive the access token, then we will set that binding value to true to notify the **AuthorizationView**. And in the **AuthorizationView**, if **isSuccessAuthorized** is **true,** we will present our **HomeView**. If it is not, then it will still be the **AuthorizationView**.

From what you have learned, you may think about using a **ZStack** and checking for an if-else condition. This is totally doable, but this is a very common situation where we want to display a new screen based on some conditions. Because of this, SwiftUI has a convenient built-in modifier for this: **.fullScreenCover(),** which receives a binding Boolean and will display the inside view with a full-screen cover.

So now, after the user grants us the authorization, we can save the received access token and redirect them to the **HomeView**. The only thing left is to call APIs to get real image data back following the Unsplash. And we already have the access token stored inside our global Singleton instance.

We will be using three APIs for this project as follows:

- Get a list of photos: **https://unsplash.com/documentation#list-photos**

- Like a photo: **https://unsplash.com/documentation#like-a-photo**

- Unlike a photo: **https://unsplash.com/documentation#unlike-a-photo**

Here is another challenge for you, based on what you have learned in this chapter. Try reading the documentation to understand the requirements of each API. Then, write the codes to implement them inside the class **APIsManager**.

Take some time, maybe some days, to try to figure it out. If you can do this by yourself, then a huge round of applause because this is kind of advance.

Now, let's jump to the solution. First, with the git list photo API:

```
// Photo API
static let basePhotoAPIURL = "https://api.unsplash.com/photos"
static let per_page = "20"
}

func fetch20Images(completion: @escaping (Result<[ImageDataModel], Error>) -> Void) {
    let urlString = Constant.basePhotoAPIURL + "?&page=1" + "&per_page=\(Constant.per_page)"
    guard let url = URL(string: urlString) else {
        completion(.failure(APIError.failedCreateURL))
        return
    }
    var request = URLRequest(url: url)                                      Step 4
    request.setValue("Bearer \(accessToken)", forHTTPHeaderField: "Authorization")
    request.httpMethod = "GET"

    let task = URLSession.shared.dataTask(with: request) { data, _, error in
        guard let data = data, error == nil else {
            completion(.failure(APIError.failedToGetData))
            return
        }

        do {
            let result = try JSONDecoder().decode([ImageDataModel].self, from: data)
            completion(.success(result))
        } catch {
            print(error.localizedDescription)
            completion(.failure(error))
        }
    }
    task.resume()
}
```

Figure 8.31: Implementation fetch list photos API

With this new API, a new base URL and query parameter key values are required. So, we add them to our Constant struct. Because this is a **GET** request, we can do string matching to create a final URL. You already learned all of this in the last chapter; the difference here is in the orange area. Now, this is the fourth step of the authorization flow, if you remember it.

4. On future requests, send OAuth Bearer access token via the HTTP Authorization header:

```
Authorization: Bearer ACCESS_TOKEN
```

Figure 8.32: *Required access token for all API requests*

That's what the new line of code you see here is doing. It embedded the access token into the HTTP Authorization header.

And if we successfully retrieve our data, we want to create a model and decode it from the data. In this API, what we have back is an array. Here is the model for it, along with the custom enumeration to present different types of errors:

```swift
import Foundation

struct LikePhotoModel: Codable {
    let photo: ImageDataModel
}

struct ImageDataModel: Codable, Hashable {
    let id: String
    let likes: Int
    let liked_by_user: Bool
    let user: UserData
    let urls: UrlsData
}

struct UserData: Codable, Hashable {
    let name: String
}

struct UrlsData: Codable, Hashable {
    let small: String
    let full: String
    let regular: String
    let thumb: String
}

enum APIError: Error {
    case failedCreateURL
    case failedToGetData
}
```

Figure 8.33: *Image data model and error enumeration*

Instead of using default data, we will replace them will real data fetched back from the API. Once again, we will implement the MVVM design pattern we learned from *Chapter 6, Tab bar, Navigation, and Compositional Layout*. Here is the ViewModel:

```swift
// Created by James Thang on 24/04/2023.
//
import SwiftUI

class ViewModel: ObservableObject {

    @Published private(set) var imageData = [ImageDataModel]()

    init() {
        fetchPost()
    }

    private func fetchPost() {
        APIsManager.shared.fetch20Images { [weak self] result in
            DispatchQueue.main.async {
                switch result {
                case .success(let data):
                    self?.imageData.append(contentsOf: data)
                case .failure(let error):
                    print(error.localizedDescription)
                }
            }
        }
    }
}
```

Figure 8.34: HomeView view model

We create a function, **fetchPost**, that will use the new API to fetch twenty photos back as an array of **ImageDataModel**. We will call this function when the view model is initialized and then save the result to the **@Published** variable named **imageData**. The final step is getting back to the **HomeView** and **ItemView** and replacing the default data with this real data:

```swift
import SwiftUI

struct ItemView: View {

    let model: ImageDataModel

    var body: some View {
        VStack(alignment: .leading, spacing: 12) {
            Image("landscape")
                .resizable()
                .aspectRatio(4/3, contentMode: .fit)
                .clipShape(RoundedRectangle(cornerRadius: 16))

            Text(model.user.name)
                .foregroundColor(.primary)
                .fontWeight(.medium)

            HStack {
                Button(model.liked_by_user ? "Unlike" : "Like") {

                }

                Spacer()

                Text("\(model.likes) likes")
                    .font(.callout)
                    .foregroundColor(.secondary)
            }
        }
    }
}
```

Figure 8.35: Refactor the ItemView with real model data

Here, the **ItemView** will receive a model **ImageDataModel** that has all the required data. We will **replace** all the default information with the real information from the model, except for the image here. It is because what we get back is the image URL, not the **data** of the image itself. Because of this, we will first have to go to that address to download the image data. We will learn how to do this in the next section. Now, let's go back to the **HomeView** and apply our just-created view model to it:

Figure 8.36: *Refactor the HomeView with real model data*

We are now using the real fetched data from the view model. As you can see from the right side of the simulator, except for the image, all the data are now real and live.

Another thing we want to point out here is the live preview is usually used to view the UI only. There are still a lot of things not working correctly on it, so you still need to build to the simulator and real device to test and see the real result. In this example, we will rebuild the app in the real simulator and reauthenticate it to see the real result.

Finally, let's learn how to load the real image to our app from a URL using **URLSession**.

Downloading images from URL using URLSession

Just like a normal API, calling to get image data is just another GET request. But instead of decoding it to our custom model, we will return the received data directly:

```swift
func downloadImage(from urlString: String, completion: @escaping ((Result<Data, Error>) -> Void) {
    guard let url = URL(string: urlString) else {
        let error = APIError.failedCreateURL
        completion(.failure(error))
        return
    }

    let task = URLSession.shared.dataTask(with: url) { (data, response, error) in
        if let error = error {
            completion(.failure(error))
            return
        }

        if let data = data {
            completion(.success(data))
        } else {
            let error = APIError.failedToGetData
            completion(.failure(error))
        }
    }

    task.resume()
}
```

Figure 8.37: *Define the download image data function using URLSession*

Inside the **APIsManager**, we will add another function for downloading an image from a URL. Now, back to the **ItemView**, we will use this new function when the view appears:

```swift
struct ItemView: View {
    let model: ImageDataModel
    @State var uiImage: UIImage?

    var body: some View {
        VStack(alignment: .leading, spacing: 12) {
            if let uiImage = uiImage {
                Image(uiImage: uiImage)
                    .resizable()
                    .aspectRatio(4/3, contentMode: .fit)
                    .clipShape(RoundedRectangle(cornerRadius: 16))
            }

            Text(model.user.name)
                .foregroundColor(.primary)
                .fontWeight(.medium)

            HStack {
                Button(model.liked_by_user ? "Unlike" : "Like") {

                }

                Spacer()

                Text("\(model.likes) likes")
                    .font(.callout)
                    .foregroundColor(.secondary)
            }
        }
        .onAppear {
            APIsManager.shared.downloadImage(from: model.urls.regular) { result in
                switch result {
                case .success(let data):
                    uiImage = UIImage(data: data)
                case .failure(let error):
                    print(error.localizedDescription)
                }
            }
        }
    }
}
```

Figure 8.38: *Calling download image data function using URLSession*

If our function succeeds, we will have the image data back. There is the built-in initializer from **UIKit** to transform the data into an image: **UIImage(data:)**. We will make this image an optional state variable. Inside our view, after unwrapping it, we can use another initializer of the image that receives a **UIImage** as its parameter: **Image(uiImage:)**.

Now, let's rebuild the app using the simulator; you should see the real images:

Figure 8.39: *Successfully load images*

With this, you almost have a real application on your hands. It certainly works but is not perfect yet. There are some remaining issues as follows:

- The scroll is cluttering because the images are not cache

- If you are offline, then you cannot use this app

We will tackle all of these in the next chapter.

Conclusion

In this chapter, we have built a real application with API services from Unsplash. During this process, we learned about OAuth 2.0 for authentication in modern applications, different HTTP methods, and distinguishing between GET requests and POST requests. We encountered a problem with the share access token and solved it using the Singleton design pattern. We also learned how to present a website inside our project using WebKit and how to download images using URLSession.

There are still some remaining problems, so we will learn how to solve them in the next chapter, where we will learn how to use local storage for persistence and how to leverage third-party libraries inside our project for better performance.

CHAPTER 9

Local Storage with UserDefaults, CoreData, and File Manager

Introduction

In the last two chapters, we have learned about Networking and how to build a beautiful application. Although the app is not working perfectly yet, there are still observed issues in it.

In this chapter, we will discuss local storage - what it means and the purpose of using it.

Local storage is a crucial aspect of iOS app development, enabling the storage and retrieval of user-specific data within an application. In SwiftUI development, various techniques and frameworks are available for local storage implementation, including UserDefaults, CoreData, and File Manager. Each of these options offers distinct features and capabilities to handle different types of data.

We will explore these three local storage options in the context of iOS SwiftUI development, discussing their benefits, use cases, and implementation techniques. By understanding these approaches, developers can efficiently manage local data storage in their applications, providing seamless user experiences and improved data management capabilities.

In this way, we will make our app adapt to local storage so that users can use it even though they do not have access to the internet.

Structure

In this chapter, the following topics will be covered:

- Persistence with Local storage

- Store simple values with UserDefaults

- Core Data in iOS app development

- A basic set of operators of a database system design CRUD

- Set up and use CoreData in real-world application

- How to store images on the device with File Manager

- Load image from device to use inside the application

Persistency with Local Storage

In the context of programming, **persistency** refers to the ability of data to persist or be retained beyond the lifetime of a program or a system. It is the concept of storing data in a permanent or semi-permanent manner, allowing it to be retrieved and used later, even after the program or system has been terminated or restarted.

Persistence is essential when you need to preserve and access data across different program executions or when the data needs to be available to other parts of the system or other systems entirely. Without persistence, data would be lost once the program terminates, making it difficult to build applications that require data storage or data retrieval.

In the context of iOS app development, persistency refers to the techniques and mechanisms used to store and retrieve data in iOS applications. iOS provides several options for persisting data, and the choice depends on the specific requirements and characteristics of your app.

- **UserDefaults**: UserDefaults is a simple and lightweight way to store small amounts of data such as user preferences, settings, or small configuration values. It uses a key-value pair approach and saves data in property list files. UserDefaults is commonly used for storing user preferences or application state.

- **Core Data**: Core Data is a powerful framework provided by Apple for managing complex data models and object graphs. It allows you to define entities and relationships and provides features like data validation, querying, and versioning. Core Data can store data in various persistent stores, including an SQLite database, XML files, or in-memory stores.

- **Realm (MongoDB)**: Realm is a popular third-party mobile database solution that can be used for persisting data in iOS app development. It is a cross-platform database engine that provides an object-oriented interface to store and retrieve data.

- **SQLite**: SQLite is a lightweight, embedded relational database engine that is widely used in iOS app development. It provides a SQL-based interface for storing and retrieving structured data. SQLite databases can be accessed directly using SQLite API or through ORM libraries like FMDB or GRDB.

- **File System**: iOS apps can store data directly in the file system. You can use various file formats, such as plain text files, XML, JSON, or binary files, to store structured or unstructured data. This approach is suitable for scenarios where you need fine-grained control over the data organization or when dealing with large files.

- **Network-based storage**: Sometimes, rather than storing data locally on the device, you might choose to persist data on a remote server or cloud-based storage. This approach is often used for applications that require data synchronization across multiple devices or for scenarios where data needs to be shared between users.

It's worth noting that iOS provides frameworks and APIs for handling different types of data persistency, and you can combine multiple approaches depending on your app's requirements. For example, you might use UserDefaults for storing user preferences, Core Data for managing a local database, and network-based storage for synchronizing data with a server.

When selecting a persistence mechanism for your iOS app, consider factors like the complexity of your data model, performance requirements, scalability, security, and ease of use. Apple's documentation and developer resources provide detailed guidance on using each of these persistence options in iOS app development.

In this chapter, we will learn and use UserDefaults, Core Data, and File System to level up our application. You can spend more time and conduct further research on other local storage topics. Remember that each topic comes with pros and cons. There is no such grand master key, and the choice of which one to use depends on different situations.

First, let's learn about the simplest and the most overly used one: UserDefaults.

UserDefaults

UserDefaults is a simple and lightweight persistence mechanism provided by Apple in iOS app development. It allows you to store small amounts of data, such as user preferences, settings, or small configuration values. **UserDefaults** uses a key-value pair approach to store data, and it saves the data in property list files.

In the last chapter, you have learned about Singleton, remember it? Well, **UserDefaults** in iOS is implemented as a singleton. A singleton is a design pattern that restricts the instantiation of a class to a single object. In the case of **UserDefaults**, it ensures that there is only one instance of UserDefaults throughout the app.

By designating **UserDefaults** as a singleton, Apple provides a shared instance of **UserDefaults** that can be accessed from anywhere within the app without the need to create a new instance. This shared instance provides a convenient way to access and manage user preferences and app settings.

To access the shared instance of **UserDefaults**, you typically use the standard **UserDefaults** class methods. For example:

```swift
// Storing a value in UserDefaults
UserDefaults.standard.set("John Doe", forKey: "username")

// Retrieving a value from UserDefaults
if let username = UserDefaults.standard.string(forKey: "username") {
    print("Username: \(username)")
}
```

Figure 9.1: Store and retrieve the value with User default

The `.standard` property of the **UserDefaults** class refers to the shared instance. By using **UserDefaults**.standard, you can access and modify the stored preferences throughout your app.

It's important to note that while **UserDefaults** is implemented as a singleton, it does not mean that it cannot be subclasses or extended. You can create your own custom subclasses of **UserDefaults** if you need to add additional functionality or encapsulate specific behavior.

However, for most use cases, accessing the shared instance of **UserDefaults** through the `.standard` property is sufficient and recommended. It provides a simple and standardized way to store and retrieve small amounts of app-specific data.

Now, let's make a simple demo to learn about persistency with **UserDefaults**:

Figure 9.2: *UserDefaults example: number game*

We created a simple app that increases or decreases the selected number. After playing and increasing the number to 6, if we swipe up, close the app, and reopen it, then our number resets to its first default state of 0:

Figure 9.3: *Number is reset back to 0 every time the app is reopened*

Certainly, some kinds of applications prefer this behavior, but most of them do not. Think about it: What if, in a shopping app, you have added some clothes to your cart but decided not to purchase them yet? Sometime later, you return and see your cart is empty. Now you have to remember what you selected and search for them again. How annoying is that! This is not accepted in any shopping apps. Or how about a game? After hours of playing hard, you are now at level 25. But the next day when you come back, you are reset to level 1.

Some data need to be remembered. Now, there are two main ways of doing this: database and local storage. When we talk about the database, it means we send the data to be stored somewhere else (a server or cloud), and then when we need that data, we will request it through APIs. You can do your own research and learn more about this topic. The most commonly used services in recent years are Firebase and AWS.

Local storage, as explained, is storing that data on the device itself.

Let's make this app remember the last number using **UserDefaults**:

Figure 9.4: *Using UserDefault to remember the number*

After increasing or decreasing the number, we then set its value to the key **storedNumber**. Then every time the app is opened, we will check and retrieve that value to use. As simple as that!

Another optimization here, since we are programmers who follow the DRY principle, we will make a new **storeNumber** function and reuse it:

```
struct ContentView: View {

    @State private var number: Int = UserDefaults.standard.integer(forKey: "storedNumber")

    var body: some View {
        VStack {
            Text("Stored Number: \(number)")
                .font(.title)

            HStack {
                Button(action: {
                    number -= 1
                    storeNumber()
                }) {
                    Image(systemName: "minus.circle")
                        .font(.largeTitle)
                        .foregroundColor(.red)
                }
                .padding()

                Button(action: {
                    number += 1
                    storeNumber()
                }) {
                    Image(systemName: "plus.circle")
                        .font(.largeTitle)
                        .foregroundColor(.green)
                }
                .padding()
            }
        }
        .padding()
    }

    func storeNumber() {
        UserDefaults.standard.set(number, forKey: "storedNumber")
    }
}
```

Figure 9.5: *Make a storeNumber to reuse when we need its functionality*

Here are the pros and cons of using **UserDefaults**:

Pros:

- **Simplicity**: **UserDefaults** is straightforward to use. It provides a simple API to set and retrieve values using keys, making it easy to store and retrieve data without much complexity.

- **Lightweight**: **UserDefaults** is designed for storing small amounts of data. It is efficient and does not require additional setup or external dependencies. It is suitable for storing simple preferences or small data sets without introducing unnecessary overhead.

- **Convenience**: **UserDefaults** is accessible throughout the app's lifecycle and can be accessed from any part of the app. This makes it convenient for accessing frequently used settings or preferences from different view controllers or components within your app.

- **Integration with Interface Builder**: **UserDefaults** can be directly integrated with Interface Builder, allowing you to bind user interface elements directly to **UserDefaults** keys. This enables seamless synchronization between user interface elements and stored preferences.

- **Persistence across app launches**: Data stored using **UserDefaults** persists even after the app is terminated or restarted. This means that the stored data will be available the next time the app is launched, providing a seamless experience for users.

Cons:

- **Limited data size and complexity**: **UserDefaults** is not suitable for storing large amounts of data or complex data structures. It is primarily designed for simple values such as strings, numbers, booleans, and small collections. Storing large data sets in UserDefaults may lead to performance issues or memory constraints.

- **Lack of data encryption**: **UserDefaults** does not provide built-in encryption for stored data. If you need to store sensitive or secure information, such as passwords or personal data, it is recommended to use other encryption mechanisms or consider using more secure persistence options like Keychain.

- **Lack of querying and indexing**: **UserDefaults** does not provide querying or indexing capabilities. It does not support complex searches or sorting based on specific criteria. If you require advanced querying or sorting operations, you may need to consider other persistence options like Core Data or SQLite.

- **Limited data sharing between apps**: **UserDefaults** data is scoped to the specific app where it is stored. It cannot be easily shared with other apps or shared across different devices. If you need to share data between apps or devices, other inter-app communication or synchronization mechanisms need to be implemented.

UserDefaults is best suited for storing simple preferences or settings that are used across your app. It is not intended for managing large data sets or complex data relationships. If your app requires more advanced data management, querying capabilities, or data synchronization, you may need to consider other persistence options such as Core Data, SQLite, or Realm.

Let's now go back to the app we built from the Unsplash APIs in the last chapter and start using **UserDefaults**. Again, every technology has its pros and cons. Based on what you have learned above, what do you think is a suitable place for using UserDefaults?

Think about it, **UserDefaults** is suitable for lightweight data only. And what is the piece of data that is better to be stored locally inside our application? Remember, not everything has to be stored locally, only the necessary things.

In case you forgot, the "access token" used in our APIs doesn't have an expiration time. This means that when we get the first one, we can use it forever. Therefore, it will be a waste of time and resources if we call the exchange API every time the app is started. Instead, the better solution here is to store the access token in local storage using UserDefaults the first time we get it. The "access token" is a simple string, so it is lightweight and fits every pros condition of **UserDefaults**. Then, for all the remaining time, we will try to retrieve and use the "access token" from the local storage. Only when we can't find it and fail to use it, then we will call the exchange "access token" API again. By doing this, we will save a significant amount of resources, which is money for our application.

Let's open up the project and make this optimization. Let's first go to the **APIsManager** file where we have all of the APIs logic:

```
// Replace
// var accessToken = ""

// With
var accessToken: String? {
    return UserDefaults.standard.string(forKey: "access_token")
}
```

Figure 9.6: Using UserDefaults to store access token (1)

Instead of an empty string, we will make it optional and retrieve the value from **UserDefaults** using the key **access_token**. It is optional because the .string method from **UserDefaults** will return an optional string. This is because it may or may not find it in the memory. In the preceding **.integer** of **UserDefaults,** we don't need to use optional because if it cannot find the value, the .integer method will return 0. Again, you can hold the **Option** key on your keyboard to read more about these built-in methods.

In Swift, where functions or computed properties have one line only, you can omit the **return** keyword. Here, we prefer to keep it there for better self-explanation.

This is the step for retrieving the value, but we still need to save it somewhere. We do this when we receive the access token from our API. This logic is in the same file:

```swift
func exchangeToken(code: String, completion: @escaping (Bool) -> Void) {
    // Get Token
    guard let url = URL(string: Constant.baseURL) else {
        return
    }

    var components = URLComponents()
    components.queryItems = [
        URLQueryItem(name: "client_id", value: Constant.acccessKey),
        URLQueryItem(name: "client_secret", value: Constant.secretKey),
        URLQueryItem(name: "redirect_uri", value: Constant.redirect_uri),
        URLQueryItem(name: "code", value: code),
        URLQueryItem(name: "grant_type", value: "authorization_code"),
    ]

    var request = URLRequest(url: url)
    request.httpMethod = "POST"
    request.httpBody = components.query?.data(using: .utf8)

    let task = URLSession.shared.dataTask(with: request) { [weak self] data, _, error in
        guard let data = data, error == nil else {
            completion(false)
            return
        }

        do {
            let result = try JSONDecoder().decode(AuthResponse.self, from: data)
            // Replace
            // self?.accessToken = result.access_token
            // With
            UserDefaults.standard.setValue(result.access_token, forKey: "access_token")
            completion(true)
        } catch {
            print(error.localizedDescription)
            completion(false)
        }

    }
    task.resume()
```

Figure 9.7: Using UserDefaults to store access token (2)

Instead of assigning it directly after successfully obtaining it from the API, we will store the access token in **UserDefaults** at this step. Then, whenever we need to use this, for example, in the **fetch20Images** function, we will unwrap to use the access token stored in **UserDefaults**:

```swift
func fetch20Images(completion: @escaping (Result<[ImageDataModel], Error>) -> Void) {
    let urlString = Constant.basePhotoAPIURL + "?&page=1" + "&per_page=\(Constant.per_page)"

    guard let url = URL(string: urlString) else {
        completion(.failure(APIError.failedCreateURL))
        return
    }

    guard let accessToken = accessToken else {
        completion(.failure(APIError.failedToGetAccessToken))
        return
    }

    var request = URLRequest(url: url)
    request.setValue("Bearer \(accessToken)", forHTTPHeaderField: "Authorization")
    request.httpMethod = "GET"

    let task = URLSession.shared.dataTask(with: request) { data, _, error in
        guard let data = data, error == nil else {
            completion(.failure(APIError.failedToGetData))
            return
        }

        do {
            let result = try JSONDecoder().decode([ImageDataModel].self, from: data)
            completion(.success(result))
        } catch {
            print(error.localizedDescription)
            completion(.failure(error))
        }
    }
    task.resume()
}
```

Figure 9.8: Using UserDefaults to store access token (3)

In this step, we return a new failure completion error called **failedToGet AccessToken**. With this, we can retry to call the API for "access token" just in case we cannot find it from **UserDefaults**.

And that's the last thing that needs to change is in the **AuthorizationView**:

```swift
struct AuthorizationView: View {

    @State private var isSuccessAuthorized: Bool =
        APIsManager.shared.accessToken != nil

    var body: some View {
        if isSuccessAuthorized {
            HomeView()
        } else {
            WebView(request: URLRequest(url:
                URL(string:
                APIsManager.shared
                .returnAuthorizationURL())!),
                isSuccessAuthorized:
                $isSuccessAuthorized)
                .fullScreenCover(isPresented:
                    $isSuccessAuthorized) {
                    HomeView()
                }
        }
    }
}
```

Figure 9.9: Using UserDefaults to store access token (4)

As mentioned earlier, since the "access token" does not expire, we do not need to recall the get access token API. It would be a waste of resources. Instead, we will set our **isSuccessAuthorized** equal to whether the **accessToken** string variable in the **APIsManager** has a value or not. If it doesn't have a value, then **isSuccessAuthorized** is **false**, and we will present the WebView to go to all the steps to get the "access token". However, if we already have the value, which is from **UserDefaults** in this case, then we go straight to the **HomeView**. So, from now on, after the first time, every subsequent time the user will go straight to the **HomeView**.

Now, you have successfully implemented the first local storage and made an improvement in the application.

Next, let's fix the cluttering behavior that occurs while scrolling. This happens because we tried to download the image and load it into the image of **ItemView** every time it appears. Since this is a scroll view, the onAppear will be triggered repeatedly every time a cell is in the displaying area. This is also unnecessary and inefficient because we only need to download and display the image once.

In the old UIKit, the most common life cycle is viewDidLoad, which will be called only once when that view is initialized, not every time it appears. This made it a perfect place to handle APIs. Unfortunately, SwiftUI's view does not come with this life cycle. However, we can easily recreate it with the help of a state value:

```swift
import SwiftUI

struct ItemView: View {

    let model: ImageDataModel
    @State var uiImage: UIImage?
    @State var isLoad = false

    var body: some View {
        VStack(alignment: .leading, spacing: 12) { ••• }
        .onAppear {
            if !isLoad {
                APIsManager.shared.downloadImage(from: model.urls.regular) { result in
                    switch result {
                    case .success(let data):
                        uiImage = UIImage(data: data)
                    case .failure(let error):
                        print(error.localizedDescription)
                    }
                }
                isLoad = true
            }
        }
    }
}
```

Figure 9.10: Implement view is loading lifecycle in SwiftUI

We make a new Boolean variable named **isLoad** and set it to **false** initially. Then, when the view appears, we will check if **isLoad** is **false,** and then call the API and set it to **true**. This will prevent recalling the API every time the view appears again because of the scrolling action.

It is very simple and handy. Now, build and run the application again and try to scroll up and down, you will notice that the cluttering behavior has disappeared. This is an improvement in both user experience and application performance.

Now, let's touch on the last thing, which is the main purpose of using local storage in mobile development: how to handle offline mode. The internet is a necessity in today's life, with some even considering it along with survival things like food and water. However, there will be many situations when you do not have access to the internet, such as in airplane mode or in some rural areas. What if users are bored and mess around with their phones and open our application for entertainment or accident?

In such instances, this will happen:

Figure 9.11: *Application state when there is no internet*

Because there is no internet, all the API calls will fail, resulting in an empty blank application. To use the application, users should have access to the internet. If that is the case, then we developers can handle a no-internet case with a UI to inform users about it. For our application, it would be great if we could display previous images for users to view again when they are in offline mode. This will make us truly stand out and reach more customers.

Again, you can already guess that the solution for this is to use local storage. However, this time, we have to store our **ImageDataModel**, which is a complex data structure. And to do this, we will learn about Apple's provided solution, CoreData, and how to implement it in SwiftUI.

Introduction to CoreData

Core Data is a framework provided by Apple that allows developers to manage the model layer objects in an application. It provides object graph management, persistence, and query functionality. Here are some of the pros and cons of using Core Data:

Pros:

- **Object-Relational Mapping**: Core Data provides an abstraction layer that allows you to work with objects in your code, while it handles the underlying data storage and retrieval. It simplifies the process of mapping objects to a persistent store, such as an SQLite database.

- **Relationships and Data Modeling**: Core Data allows you to define complex relationships between entities, including one-to-one, one-to-many, and many-to-many relationships. It also supports inheritance and can handle complex data models.

- **Caching and Performance**: Core Data includes an object cache that can improve performance by reducing the need to fetch data from the persistent store. It also supports various performance optimizations, such as faulting and batching fetch requests.

- **Undo and Redo**: Core Data provides built-in support for undo and redo functionality, allowing users to revert changes or redo previous actions.

Cons:

- **Learning curve**: Core Data has a steep learning curve, especially for developers who are new to the framework. It has a complex API and can be challenging to understand and use correctly.

- **Complexity of migration**: If you need to make changes to your data model after your app has been released, Core Data migration can be a complex process. It requires careful planning and handling of data migration scenarios.

- **Platform limitations**: Core Data is primarily designed for Apple platforms (iOS, macOS, watchOS, and tvOS) and may not be the best choice if you're developing a cross-platform application.

`CoreData,` as well as many topics in this book alone, is a huge domain and cannot be covered in a book, let alone a section of one chapter. So, based on the generational ideas above, we encourage you to conduct further research and exploration on your own besides what is discussed in this chapter.

Luckily, for us, both `CoreData` and `SwiftUI` are solutions from Apple, and they have learned a lot from the past when `CoreData` was used with UIKit. With SwiftUI, the integration with `CoreData` works seamlessly with a very declarative syntax.

Before jumping to implementation, let's get familiar with the basic operators used in a database system. Previously, we learned how to save and retrieve data from `UserDefaults`, which are two different actions. However, a real-world database system, whether it's online or offline, is much more complex than that. There must be more actions that can be performed, and the most fundamental operations are called CRUD.

CRUD is an acronym that stands for **Create, Read, Update, and Delete**. It is a set of basic operations commonly used in programming and database systems to manage and manipulate data. CRUD represents the fundamental actions that can be performed on data stored in a database or any other persistent storage.

Here's a breakdown of each operation:

- **Create (C)**: This operation involves creating or adding new data to a system. It typically corresponds to an **INSERT** operation in a database, where new records are added to a table or collection.

- **Read (R)**: This operation involves retrieving or reading existing data from a system. It corresponds to a **SELECT** operation in a database, allowing you to fetch records or data from a specific table or collection.

- **Update (U)**: This operation involves modifying or updating existing data in a system. It corresponds to an **UPDATE** operation in a database, enabling you to change the values of specific fields within a record.

- **Delete (D)**: This operation involves removing or deleting data from a system. It corresponds to a **DELETE** operation in a database, allowing you to remove specific records or data from a table or collection.

These four operations collectively cover the essential functionalities needed to perform data manipulation in various programming contexts. They form the basis for most data-driven applications and are widely used in web development, software development, and database management.

Similar to **UserDefaults**, we will only use two basic operators for our app with **CoreData: create** and **read**. However, you can do more to manipulate the database for your application features. We highly suggest that you conduct further research and continue exploring this topic after reading this book.

Setting up CoreData in SwiftUI

Now, let's get back to our application. Before we can use **CoreData** to create or read data, we need to do some setup first. Just like before, we created an **APIsManager** to manage all the issues related to APIs. With **CoreData**, we will create a **DataController** file that manages our database:

```
//  Created by James Thang on 18/02/2023.
//

import Foundation
import CoreData

class DataController: ObservableObject {
    let container = NSPersistentContainer(name: "ImageModelCoreData")

    init() {
        container.loadPersistentStores { description, error in
            if let error = error {
                print("Core Data failed to load: \(error.localizedDescription)")
            }
        }
    }
}
```

Figure 9.12: Defining CoreData controller

Firstly, we need to import CoreData. Then, we will mark this class as **ObservableObject**, just like we did with our view model. You might ask why we do this. It's because later, we will initialize our controller as a StateObject and leverage the power of Environment Object; this database will be shared and live updated between all views within the application. Inside this class, we'll add a single property of type **NSPersistentContainer**, which is the Core Data type responsible for loading a data model and giving us access to the data inside.

The code instructs Core Data to utilize the **ImageModelCoreData**, which is our local version of the **ImageDataModel**. However, it does not exist yet, and we will define this next. Here, it doesn't load the model itself yet; it simply prepares Core Data to load it by defining the properties and attributes as previously specified.

To load the data model, we need to invoke the **loadPersistentStores()** method on our container. This instructs **CoreData** to access the saved data based on the data model defined in **ImageModelCoreData**. However, it doesn't load all the data into memory simultaneously to avoid unnecessary resource consumption. Nevertheless, Core Data gains visibility into all the available information.

There is a possibility that loading the saved data encounters errors, such as data corruption. In such cases, there isn't much that can be done other than displaying an error message to the user and hoping that relaunching the app resolves the issue.

In any case, we'll create a small initializer for the DataController class that immediately loads our stored data. If any problems arise—which are unlikely but not impossible—we'll output a message to the Xcode debug log.

The **DataController** is now complete, and the final step is to create an instance of it and pass it into the SwiftUI environment. You might already be familiar with the **@Environment** feature in SwiftUI, which not only allows us to dismiss views but also stores other valuable data such as the time zone and user interface appearance.

In the context of Core Data, since most apps typically work with a single Core Data store at a time, instead of each view trying to create its own store individually, we create it once when the app starts and store it within the SwiftUI environment. This way, every other part of our app can access and utilize the same store.

To achieve this, navigate to the root view of the application and add the following property to the struct:

```swift
//  Created by James Thang on 11/05/2023.
//

import SwiftUI

@main
struct Chapter8_SwiftUIBookApp: App {

    @StateObject private var dataController = DataController()

    var body: some Scene {
        WindowGroup {
            ContentView()
                .environment(\.managedObjectContext, dataController.container.viewContext
        }
    }
}
```

Figure 9.13: *Injecting CoreData controller as an environment object*

Here, we have used the concept of Environment Object to inject the context of Core Data into the environment key called **managedObejctedContext**. This special key is used for type **NSPersistentStoreContainer,** which is the context of the container defined in the **DataController**.

The **NSPersistentStoreContainer** handles loading the actual saved data on the user's device. Now, you'll be introduced to the second crucial component of Core Data: managed object contexts. These contexts represent the **live** version of your data. When you load objects and make changes to them, those changes exist only in memory until you explicitly save them back to the persistent store.

The purpose of the view context is to allow us to work with all our data in memory, which is much faster than constantly reading from and writing to the disk. When we are ready, we still need to write the changes to the persistent store if we want them to persist for the next run of our app. However, we also have the option to discard changes if we do not wish to keep them.

So, we already have the container and the context. The last setup required is to define the **CoreData** version of our **ImageDataModel**, which will store the definitions of the entities and attributes that we want to use:

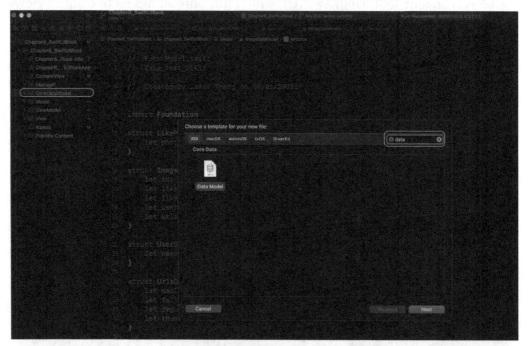

Figure 9.14: *Create CoreData model*

We will create a new folder and call it **CoreDataModel** to separate it from the **Model** folder that contains all the models used inside our application before. Create a new file, but this time, for **CoreData,** you need the specific type of file named **Data Model**. Search for it under the iOS category then click *Next*. Make sure that you named it the same as the string named used in the **DataController**. Here, we named this file **ImageModelCoreData**.

Here is our new file. Unlike the .swift file before, this data model file Xcode provides us with an interface to define our entities and their attributes. Now to be simple for Core Data, an entity will be equal to our model, which is a struct, and its attributes are equal to our models' properties. This is a new interface you will see after creating it:

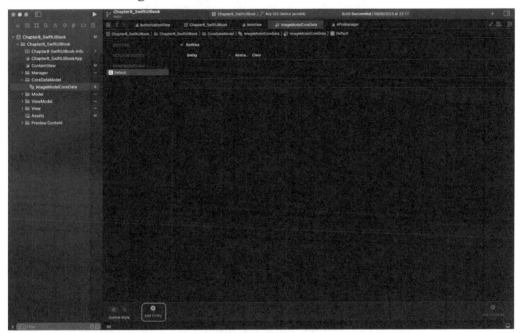

Figure 9.15: *CoreData model interface*

We will use the **Add Entity** button at the bottom to create a new entity and then define its attributes. Let's take a look back at our **ImageDataModel** to see what it contains:

```
// Created by James Thang on 09/01/2022.
//

import Foundation

struct ImageDataModel: Codable, Hashable {
    let id: String
    let likes: Int
    let liked_by_user: Bool
    let user: UserData
    let urls: UrlsData
}

struct UserData: Codable, Hashable {
    let name: String
}

struct UrlsData: Codable, Hashable {
    let small: String
    let full: String
    let regular: String
    let thumb: String
}
```

Figure 9.16: *Image model required data*

We will recreate the same architecture with the same attributes inside our **ImageModelCoreData**. Firstly, we observed that there are three models here, so in correlation, there will be three entities. Click the plus button, and you will see the new entity is added, then double click on it to rename it. We created three entities and named them **ImageCoreData**, **UrlsCoreData,** and **UserCoreData**:

Figure 9.17: *CoreData Entity interface*

For each entity, there are three sections here, but we will focus on the first two: **Attributes** and **Relationships**. With the plus button at the end of the **Attribute** section, we can define the attributes required for that entity. Then, we will state the relationship between our three entities by adding a relationship in the **Relationships** section for them:

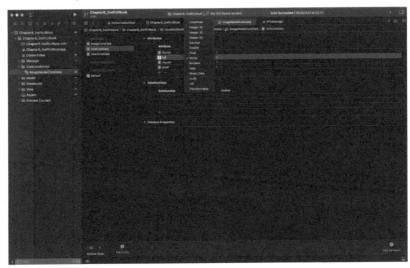

Figure 9.18: Adding attributes to the entity UserCoreData

Click the plus in the **Attribute** section to add new attributes. Let's name them the same as what we used before. Make sure that the type is also the same; click the dropdown and you will see all the available types for it. The **UrlsCoreData** is the same version as **UrlsData**, so it will have four attributes: **small**, **regular**, **full,** and **thumb**, all of which will be of type string. The same goes for **UserCoreData**; it will only have one string attribute, which is **name**.

The interesting thing will happen in the **ImageCoreData** entity:

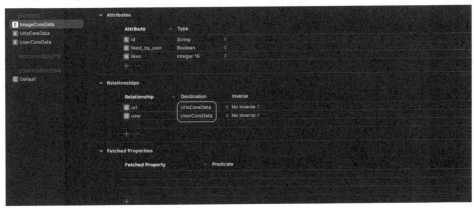

Figure 9.19: Adding attributes to the entity ImageCoreData

Here, we have three attributes: **id**, **liked_by_user,** and likes, which are string, Boolean, and integer, respectively. Integer 16 is just a type of integer in Swift used to store small integers for better memory management.

Now to set up the relationship of this with the other two entities, we need to add two relationships because these two entities will be the children of **ImageCoreData**. We will name them **url** with the destination to be **UrlsCoreData** and **user** with the destination to be **UserCoreData**. However, we are not done yet because the relationship has to be set in two ways:

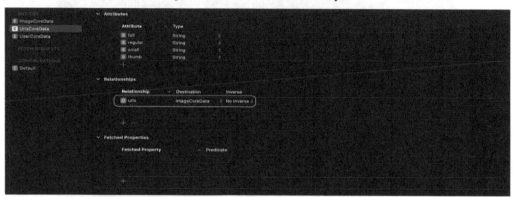

Figure 9.20: *Finish setting the relationship of UrlsCoreData*

Now, let's get back to the **UrlsCoreData** entity. We need to add a new relationship to confirm it with what was set up in the **ImageCoreData**. The name here will be the same, but the destination will point back to the **ImageCoreData**. The same goes for the **UserCoreData** entity:

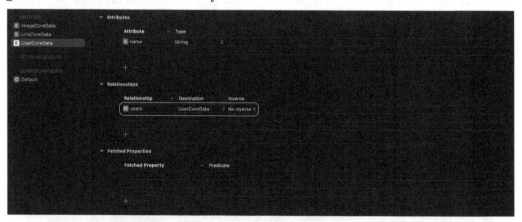

Figure 9.21: *Finish setting relationship of UserCoreData*

And we are done with the setting up of CoreData in SwiftUI. At this stage, we have created our Core Data model, loaded it, and prepared it for integration with SwiftUI. However, two essential aspects remain: reading data (Read) and writing data (Create, Update, or Delete).

You may wonder what the last section of *Fetched Properties* is about. It is for sorting the data when it's returned, but we can do this from the code inside our views.

Read and write data with CoreData in SwiftUI

To retrieve information from Core Data, we utilize a fetch request. We specify our desired criteria, such as sorting preferences and any applicable filters, and Core Data provides us with all the matching data. It is crucial to ensure that this fetch request remains up to date over time so that our user interface stays synchronized as students are created or removed.

Fortunately, SwiftUI offers a solution for this, and it comes in the form of another property wrapper. This time, it's called **@FetchRequest**, and it requires at least one parameter to define the desired sorting of results. The **@FetchRequest** property wrapper has a specific format, so let's proceed by adding a fetch request for our images.

Please add the following property to the **HomeView** now:

```
//  Created by James Thang on 11/05/2023.
//

import SwiftUI

struct HomeView: View {

    @StateObject private var viewModel = ViewModel()
    @Environment(\.managedObjectContext) var context
    @FetchRequest(sortDescriptors: [SortDescriptor(\.likes)],
                  predicate: NSPredicate(format: "id != %@", "")) var imageDataLocal: FetchedResults<ImageCoreData>
    @State var isLoad = false

    var body: some View {
        NavigationStack { ··· }
        .onAppear {
            if !isLoad {
                print(imageDataLocal.count)
                isLoad = true
            }
        }
    }
}
```

Figure 9.22: fetch local data inside the HomeView

Here, first, we get our context from the environment and call it **context**. Then, we used the **@FetchRequest** property wrapper to fetch all the data of type

ImageCoreData, which is the entity that resembles our image model from local storage. Remember we discuss that we can add filters to the return data. Here, in this example, with the help of **sortDescriptors** and **predicate**, we will be able to filter out all the items where the ID is empty and sort them in the order of **likes**. This is convenient because it eliminates the need to write the functions and perform them after retrieving data. This is facilitated by the **@FetchRequest** property wrapper.

We then use a state isLoad, so that we call this once when this view is initialized. This time, we will print out the number of items that we can get from the local storage. If you build and run this now, you will see that the number printout is 0. This is because we have never saved anything to our local storage yet. So yes, with this, we have successfully retrieved and read all the **ImageCoreData** entities in our storage, even though we don't have any yet.

Let's consider when and where we should save the image data to the local storage. The answer is right when we have that data, which is in our API call **fetch20Image** in the view model. So, after getting data back from the API, we will do another step than just assigning those data back to the **imageData** publisher; this saves those data locally.

Inside our view model, add these two functions:

```swift
private func saveDataToLocal(data: [ImageDataModel], context: NSManagedObjectContext) {
    data.forEach { imageData in
        let newLocalData = ImageCoreData(context: context)
        newLocalData.id = imageData.id
        newLocalData.liked_by_user = imageData.liked_by_user
        newLocalData.likes = Int16(imageData.likes)

        let userData = UserCoreData(context: context)
        userData.name = imageData.user.name
        newLocalData.user = userData

        let urlData = UrlsCoreData(context: context)
        urlData.small = imageData.urls.small
        urlData.full = imageData.urls.thumb
        urlData.regular = imageData.urls.regular
        urlData.thumb = imageData.urls.thumb
        newLocalData.url = urlData

        do {
            try context.save()
        } catch {
            print(error.localizedDescription)
        }
    }
}

private func deleteAll(data: FetchedResults<ImageCoreData>, context: NSManagedObjectContext, completion: @escaping
(Bool) -> ()) {
    for item in data {
        context.delete(item)
    }
    do {
        try context.save()
        completion(true)
    } catch {
        completion(false)
    }
}
```

Figure 9.23: *Create and delete with CoreData*

Remember that we need a context of type **NSManagedObjectContext** to be able to perform any writing actions with Core Data. This is the context that we passed from the root view through the environment object and is originally from the container inside the **DataController**.

For the **save** function, since the API returns an array of **ImageDataModel**, we will use the for each block to go through every item, each creating a new parallel **ImageCoreData** entity and saving it to the local storage. The important thing here is that for any entity in our code, we need to initialize it with the context. Then, the rest of the code is for mapping property values. Once this is completed, we must use the .save() from the context to confirm saving this data to local storage. Of course, this can fail, so we can either use a do try block or an option try.

For the **delete** function, we will be passing the deleted item as a parameter to the context. And importantly after that, we will need to confirm that action by calling **.save()** as well.

These are the logic behind performing writing data with **CoreData**. You might wonder why we need to write a delete all function here too. This is because data can be duplicated each time the API is called. So, here, we will first delete all existing local data, and then save the newly received data to our local storage. Let's rewrite our **fetchPost** function:

```swift
//  Created by James Thang on 24/04/2023.
//

import SwiftUI
import CoreData

class ViewModel: ObservableObject {

    @Published private(set) var imageData = [ImageDataModel]()

    init() {}

    func fetchPost(context: NSManagedObjectContext, oldLocalData: FetchedResults<ImageCoreData>) {
        APIsManager.shared.fetch20Images { [weak self] result in
            guard let this = self else { return }
            DispatchQueue.main.async {
                switch result {
                case .success(let data):
                    this.imageData.append(contentsOf: data)
                    this.deleteAll(data: oldLocalData, context: context) { _ in
                        this.saveDataToLocal(data: data, context: context)
                    }
                case .failure(let error):
                    print(error.localizedDescription)
                }
            }
        }
    }
}
```

Figure 9.24: Adding saving and deleting local storage local to the API call

After successfully retrieving data, we will first call the function to delete all local data. Once it is completed, we will save all the newly received data to local storage. Due to this, our fetch function needs two more parameters: the context and the old deprecated data. However, we do not have access to these two from our view model, so we cannot call it in the initializer like before. Instead, we will call it when our view appears the first time, you already know how to do this.:

```swift
// Created by James Thang on 11/05/2023.
//

import SwiftUI

struct HomeView: View {

    @StateObject private var viewModel = ViewModel()
    @Environment(\.managedObjectContext) var context
    @FetchRequest(sortDescriptors: [SortDescriptor(\.likes)],
                  predicate: NSPredicate(format: "id != %@", "")) var imageDataLocal: FetchedResults<ImageCoreData>
    @State var isLoad = false

    var body: some View {
        NavigationStack { ... }
            .onAppear {
                if !isLoad {
                    viewModel.fetchPost(context: context, oldLocalData: imageDataLocal)
                    print(imageDataLocal.count)
                    isLoad = true
                }
            }
    }
}
```

Figure 9.25: *Calling the API in view appears instead*

With this, now rebuild the project again and run it twice. You will see the number 20 printout in the debug console. The first time will still be 0 because there is no data during the first launch.

If you turn off your Wi-Fi and 4G now, nothing will be displayed, just as before. This is because we haven't done the layout for it yet.

To separate the view for online mode, we will create a new view for offline mode and call it **ItemLocalView**:

```swift
// Created by James Thang on 04/06/2023.
//

import SwiftUI

struct ItemLocalView: View {

    let model: ImageCoreData
    @State var uiImage: UIImage?
    @State var isLoad = false

    var body: some View {
        VStack(alignment: .leading, spacing: 12) {
            if let uiImage = uiImage {
                Image(uiImage: uiImage)
                    .resizable()
                    .aspectRatio(4/3, contentMode: .fit)
                    .clipShape(RoundedRectangle(cornerRadius: 16))
            }

            Text(model.user?.name ?? "")
                .foregroundColor(.primary)
                .fontWeight(.medium)

            HStack {
                Button(model.liked_by_user ? "Unlike" : "Like") { }

                Spacer()

                Text("\(model.likes) likes")
                    .font(.callout)
                    .foregroundColor(.secondary)
            }
        }
    }
}
```

Figure 9.26: *Making new View for offline mode*

Here, we will use the CoreData entity as the model. Since all of the properties are still the same, we do not need to change much. The main difference here is that we won't call the **downloadImage** API when this view appears. Even though we already have the image URL, it is not useful here because we do not have an internet connection; it would fail anyway. In the next section, we will learn about File Manager and learn how to store the image data on our phone to solve this problem.

An important thing to note here is that instead of making a new **ItemLocalView**, we can reuse the old **ItemView** by writing a function to map **ImageCoreData** to **ImageDataModel**. In programming, we called this by the name Mapper layer. This will save us from creating a new view for any new **CoreData** models. In this example, we will make a new view for better visualization of the separation between local storage and the normal online logic.

Now, let's get back to the **HomeView** and add a condition for displaying depending on whether the application is online or offline. While there is actually a frame solution to check this, we do not need it here. We can simply check if the **imageData** in our view model is empty, and then we will present the data from our local storage. This is a more general solution since it will be the case where we are online but the API call fails because of server issues:

```swift
import SwiftUI

struct HomeView: View {

    @StateObject private var viewModel = ViewModel()
    @Environment(\.managedObjectContext) var context
    @FetchRequest(sortDescriptors: [SortDescriptor(\.likes)],
                  predicate: NSPredicate(format: "id != %@", "")) var imageDataLocal: FetchedResults<ImageCoreData>
    @State var isLoad = false

    var body: some View {
        NavigationStack {
            ScrollView(.vertical) {
                LazyVGrid(columns: [GridItem(.flexible())]) {
                    if viewModel.imageData.isEmpty {
                        ForEach(imageDataLocal, id: \.self) { data in
                            ItemLocalView(model: data)
                        }
                    } else {
                        ForEach(viewModel.imageData, id: \.self) { data in
                            ItemView(model: data)
                        }
                    }
                }
                .padding(.horizontal)
            }
            .navigationTitle("Galerry").navigationBarTitleDisplayMode(.inline)
        }
        .onAppear {
            if !isLoad {
                viewModel.fetchPost(context: context, oldLocalData: imageDataLocal)
                print(imageDataLocal.count)
                isLoad = true
            }
        }
    }
}
```

Figure 9.27: Handle contents displaying for both online and offline modes

Inside our **LazyVStack** here, we add an if-else check. If we are in offline mode, we will retrieve data for the local storage and show them using the **ImageLocalView** instead.

Rebuild this, run the application on your phone, and then turn off Wi-Fi and 4G, you will now see that we already have the data, but no images:

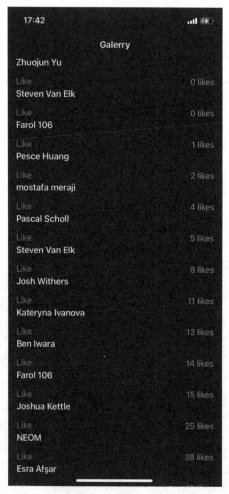

Figure 9.28: *Handle contents displaying for both online and offline modes*

As we have discussed, this is because we have the image URL, but to download, we need the internet. In this situation, we need to change to another local storage approach. For images, we will permanently store them on the user's phone and retrieve them when needed. There is a solution provided to us by Apple called File Manager.

Storing images inside users' phones with File Manager

In iOS app development, a File Manager is a component or feature that allows you to interact with the file system on an iOS device. It enables you to perform various operations such as browsing, creating, deleting, moving, and copying files and directories.

The File Manager in iOS provides an interface to access both the app's sandboxed file system and external storage locations, such as iCloud Drive and third-party cloud storage providers. It allows you to manage files and directories within your app's designated folders and perform file-related tasks.

In iOS, an app's sandboxed file system refers to the restricted storage environment in which an application operates. Each iOS app is given its own isolated file system, or "sandbox," which is separate from the rest of the device's file system. This means that an app can only access and modify files within its designated sandbox directory and cannot directly access files from other apps or the system.

The main purpose of sandboxing is to enhance security and protect user data. By restricting an app's access to its own sandbox, the risk of unauthorized access or manipulation of sensitive user data is significantly reduced. This security measure helps prevent malicious apps from tampering with other apps' data or interfering with the device's operating system.

Some common tasks that can be accomplished using a File Manager in iOS app development include:

- **Browsing**: You can navigate through the file system to locate files and directories within the app's sandbox or external storage locations.

- **Creating and Deleting**: You can create new files and directories programmatically or delete existing ones.

- **Moving and Copying**: You can move files and directories from one location to another within the file system or make copies of files.

- **Reading and Writing**: You can read the content of files and write data to files, allowing you to perform operations such as reading configuration files or saving user-generated content.

- **Metadata and Attributes**: You can access file metadata, such as file size, creation/modification dates, and file permissions. You can also modify attributes like file permissions or extended attributes.

- **Sharing**: You can utilize the File Manager to share files with other apps or export them to different locations.

The iOS File Manager APIs provide a set of classes and methods to interact with the file system, such as **FileManager** and **URL**. These APIs allow you to perform file-related operations and handle file system tasks efficiently within your iOS app.

Overall, the File Manager in iOS app development is a crucial component that empowers you to manage files and directories, providing users with a seamless and intuitive file management experience within your app.

We will use this to save our photo image to the user's phone and retrieve it back to use for the offline mode.

Because this is a new stand-alone login, we will create a new manager and call it **ImageManager**:

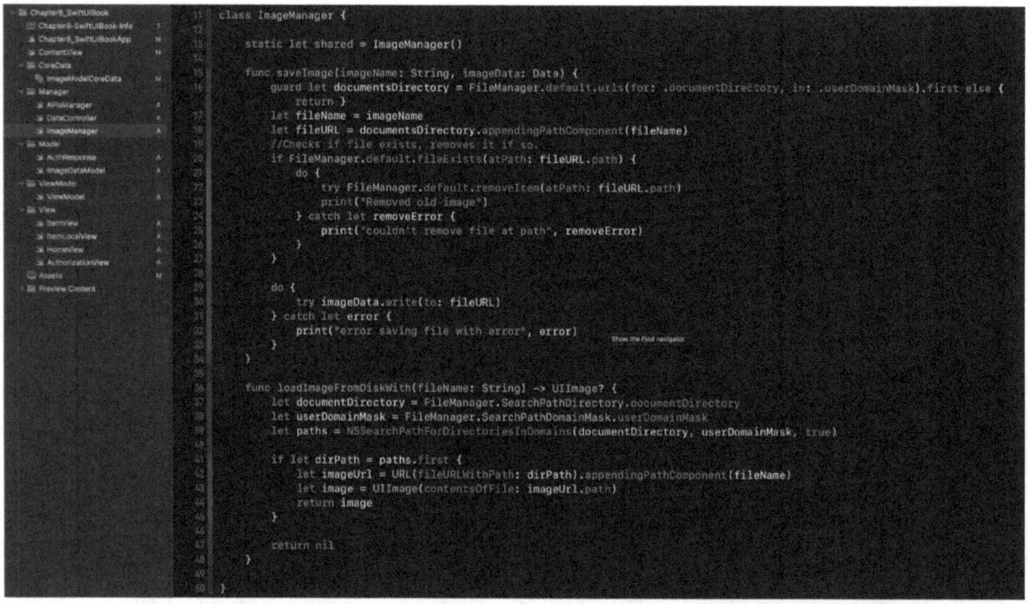

Figure 9.29: *Image Manager to store and load images to the user's device*

Just like with **UserDefaults** previously, we need a unique key for each value to keep track of where we store data and retrieve it when needed. For File Manager, we often refer to it as file URL, which is an address inside the device to store that piece of data.

In this newly created manager, we have two functions to save and load our images. Both require the file URL to save and retrieve data when needed. The **saveImage** requires another parameter, which is the data we want to store. And in the **loadImage** function, once we successfully get that data, we can try to turn it into a **UIImage** and return it. Also, in the saveImage function, we can add the logic to remove duplicate files in the same address to remove outdated images.

So, the next question to think is how should we name this URL address so that we can later know which image belongs to a specific **ItemCoreData**. Well, we need something unique for each image, and it better belong to the **ItemCoreData**. And this is what the **id** property is about, a unique ID for each instance.

The final question here is where should we call these two functions? For the **saveImage**, the best place to call it is when we get back the image data, which occurs in the downloadImage from the **APIsManager**:

```swift
class APIsManager {
    func downloadImage(from urlString: String, imageId: String, completion: @escaping (Result<Data, Error>) -> Void) {
        guard let url = URL(string: urlString) else {
            let error = APIError.failedCreateURL
            completion(.failure(error))
            return
        }

        let task = URLSession.shared.dataTask(with: url) { (data, response, error) in
            if let error = error {
                completion(.failure(error))
                return
            }

            if let data = data {
                ImageManager.shared.saveImage(imageName: imageId, imageData: data)
                completion(.success(data))
            } else {
                let error = APIError.failedToGetData
                completion(.failure(error))
            }
        }

        task.resume()
    }
}
```

Figure 9.30: *Save image data to user's device*

Just when we get back data from the APIs along with the image URL, we save it to the user's device and then return the data for use. Remember, the important thing here is to pass the image ID as a file URL. Now, to load it, we will perform the same logic from the **ItemView** to the **ItemLocalView**. The difference is this time instead of fetching the image using the image URL, we will load it from the user's device using the image ID from the **ImageCoreData** model:

```
// Created by James Thang on 04/06/2023.
//

import SwiftUI

struct ItemLocalView: View {

    let model: ImageCoreData
    @State var uiImage: UIImage?
    @State var isLoad = false

    var body: some View {
        VStack(alignment: .leading, spacing: 12) { ••• }
        .onAppear {
            if !isLoad {
                if let imageId = model.id {
                    uiImage = ImageManager.shared.loadImageFromDiskWith(fileName: imageId)
                }
                isLoad = true
            }
        }
    }
}
```

Figure 9.31: *Load image data from user device*

Now, for the moment of truth, rebuild the application and run it on the Internet. Then, turn off all the Wi-Fi and 4G or any source of the Internet:

Figure 9.32: *Application when there is no Internet*

Our application is now functioning in both online and offline modes. And it works beautifully and seamlessly, thanks to **UserDefaults**, **CoreData**, and File Manager. This is a great achievement for every mobile application.

Conclusion

Local storage is an essential aspect of iOS SwiftUI development, enabling applications to store and retrieve user-specific data efficiently. In this chapter, we explored three popular local storage options: UserDefault, CoreData, and File Manager.

UserDefault offers a lightweight key-value store suitable for storing simple data types. CoreData provides a powerful object-oriented framework for managing complex data models and relationships. File Manager allows direct file manipulation for advanced data handling requirements, such as saving and loading images to user's device.

Throughout this chapter, we have used all this new knowledge to improve our applications in performance, save resources, and improve user experience by allowing offline mode.

By understanding the strengths and use cases of each option, you can make informed decisions about which approach best suits your application's needs. Whether it's a small-scale project or a large-scale application, having a solid understanding of local storage techniques is vital for providing a seamless user experience and efficient data management.

With the knowledge gained from this chapter, we hope you can confidently implement local storage solutions in your iOS SwiftUI apps and enhance the overall functionality and performance of your future applications.

That's all for this chapter. In the next chapter, we will introduce you to a new API available from iOS 16: Swift Charts. This is a new declarative way to build beautiful charts natively. See you there!

CHAPTER 10
Construct Beautiful Charts with Swift Charts

Introduction

We have reached the final chapter of this book. It has been quite a great journey, and we hope that you have realized the power of SwiftUI in developing native iOS applications.

In this final chapter, we want to introduce you to a new powerful framework that has been available lately: Swift Charts. Charts are one of the most common and widely used forms of data visualization. They have been used in various applications with multiple use cases. As a developer, it is crucial and an advantage to be able to draw charts with our applications. However, creating a custom chart from scratch can be challenging and time-consuming. Previously, there were many frameworks and third-party libraries made to solve this problem, but all of them have flaws.

With iOS 16, Apple introduced their solution built in SwiftUI to make charts. This framework works seamlessly combining SwiftUI with the declarative syntax. Furthermore, in this year, it has even received more updates with iOS 17.

In this chapter, we will explore Swift Charts and recreate some of the most commonly used charts, ranging from bar charts, line charts, pie charts to donut charts. During the process, we will make a simple application of expense tracking, which will visualize the spending data in different kinds of charts.

Please note that unlike the previous nine chapters, which required iOS16, this chapter requires you to develop on iOS 17.

Structure

In this chapter, the following topics will be covered:

- Swift Charts
- Bar Char
- Line Chart
- Pie Chart
- Donut Chart

Introduction to Swift Charts

Swift Charts is an efficient and compact SwiftUI framework that allows you to convert your data into meaningful visual representations. It was introduced in WWDC 2022 and is available to use from iOS 16. By utilizing Swift Charts, you have the ability to construct impactful and adaptable charts with minimal coding effort. This framework offers various fundamental elements such as marks, scales, axes, and legends, which can be combined to create a diverse array of charts driven by data:

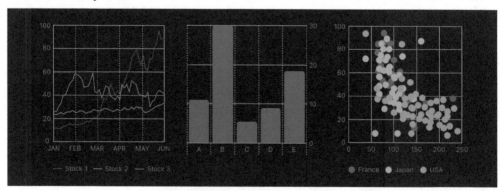

Figure 10.1: *Swift Charts examples*

Swift Charts offer numerous methods to effectively convey patterns and trends within your data. With this framework, you have the flexibility to generate an assortment of chart types such as line charts, bar charts, and scatter plots, as exemplified previously. When constructing a chart using Swift Charts, it conveniently generates scales and axes that are tailored to suit your data automatically.

Swift Charts is equipped with localization and accessibility capabilities, ensuring support for different languages and accessibility requirements. Additionally, the framework allows you to override default behavior through the use of chart modifiers, enabling extensive customization of your charts. For instance, you can enhance the user experience by incorporating animations into your charts, creating a dynamic and visually engaging presentation.

Now, let's get to know the fundamentals of Swift Charts.

Swift Charts foundations

Let's take a moment to acquaint ourselves with the fundamental components of any Swift chart: chart view, marks, properties, modifiers, and data.

- **Chart View**: It is the container view for the chart that contains all the marks inside. It is the same idea as NavigationView that you have learned in Chapter 6, *Tab bar, Navigation, and Compositional Layout*. NavigationView is a container that wraps all the NavigationLink, but, here, Chart is the container view that wraps all the Marks.

- **Marks**: Marks are the graphical elements that represent the data in a chart. They can take various forms such as points, bars, lines, or wedges in pie charts. Marks visually convey the information contained in the data.

- **Properties**: Properties define the visual characteristics of the chart and its components. They include attributes like he, sizes, shapes, and styles that determine how the chart and its marks are displayed.

- **Modifiers**: Modifiers are used to customize the behavior and appearance of the chart. They enable you to override default settings and apply specific transformations or enhancements to the chart and its elements. Modifiers can be used to add animations, adjust interactivity, or modify visual aspects.

- **Data**: Data is the core information that drives the chart. It consists of the values and labels that define the content and structure of the chart. Typically, data is provided in an organized format, such as arrays or dictionaries, and is used to populate the marks in the chart.

By understanding and manipulating these building blocks—marks, properties, modifiers, and data—you can create and customize Swift charts to effectively represent and visualize your data.

Let's talk more about Marks and Properties here since they are quite interesting. A mark is a graphical element that represents data; for example, the rectangular bars in a bar chart.

Swift charts include the following marks by default:

- BarMark

- PointMark

- LineMark

- AreaMark

- RuleMark

- RectangleMark

- SectorMark (new in iOS 17)

You may have guessed it based on their name. Each mark here is representative of a different kind of chart. We will soon meet some of them. Marks are extensive, so you can create a custom mark too.

In this chapter, you'll use properties to provide data and customize their appearance and interaction with modifiers.

Swift Charts support three types of data as follows:

- **Quantitative**: It represents numerical values, such as temperature, inches of snowfall, and so on.

- **Nominal**: These values are discrete categories or groups, such as a city, the name of a person, and so on. This data type often becomes the labels.

- **Temporal**: It represents a point or interval in time, such as the duration of a particular day part.

There is more to learn, but this is enough to get started. From here to the end of this chapter, you will develop and make several kinds of charts.

Now, open up Xcode, and let's get started.

Setting up the project

Just as with all the previous applications, we will adapt the MVVM Model for this project.

Let's begin with the models.

Firstly, we will tackle four different kinds of charts, and to distinguish them, we will use an enumeration. Here, we create a **GraphType** enumeration that has four cases representing four types of charts. We also adapt it to **String** and **CaseIterable** protocols so that we can use them inside the **ForEach** container later:

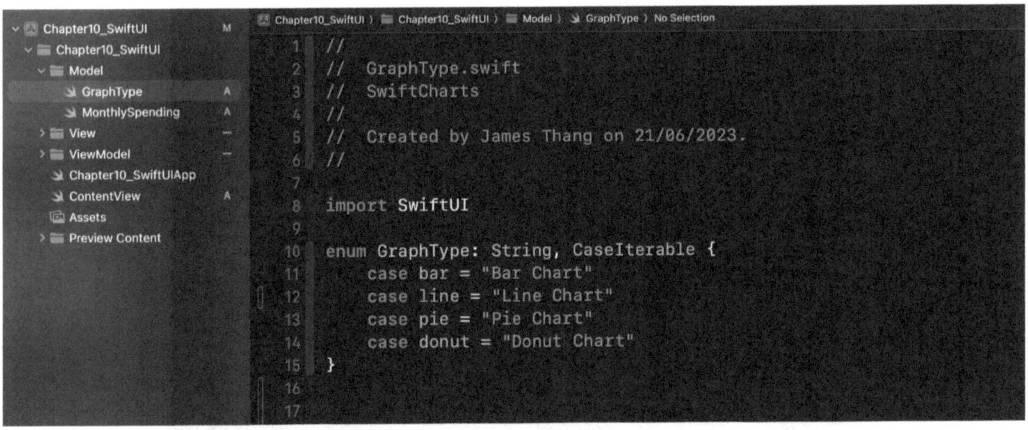

Figure 10.2: *Define different types of charts with custom enumeration*

Next, let's move on to the main model that will be used inside the application. In this application, we will represent and compare spending for different months of the year. So, we'll make a new model and name it **MonthlySpending**:

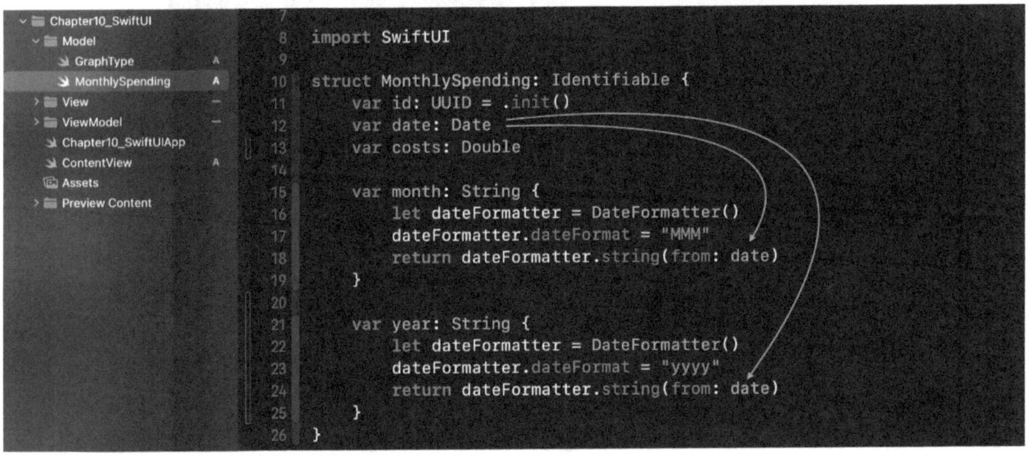

Figure 10.3: *Define the monthly spending model*

Our model has five properties. Each instance needs a unique ID so that we can distinguish them and be able to query through. The main information for each instance will be the **date,** which represents the period that was taken in and the total spending **cost** for that period.

The two remaining properties, **month** and **year,** are for chart representation later. These two are computed properties that will extract the month and year components from the **date** and return them as a string.

For more convenience later, we will make two extensions to use here:

```swift
extension [MonthlySpending] {
    func findCosts(_ on: String) -> Double? {
        if let cost = self.first(where: {
            $0.month == on
        }) {
            return cost.costs
        }

        return nil
    }

    func index(_ on: String) -> Int {
        if let index = self.firstIndex(where: {
            $0.month == on
        }) {
            return index
        }

        return 0
    }
}

extension Date {
    static func createDate(_ day: Int, _ month: Int, _ year: Int) -> Date {
        var components = DateComponents()
        components.day = day
        components.month = month
        components.year = year

        let calendar = Calendar.current
        let date = calendar.date(from: components) ?? .init()

        return date
    }
}
```

Figure 10.4: Define convenient extensions

In Swift, an **extension** is a language feature that allows you to add new functionality to an existing class, structure, enumeration, or protocol type. It provides a way to extend the behavior of a type without modifying its original implementation. Extensions are particularly useful when you want to add methods, properties, or initializers to a type that you don't have direct access to or want to keep the code organized by grouping related functionality.

Here, we create two extensions: one on the swift built-in type **Date** and another on an array of our newly created model, **MonthlySpending**: **[MonthlySpending]**.

The first extension will be used later when we create all of our charts. Since all of the chart input data will be an array of **MonthlySpending**, we make an extension for this type, so that we can conveniently have access to the two new functions to find the cost of the month and the index of those cost items. It is because later we will make four different views for four of our charts. With this extension, we don't have to repeatedly define them in different views. You can of course define these two functions inside the view model. But again, what if another different view model needs one of these somewhere else? Extensions offer a better and more scalable solution.

The second **extension** on the **Date** type is for a fast and convenient initialization of the date. With this new function, we can pass in the numeric number to initialize the date. Let's make our view model using sample data for our application:

```
//
// Created by James Thang on 25/06/2023.
//

import SwiftUI

class ChartViewModel: ObservableObject {

    var thisYearSpending: [MonthlySpending] = [
        .init(date: .createDate(1, 1, 2023), costs: 2500),
        .init(date: .createDate(1, 2, 2023), costs: 3500),
        .init(date: .createDate(1, 3, 2023), costs: 1500),
        .init(date: .createDate(1, 4, 2023), costs: 9500),
        .init(date: .createDate(1, 5, 2023), costs: 1950),
        .init(date: .createDate(1, 6, 2023), costs: 5100),
    ]

    var lastYearSpending: [MonthlySpending] = [
        .init(date: .createDate(1, 1, 2022), costs: 2800),
        .init(date: .createDate(1, 2, 2022), costs: 1500),
        .init(date: .createDate(1, 3, 2022), costs: 5500),
        .init(date: .createDate(1, 4, 2022), costs: 6500),
        .init(date: .createDate(1, 5, 2022), costs: 3950),
        .init(date: .createDate(1, 6, 2022), costs: 2100),
    ]

    init() { }
}
```

Figure 10.5: *Define our view model with sample data*

In our view model, we will create two new arrays of data representing spending in the first six months of 2023 and 2022. This will be used and visualized in our chart views. Don't forget to adapt to **ObservableObject**:

Now, let's build the last part, which is our application's main view:

```
struct ContentView: View {

    // View Properties
    @State private var graphType: GraphType = .bar
    @StateObject private var viewModel = ChartViewModel()

    var body: some View {
        NavigationView {
            VStack {
                // Segment Picker
                Picker("", selection: $graphType) {
                    ForEach(GraphType.allCases, id: \.rawValue) { type in
                        Text(type.rawValue)
                            .tag(type)
                    }
                }
                .pickerStyle(.segmented)
                .labelsIsHidden()

                switch graphType {
                case .bar:
                    BarChartView(viewModel: viewModel)
                case .line:
                    LineChartView(viewModel: viewModel)
                case .pie:
                    PieChartView(viewModel: viewModel)
                case .donut:
                    DonutChartView(viewModel: viewModel)
                }

                Spacer(minLength: 0)
            }
            .navigationTitle("Swift Charts")
            .padding(.top, 10)
            .padding()
        }
    }
}
```

Figure 10.6: *Application main view*

Here, we leverage the power of enumeration and use it to present a Picker, which will bind to the local state **graphType**. When it is updated, we will change the presented chart view. By adopting the CaseIterable previously, we can loop to all its cases to provide data input for the Picker view here.

We are initializing our view model here and passing it into all four chart views. Now, let's take a look at them, starting with the most common one: bar chart.

Creating a Bar chart

It's important to choose the appropriate chart type based on the nature of your data and the story you want to tell.

Bar charts are best used for visualizing and comparing categorical data or discrete values. They are particularly effective in the following scenarios:

- **Comparing data**: Bar charts allow you to compare different categories or groups by representing their values as individual bars. The length or height of each bar represents the magnitude of the data, making it easy to visually compare values across different categories.

- **Showing trends over time**: Bar charts can be used to display changes in data over time by representing different periods on the x-axis and the corresponding values on the y-axis. This allows viewers to observe trends, identify patterns, and analyze the data's progression.

- **Displaying rankings**: Bar charts are useful for displaying rankings or ordering data based on their values. You can arrange the bars in descending or ascending order to highlight the highest or lowest values, enabling quick comparisons and identification of the most significant factors.

- **Presenting survey or poll results**: Bar charts are commonly used to present survey data, poll results, or responses to multiple-choice questions. Each response option is represented by a separate bar, making it easy to visualize the distribution of responses and identify the most popular or least popular choices.

- **Comparing performance metrics**: Bar charts are effective in comparing performance metrics for different entities, such as sales figures for different products or revenue generated by different departments. The bars allow for a quick visual assessment of the relative performance of each entity.

- **Visualizing proportions**: Bar charts can be used to represent proportions or percentages of a whole. Each bar represents a category, and the length or height of the bar corresponds to the proportion or percentage it represents. This helps viewers understand the relative contribution of each category to the total.

Making charts with Swift Charts APIs is very simple. Here is how it is for the bar chart:

Figure 10.7: *Making a bar chart with SwiftUI*

First, we have to import Charts, which are the new APIs Swift Charts provided by Apple.

Next, remember that everything in Swift Charts must be wrapped inside the Chart container view to use them.

For bar charts, we will use BarMark to visualize our data. Using a ForEach block looping through all data from this year (2023), we will pass the **month** string value as the x-value and the corresponding cost as the y-value.

And as simple as that, we have our clear bar chart data on the right side. It takes less than 10 lines of code to make such a beautiful bar chart! This used to be painful with huge configurations back then. However, with SwiftUI, starting from iOS 16, you can have it right out of the box.

Now, let's add more modifiers to make our chart stand out:

Figure 10.8: *Improve our bar chart with modifiers*

Available out of the box, we can make our bar chart rounded with the `.cornerRadius()` modifier. Similar to how all SwiftUI view has a `.foreground()` modifier, here you can use `.foregroundStyle()` to distinguish between different items in the axis. Here, we specify that the style will be different based on the *x*-axis value, which is our months.

That's it, and now we have a beautiful bar chart on the right side, looking much better than the previous default one.

Next, let's see the difference in spending in the first six months between 2022 and 2023. The chart best suited for this comparison is the line chart.

Creating a Line chart

Line charts are best used for visualizing and tracking trends in data over time. They are particularly effective in the following scenarios:

- **Displaying trends**: Line charts are ideal for illustrating the change or progression of a variable over a continuous period. By plotting data points and connecting them with a line, line charts provide a clear visual representation of how a value fluctuates, rises, or falls over time.

- **Comparing multiple variables**: Line charts allow for the simultaneous comparison of multiple variables on the same graph. By plotting multiple lines on a single chart, you can easily compare and contrast the trends and patterns of different variables.

- **Identifying patterns and cycles**: Line charts are effective in identifying patterns, cycles, and seasonality in data. By examining the peaks, valleys, or recurring trends in the lines, you can gain insights into the cyclical nature of the data and make informed predictions or decisions.

- **Analyzing correlations**: Line charts can help visualize the correlation between two variables. By plotting both variables on the same chart, you can observe how changes in one variable correspond to changes in the other. Positive correlations show an upward trend, while negative correlations show a downward trend.

- **Tracking progress towards a goal**: Line charts are useful for tracking progress towards a specific goal or target over time. By plotting the actual values against the desired target, you can easily see if the progress is on track or if adjustments need to be made.

- **Showing continuous data relationships**: Line charts are effective for displaying continuous data, such as temperature, stock prices, or population growth. The continuous line allows for a smooth representation of the data points, making it easier to identify trends and patterns.

Line charts are versatile and widely used for visualizing time series data. Let's take a look at the difference in spending in the first six months between 2022 and 2023:

Top of Form

Bottom of Form

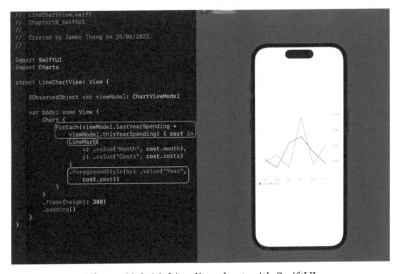

Figure 10.9: *Making line chart with SwiftUI*

In Swift, it is very convenient when you want to merge two arrays into one; just use the "+" sign, and you have it. Here, we merge the data of the current year's spending, 2023, and the last year, 2022.

Then, everything is almost the same. We just have to replace **BarMark** with **LineMark** to make a line chart. Also, in the **.foregroundStyle()** modifier, instead of distinguishing them in months, we will distinguish them in years to compare the trend of spending between two years.

It already looks great, but we can make it even better. To visualize the point of each month, we can use another mark from Swift Charts: **PointMark**:

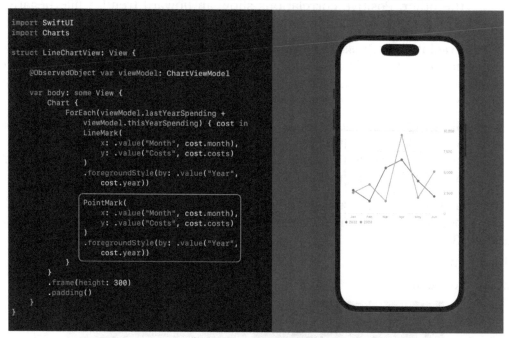

```
import SwiftUI
import Charts

struct LineChartView: View {

    @ObservedObject var viewModel: ChartViewModel

    var body: some View {
        Chart {
            ForEach(viewModel.lastYearSpending +
                viewModel.thisYearSpending) { cost in
                LineMark(
                    x: .value("Month", cost.month),
                    y: .value("Costs", cost.costs)
                )
                .foregroundStyle(by: .value("Year",
                    cost.year))

                PointMark(
                    x: .value("Month", cost.month),
                    y: .value("Costs", cost.costs)
                )
                .foregroundStyle(by: .value("Year",
                    cost.year))
            }
        }
        .frame(height: 300)
        .padding()
    }
}
```

Figure 10.10: *Add a Point mark to visualize each month's data*

Adding **PointMark** for each cost will present a point for that data, and here it is sitting above our line, making a beautiful descriptive chart. Remember to apply the same **.foregroundStyle()** as the **LineMark**.

Now, there is still a very interesting modifier to add here:

```swift
import SwiftUI
import Charts

struct LineChartView: View {

    @ObservedObject var viewModel: ChartViewModel

    var body: some View {
        Chart {
            ForEach(viewModel.lastYearSpending +
                viewModel.thisYearSpending) { cost in
                LineMark(
                    x: .value("Month", cost.month),
                    y: .value("Costs", cost.costs)
                )
                .foregroundStyle(by: .value("Year",
                    cost.year))

                PointMark(
                    x: .value("Month", cost.month),
                    y: .value("Costs", cost.costs)
                )
                .foregroundStyle(by: .value("Year",
                    cost.year))
                .annotation(position: .overlay,
                            alignment: .bottom,
                            spacing: 10) {
                    Text("\(Int(cost.costs))")
                        .font(.caption)
                }
            }
        }
        .frame(height: 300)
        .padding()
    }
}
```

Figure 10.11: Adding annotations for line chart

With the `.annotation()` modifier, we can show the cost of each month in our line chart, looking just like a professional application, isn't it?

We are able to make this with less than 20 lines of code in Swift Charts. How powerful is that!

With the new updates in iOS 17, we can now implement a pie chart with SectorMark. Let's explore it.

Creating a Pie chart

Pie charts are best used for visualizing the composition or distribution of categorical data. They are particularly effective in the following scenarios:

Showing proportions: Pie charts are ideal for representing the relative proportions or percentages of different categories within a whole. The entire pie represents 100% of the data, and each category is represented by a slice, the size of which corresponds to its proportion or percentage.

Comparing categories: Pie charts allow for quick visual comparisons between categories. By comparing the sizes of the slices, you can easily identify which categories are larger or smaller in relation to each other.

Highlighting dominant categories: Pie charts can effectively highlight dominant or significant categories. The largest slice in the pie stands out and draws attention, making it easy to identify the most prominent category.

Presenting simple data sets: Pie charts work best when you have a relatively small number of categories (typically less than 6 or 7) and clear proportions. They are especially useful when the data is divided into a few distinct categories, and you want to show the distribution in a visually appealing and easily understandable way.

Displaying percentages: Pie charts can be used to show the percentage contribution of each category to the whole. The slices are often labeled with the corresponding percentages, allowing viewers to understand the precise proportion of each category.

However, it's worth noting that pie charts have some limitations and can be less effective in certain situations. For instance:

- They can become cluttered and difficult to interpret when there are too many categories or when the proportions are similar.

- It can be challenging to accurately compare the sizes of different slices, especially when they are close in size.

- Pie charts do not work well for displaying trends over time or comparing values between different data sets.

Let's make the pie chart from the current year's (2023) spending:

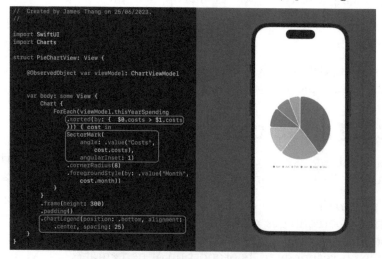

Figure 10.12: *Making a pie chart with SwiftUI*

Here, first, we will sort our data in descending order because the nature of the pie chart is usually present in data order.

Next, we will use the new **SectorMark**, making use of two properties: the **angle** passing the value, which will be used to draw the chart here (which will be the monthly cost), and the **angularInset** to have some space between each pie, set to a 1-pixel value.

The corner radius and foreground style will be the same as in the previous chart. Now every chart by default comes with a chart legend, and it is positioned at the bottom leading side. However, we can modify it too with the **.chartLegend()** modifier on the Chart view. Here, we align it to the center and add some more space to the pie chart.

Now, the last one is just a variable of the pie chart, which just adds one more property. Let's explore the donut chart.

Creating a Donut chart

A donut chart, also known as a doughnut chart, is a type of circular chart used to represent data in a visually appealing way. It is similar to a pie chart but has a hole in the center, creating a "donut" shape. The chart is divided into segments, where each segment represents a proportion or percentage of the whole.

Donut charts are useful for displaying categorical data with a few distinct categories and comparing their relative sizes. The outer edge of the chart represents 100% or the total value, and each segment's size is proportional to its corresponding value or percentage. The segments are typically labeled to indicate the category they represent.

The central hole in the donut chart can be used for additional information or to enhance the visual appeal. It can display a summary or a total value related to the data, or it can be left empty for a more minimalist design.

Donut charts are commonly used in business presentations, reports, and dashboards to convey data in an easily understandable and visually appealing manner. However, it's important to note that donut charts can sometimes be less effective than other chart types, such as bar charts or stacked bar charts, especially when dealing with complex or numerous categories, as the segments can become difficult to compare accurately:

```
// Created by James Thang on 25/06/2023.
//

import SwiftUI
import Charts

struct DonutChartView: View {

    @ObservedObject var viewModel: ChartViewModel

    var body: some View {
        Chart {
            ForEach(viewModel.thisYearSpending
                .sorted(by: { $0.costs > $1.costs
            })) { cost in
                SectorMark(
                    angle: .value("Costs",
                        cost.costs),
                    innerRadius: .ratio(0.61),
                    angularInset: 6)
                .cornerRadius(8)
                .foregroundStyle(by: .value("Month",
                    cost.month))
            }
        }
        .frame(height: 300)
        .padding()
        .chartLegend(position: .bottom, alignment:
            .center, spacing: 25)
    }
}
```

Figure 10.13: *Making a donut chart with SwiftUI*

Inside **SectorMark**, you can create a new and strange chart simply by adding another built-in property, **innerRadius**. Here, we will specify that the ratio of the empty inner circle is 61 percent. You can make your choice and go with it. Also, let's increase the spacing between the pie by more than 6 pixels.

So now, we are having four different kinds of charts to visualize our spending data:

```
var body: some View {
    NavigationView {
        VStack {
            // Segment Picker
            Picker("", selection: $graphType) {
                ForEach(GraphType.allCases, id:
                    \.rawValue) { type in
                    Text(type.rawValue)
                        .tag(type)
                }
            }
            .pickerStyle(.segmented)
            .labelsHidden()

            switch graphType {
            case .bar:
                BarChartView(viewModel:
                    viewModel)
            case .line:
                LineChartView(viewModel:
                    viewModel)
            case .pie:
                PieChartView(viewModel:
                    viewModel)
            case .donut:
                DonutChartView(viewModel:
                    viewModel)
            }

            Spacer(minLength: 0)
        }
        .navigationTitle("Swift Charts")
        .padding(.top, 10)
        .padding()
    }
}
```

Figure 10.14: *Four kinds of charts in our application*

With this, we are done with this application. There are four different kinds of charts, and you can easily switch between them with the picker.

Although this is a new framework available only starting from iOS 16, it completely changes everything, and so off the power of SwiftUI with declarative programming.

There is still much more to explore, such as other marks like **AreaMark**, **RuleMark**, **RectangleMark**, and other interesting modifiers to make your charts stand out.

Just like all of the other chapters in this book, everything does not end here, and there will be more for you to explore. What we are trying to provide is a basic foundation.

Conclusion

Swift Charts provides a powerful and user-friendly solution for visualizing data in SwiftUI. With its introduction in WWDC 2022 and availability from iOS 16, this efficient and compact framework has proven to be a valuable tool for developers.

By offering a wide range of chart types, such as line charts, bar charts, and scatter plots, Swift Charts allows for the creation of diverse and impactful visual representations of data. The framework's ability to automatically generate scales and axes tailored to the data simplifies the chart construction process, requiring minimal coding effort.

In this chapter, we have explored four different charts: bar chart, line chart, pie chart, and donut chart. During the process, we used four different marks: BarMark, LineMark, PointMark, and SectorMark. With this, we have built a beautiful visualization for our cost-tracking application. However, this framework or any other concepts mentioned in this book are just the beginning. There is so much more waiting for you to explore on your own.

Overall, Swift Charts empowers developers to effortlessly transform data into meaningful visualizations, making it a valuable asset in the SwiftUI ecosystem.

iOS 17 Appendix

With Swift 5.9 and Xcode 15, we can leverage **Macros** in Swift. **Macros** transform your source code when you compile it, letting you avoid writing repetitive code by hand.

Macros can either be written with a "@" prefix or with a "#" prefix, depending on where they›re being used. Here are 2 things that can be done differently:

1. Showing Preview with **#Preview** Macro:

   From XCode 15, there is a new shorter way to show the live Preview.

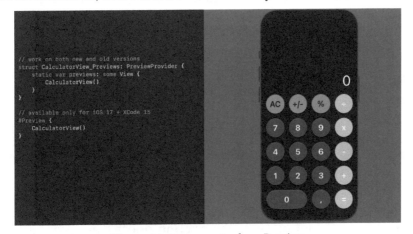

Figure A.1: *New way to show Preview*

From Xcode 15, developers will be greeted with a welcome enhancement: a new, more concise syntax for displaying previews **#Preview**. This streamlined approach not only makes the code cleaner and easier to read but also boosts efficiency by reducing the keystrokes needed to achieve the same result.

The best part is that while this new syntax offers convenience and modernity, the old method still works seamlessly.

This thoughtful compatibility ensures that developers can transition at their own pace and continue to work with their familiar workflows, all while having the option to embrace the improved brevity of the new Preview syntax whenever they're ready.

2. Observable Macro with **@Observable** Macro:

   Embracing Observation offers your application a range of advantages, including:

   - Monitoring options and collections of items, a capability that is not available when employing **ObservableObject**.

   - Utilizing established data flow tools like **@State** and **@Environment** rather than object-oriented counterparts like **@StateObject** and **@EnvironmentObject**.

   - Ensuring that views respond to alterations in observable properties that are explicitly read within a view's content, as opposed to tracking changes in any property of an observable object. This can contribute to enhancing your app's overall performance.

To implement Observation in an app that already exists, start by substituting the **ObservableObject** in your data model type with the **@Observable** macro. This macro generates code during compilation, which introduces support for observation of the type.

```
// BEFORE
import SwiftUI

class Library: ObservableObject {
    // ...
}
```

```
// AFTER
import SwiftUI

@Observable class Library {
    // ...
}
```

Figure A.2: *Migrating to the new @Observable macro*

Next, eliminate the **@Published** property wrapper from your observable properties. It's worth noting that **Observation** doesn't necessitate a property wrapper to render a property observable. Instead, the property's observability is determined by its accessibility concerning an observer, such as a view.

```
// BEFORE
@Observable class Library {
    @Published var books: [Book] = [Book(), Book(
}
```
```
// AFTER
@Observable class Library {
    var books: [Book] = [Book(), Book(), Book()]
}
```

Figure A.3: *Removing @Published property wrapper*

To fully adopt Observation, replace the use of **@StateObject** with **@State** in the View layer after updating our View Model.

```
// BEFORE
@main
struct BookReaderApp: App {
    @StateObject private var library = Library()

    var body: some Scene {
        WindowGroup {
            LibraryView()
                .environmentObject(library)
        }
    }
}
```

```
// AFTER
@main
struct BookReaderApp: App {
    @State private var library = Library()

    var body: some Scene {
        WindowGroup {
            LibraryView()
                .environment(library)
        }
    }
}
```

Figure A.4: *Replacing @StateObject with @State*

Now that the Library no longer conforms to **ObservableObject**, the code can change to use **@State** instead of **@StateObject** and to add a library to the environment using the environment(_:) modifier.

Just like before, this new syntax offers convenience and reduces boilerplate code, but the best part is the old method still works seamlessly.

Developers will have time to adapt. Macros are great features but they are only available from Swift 5.9 with XCode 15, so it will take time to transition into it.

Reference

https://docs.swift.org/swift-book/documentation/the-swift-programming-language/macros/

https://developer.apple.com/documentation/swiftui/migrating-from-the-observable-object-protocol-to-the-observable-macro

Index

Made in United States
Troutdale, OR
12/29/2023

16542686R10157